T0278224

A Long
Season *of*
Ashes

A Long Season *of* Ashes

a memoir

SIDDHARTHA GIGOO

PENGUIN

VIKING

An imprint of Penguin Random House

VIKING

USA | Canada | UK | Ireland | Australia
New Zealand | India | South Africa | China | Singapore

Viking is part of the Penguin Random House group of companies
whose addresses can be found at global.penguinrandomhouse.com

Published by Penguin Random House India Pvt. Ltd
4th Floor, Capital Tower 1, MG Road,
Gurugram 122 002, Haryana, India

Penguin
Random House
India

First published in Viking by Penguin Random House India 2024

Copyright © Siddhartha Gigoo 2024

All rights reserved

10 9 8 7 6 5 4 3 2 1

This book is a memoir based on the author's own imperfect recollections of events
that have long since transpired. For the purposes of narrative flow, some dialogue
has been recreated and must not be treated as representing word-for-word renditions.
Rather, the author has retold them in a way that evokes the feeling of what was said
while preserving the essence of the speaker's version. While the stories in this book
are true, some names and identifying details have been changed to protect the privacy
of the people involved. The views expressed in the book are the author's own and
the facts are as reported by him, which have been verified to the extent possible. The
publisher assumes no responsibility for errors, inaccuracies, omissions or any other
inconsistencies herein and is in no way liable for the same. The intention of this book
is not to hurt anyone's sentiments or be biased in favour of or against any particular
person, community, profession, region, linguistic identity, caste, religion or gender.

ISBN 9780670098262

Typeset in Sabon by Manipal Technologies Limited, Manipal
Printed at Replika Press Pvt. Ltd, India

www.penguin.co.in

MIX
Paper from
responsible sources
FSC® C016779

For Babi and Babuji

Let us rejoice for the dead
and grieve for the living
as we go
from ashes to ashes

'The light of memory, or rather the light that memory lends to things, is the palest light of all. I am not quite sure whether I am dreaming or remembering, whether I have lived my life or dreamed it. Just as dreams do, memory makes me profoundly aware of the unreality, the evanescence of the world, a fleeting image in the moving water.'

—Eugène Ionesco

'Night has fallen, the day's work is done. I return like a mole to my home, the ground. Not because I am tired and cannot work. I am not tired. But the sun has set.'

—Nikos Kazantzakis, *Report to Greco*

Contents

Prologue

On 23 October 1992, Imre Kertész, a Hungarian writer of Jewish descent, delivered an address at the University of Vienna on what it meant for an entire generation to bear the burden of the Holocaust. The lecture titled 'The Holocaust as Culture' was a seminal text on the atrocities suffered by the European Jews. Towards the end of the lecture, Kertész asked an important ethical question: Can the Holocaust give rise to values? The forced deportation from his home in Budapest, Hungary, followed by serving time in a Nazi extermination camp in Germany at the age of fourteen, had led Kertész to a deeper understanding of his own condition, intellectually as well as spiritually. The crisis led to the awakening of knowledge within him about the human spirit in times of horror.

Around the same time, in 1992, when Kertész was delivering lectures and writing about the role of the Holocaust in shaping his identity as a writer, about half a million displaced Hindus of Kashmir were battling alienation and deprivation in horrid migrant camps in the Jammu province of the Jammu and Kashmir state.

My family and I were among these people. Two years had passed since our enforced ouster from Kashmir, our homeland for centuries. We never abandoned hope despite being forced to live impoverished lives in camps that lacked the most basic amenities. Every day, people perished because of a lack of proper rations, water, medical care and sanitation. Nearly all deaths were unnatural and untimely, with hitherto unknown diseases striking down the young and the old.

We thought that our exile was going to be temporary and that we would soon be able to return to our homes in Kashmir. Little did we know that our fate had been sealed.

What followed was a long, dark time—a 'camp' existence and a struggle for survival.

Nobody paid heed to what we, the exiles, were made to go through in these camps. A tent kept a homeless family alive in inclement conditions. A tattered tent!

Imagine living in a camp for twenty-four years—in tents for the first twelve years and one-room tenements (ORTs) for the next twelve. These camps, which are now no better than housing ghettos, still exist in Jammu. In such ghettos, there can never be either a sense of belonging or a sense of identity. There is only a deep sense of betrayal and hurt.

Those of us who survived were perhaps not meant to survive. We were just fortunate.

I was among the fortunate, but Babuji, my grandfather, wasn't. A strange affliction gripped him and took him away from us. The tiny bridges running across the islands of his memory collapsed one by one until one island didn't know the whereabouts of another. And then, memory became unmemory, space became unspace and time became untime.

I never wanted my grandfather to die the way he did—such a death shouldn't be any human's fate. Towards the end, Babuji didn't remember that he was married to a woman who loved him the most and was still alive. Unable to bear his pain and her own pain, Babi, my grandmother, wished him deliverance every moment. She couldn't come to terms with his strange and horrifying mental condition that made him mistake his own granddaughter for his wife, his wife for his granddaughter, her only son and grandson for his grandfather and others for some other people, some known and some unknown. Babi also wished him life, but she wished him life at home! Such was the bond they shared that no matter where they lived and spent their lives and under whatever circumstances, they should and would only die in their ancestral home. Babuji spent his last years in a place very far away from where he wanted to live and die. From our perspective, the place didn't even exist.

When he died in exile, pining for his home in Kashmir, I cried out of relief. He set us free from pain. The pain of having lost everything. The pain of not being able to return home and die there.

Little did I realize that a day would come when his entire life as well as his death would bear testimony to a forgotten chapter in the history of modern India. A chapter on what around half a million Kashmiri Pandits have had to endure for over three decades after their enforced exodus from Kashmir. What we were made to go through in camps is a blot on the collective conscience of a nation whose constitution guarantees justice, liberty, equality and fraternity to all citizens.

The grandparents of thousands of people like me went through an ordeal of unimaginable proportions, while the rest of India didn't even notice.

'For us, history had stopped,' says Primo Levi about his time in Buna (a sub-camp of Auschwitz). For over a quarter of a century, we saw the end of history, too. A people with a 5000-year history witnessed an endless pause once more in

1990[1] when they were banished from their land for the seventh time and condemned to a miserable exile. The land that for centuries had welcomed and sheltered zealots, scholars, mystics, conquerors, missionaries, atheists, agnostics and warriors, and allowed them to profess and practise their ideas and beliefs, had no place for its original inhabitants any more.

Quoting Jean Améry, the Austrian writer who survived internments in Auschwitz and Buchenwald and later took his own life, Kertész likened the survivor to an accident, requiring justification, although the survivor was, in fact, unjustifiable. 'Survival seems unimaginable, but it is the camps that should seem unimaginable,' he said.

The losses we Kashmiri Pandits have been forced to incur are unimaginable. How must we measure these losses? How must we look at the entire odyssey from paradise to hell and back? From the days of glory, happiness and contentment to the days of persecution, banishment, horror, annihilation and suffering. How must we reconcile our fate with this civilizational paralysis that has gripped us as a result of the nation's apathy?

Even today, thirty-four years after being forced out of Kashmir due to cross-border insurgency, separatism and religious persecution, we haven't even been accorded the status of internally displaced persons (IDPs) and are still referred to as 'migrants' as if we left out of our own volition.

Not a single judicial commission of inquiry has been instituted to investigate the crimes committed against us. Not a single testimony has been recorded and entered in any of the official documents of either the state or the central government. We haven't even been given a hearing by the government. The Supreme Court of India, too, has dismissed plea after plea seeking a probe into our genocide, saying that the matter is three decades old and that there won't be any witnesses to testify.[2] What else are we collectively, if not witnesses to our own persecution and to surviving the horror of 1990 in Kashmir and in the camps outside it?

We are the living testimony of the crimes committed against us. And the multidimensional impact of these crimes now threatens our own existence and future.

Thousands of Kashmiri Pandits died with longing in their hearts—the longing to go back to their homes and live and die there. They didn't want to die anywhere else but in their homes. Definitely not in the horrid camps. No one should ever die in a displacement camp. Those lonely deaths are punishments that no human deserves.

Writers such as Jean Améry, Imre Kertész, Primo Levi, Eli Wiesel and Tadeusz Borowski help us understand our own condition, including the possibility of return and the possibility of giving rise to a new us; of reconciling our past and preserving our memory to craft our present and future.

Those who yearned to return to their homes in Kashmir are long dead. An entire generation was wiped out in the camps. What's left now is residue. This residue has now begun to cast a long shadow on our own personal histories.

But history never dies. History speaks through those who were trampled by it.

The questions I ask are: Who am I? What happened to us? What will become of us years from now? How should we live? How should we understand our history and its impact on us?

I must pause here . . . I can't go on . . .

But I must go on . . . no matter what . . . I will go on . . . I will tell you everything. Stories, accounts and incidents that should never have to be told for the deep suffering that they hold—the kind of suffering that no human has the capacity to face or bear. But, humanity and even beauty, are born out of such suffering.

1

At Least We Are Safe

Evening
March 1990
Jammu

The truck pulls over by the roadside of this strange place that I've never wanted to go to. Behind me is the setting sun, which shone brightly over the dew in the courtyard of my ancestral house earlier that day.

In the morning, we were in our home in Srinagar, Kashmir. Now, ten hours later, we are here, in this unknown and unfamiliar city.

In the truck is the Koul family: Ratni Aunty, Chaman Lal Uncle, his father, Baisaab (the retired police constable), their two daughters and son—Babli Didi, Choti Didi and Kuka Bhaiya, Henna and me.

What are we going to do? What is going to happen to us? Where are we going to go? Can't we just turn back? Can't we just go back home? What if I close my eyes and open them again? Maybe this bad dream will end then. And when I wake up, I will be in my room, happy and about to go to bed.

Throughout the journey, I kept praying with my eyes closed that this is just a ride and that we will turn back after the next milestone. Now that we are here, all my efforts to dismiss this reality as a bad dream have gone in vain.

The 'there-is-no-turning-back-now' expression on some people's faces crushes all my hopes. This is reality. It won't go away even if I close my eyes or look the other way. What do I do now?

Henna is still asleep. She will likely become hysterical when she wakes up and finds herself in a truck in a strange place. What do I tell her? What will I do when she asks for Ma and Pa? She is not even ten. How am I supposed to look after her when I am lost and clueless myself? But I'm all she has here. I am her big brother and I must perform my duty, not only as her brother but also as her sole caretaker and guardian. This is what Ma told me.

People surround our truck and start examining us curiously as if we are an exotic species. The expressions on the faces of some seem to indicate, 'One more family. Safe and sound. Lucky people.'

'We have reached, Panditji,' says the driver, sensing our confusion. 'Get hold of a labourer and get your luggage off the truck quickly so that I can leave before it gets dark. I must reach home before midnight. Look at this chaos here. This is an everyday affair now.'

'Where are we? Which place is this?' asks Baisaab.

'Jom,' says Kuka Bhaiya.

'But you had said we would be back home by evening. This doesn't seem like home. Where have you brought me?'

'Where do you want to go, Panditji?' asks the driver. 'You have somewhere to go?'

Eyes meet eyes, faces meet faces! An expression of relief on the faces of some, and a shadow of horror and disbelief on the faces of others.

Soon, it becomes clear to us that these people are searching for familiar faces—loved ones, acquaintances, neighbours, relatives, people they have known and heard of.

Strange questions are thrown at us.

'What took you so long? You could have been killed like the others . . .'

'Have you seen Rattan Lal Koul and his family? From Anantnag? They were supposed to leave this morning and should have been here by now . . .'

'Are you from Baramulla? Are there any Pandits left there?'

'You are from Srinagar? How many were killed yesterday? Is it true that the city has been taken . . . ?'

There is a man sitting on the pavement; his gaze is fixed on the trucks lined up by the road. He is counting using his fingers.

Twenty-six . . . twenty-seven . . . thirty-two . . . forty-eight . . . hundred and nine . . .

'You should have come here in January itself. There is not an inch left anywhere here. Where will you go now?'

'Stop panicking. The government will help us . . .'

Some bystanders and local shopkeepers pitifully gape at the chaos that has ensued. Their stares are terrifying, but laden with questions: 'Look at these poor, hapless people. They look more dead than alive. What's going to happen to them? Where will they go?'

At a distance, hundreds of trucks carrying Pandit families line up one after another by the highway. Labourers and porters emerge out of nowhere and offer their services.

A Pandit woman says to her son: 'Where are we? Which place is this? Let's go back home. It is time for dinner. I kept everything ready in the morning itself. Gasha, please take me back home. I beg you. Take me back. Let's all go back . . .'

A husband to his wife: 'Stop blabbering. At least we are safe. At least we will have a place to hide. Look at these people . . .'

A son to his mother: 'At least we haven't been killed . . . Your son is still alive. Think of your brother, whose only son was . . .'

'Rs 10 to Geeta Bhavan and Rs 40 to the camp.'

'Camp . . .' I wonder. 'What is a camp?'

Some more people start screaming and complaining about the ordeal: 'Don't believe a word of what these people are saying . . . The camps are full! There is no room left in any of the camps . . .'

'We have been stranded here for days now . . . We camped up here at the bus terminus last month. At least we have a roof there over our heads . . . Some families are at the railway station . . .'

'But the railway platforms are full, too. They want to throw us out of there as well . . .'

'The authorities are heartless and cruel. There is no end to our woes now . . .'

'But the Dogras . . . They are Hindus . . . They ought to help us . . .'

'There, we had the Muslims to persecute us. And here, these Dogras have neither pity nor sympathy for their fellow Hindus . . .'

'What a shame it is to have nowhere to go in your own country? Where shall we go now? We have gone from one end of the city to another. There isn't an inch left for us to rest our tired limbs . . .'

'These locals have upped the rental fees. For them, we are just bodies, worse than cattle. This is hell . . .'

'Even the school complexes are full . . . The only place left is the stadium . . . It can accommodate a few more people . . .'

'No, no, stop misleading people. There was some room in the stadium until last week. It is overcrowded now. Going there will be a waste of time. Trust me . . .'

'Where are the authorities? Where is the government?'

'The Vishva Hindu Parishad [VHP] people are helping. They are coming in some time.'

'Chai and bread for Rs 2!' an errand boy screams from a roadside tea shop.

'Geeta Bhavan is walking distance from here,' someone says out loud. 'Take your luggage and go there . . . You can spend the night in the temple compound . . .'

'We have no money. How will we carry these trunks?' asks a Pandit man who doesn't know what to do now that they have reached the destination. The expression on his face is one of 'where do we go from here?'

'At least you managed to salvage your things. You have these trunks. We have nothing. We had to leave everything behind.'

Beggars close in on us. A man with a limp is staring at me. Nearby, a squabble erupts among minibus drivers and truck conductors over causing a traffic snarl on the road. Some hawkers push their handcarts closer to the trucks and buses. Crowds of people jostle around.

It seems these tea shops and hawkers have been anticipating this—as if the preparations have been going on for days.

The shops are full of snacks. Sugarcane juice vendors are busy extracting juice and sending errand boys with brimming glasses to customers. There are dirty flies all around the juice carts.

'I am thirsty,' says Henna. 'Can you get me a cola?'

'The houses here seem to have lost their roofs,' an old man points out to his wife, noticing that the houses don't have tin roofs like the ones in Kashmir.

Another old man peeps through the window of a truck that is slowing down to park somewhere on the side of the overcrowded road. 'Have we reached the destination? Do we get off here?' he asks.

Another man is a statue. Even the look on his face is blank. He's not even blinking. It's like the face of a dead man.

Some Pandit youth who seem to have arrived earlier get off a minibus with buckets full of water and bread rolls wrapped in old newspapers. They attempt to bring some order to the descending chaos. Everyone is directionless and dazed.

'How many Pandits were killed today?' asks one man, whose only interest seems to be in knowing the count of the dead. He's been repeating the same question over and over again, despite carrying a newspaper in his hand.

'Don't you know?' says another man standing next to him. 'It's in the newspaper. Read the headline.'

'I am not going to read this wretched newspaper.'

Kuka Bhaiya is talking with some people. We wait and wait.

'We might have to spend the night in a temple complex,' he says. 'But someone is saying we should try our luck in Talab Tillo. We have to wait longer. Meanwhile, you fill the bottles with water and eat. You never know how long we will be waiting.'

Aunty takes some rotis out of a cloth bag and offers one to each of us along with some pickle.

A girl sitting on the pavement looks at us while we munch on the rotis. Her mother gently slaps her, dissuading her from looking at us. 'You ate just now, didn't you?' she whispers.

Around 10 a.m., when our truck briefly stopped to fill up on diesel at Qazigund, Muslim families were assembled along the highway, offering sheer chai* and lavasas to fleeing

---

* Salty tea.

Kashmiri Pandits. A Muslim family wished us a happy journey while offering us breakfast.

We should not have left home in the first place. Or, at the very least, we shouldn't have come to Jammu. It would have been better to go to Delhi. To Nanaji's house there. But what is the point of thinking about all this now? We should have done this. We should have done that. We should not have done this. We should not have done that. For now, I just want to lie down somewhere.

'Register your family immediately,' someone says. 'Only then will you be allotted a tent. You are late . . .'

'They are allotting tents? Where?'

'Don't even think about tents,' says another person. 'They are in pathetic condition. They are all old, used tents . . .'

'At least some have tents . . . What about the rest of us who have nowhere else to go?'

'They are organizing more tents. No one will die here. We are safe here. This is the land of our Hindu brethren.'

'Everyone will be taken care of. Don't panic.'

'Don't worry! Things are being taken care of,' Kuka Bhaiya reassures us once again. 'Someone I know is organizing something for us.'

Ratni Aunty is desperate to settle somewhere.

'Hurry, get back inside the truck,' someone instructs. 'All of you, get back. We need to leave immediately.' The man hops into the driver's cabin and starts giving driving directions.

'If you choose to forgo it, some other family will take it,' he warns. 'Grab the place quickly or else be prepared to spend some more days on the roads of Jammu.'

'Where are we headed?'

'Talab Tillo!'

'How far?'

'Thirty minutes.'

'But I need to leave right now,' says the truck driver. 'You must make alternative arrangements. I can't take you anywhere else . . .'

'Where will we go at this hour, Sardarji? You can see with your own eyes what is going on here. You have seen everything so far. Will you leave us here like this? You have a heart of gold. You saved us and brought us here. Had you not come this morning, we would have been . . . Please don't leave us here on this road. We will be grateful . . .'

In an instant, the driver hops back in, grabs the steering wheel, turns the ignition key, applies the gear, presses the accelerator pedal and gives us a pitiful, comforting look.

'You didn't need to say all this, brother. I won't leave you in the lurch. I won't leave until you have reached some decent place, and are safe and sound.'

'Are we going home now?' asks Baisaab. The sparkle is back in his grey eyes.

'Yes, we are going home,' Kuka Bhaiya replies.

'Don't lie to him,' Aunty urges.

'You tell him the truth . . .'

'Stop, stop,' Kuka Bhaiya says to the driver after what appears to be several minutes. 'Next to that gate . . . over there . . .'

The truck stops next to a large building that looks like a factory.

'Second floor. Hurry!' the man says.

I hear whispers: 'Who are these people now? More people . . . Where is the room for more?'

Some other people are whispering: 'Don't say such things in front of them. We will do something. Remember when you arrived, we made space for you . . .'

The man begs some youngsters to help take the things out of the truck. There isn't much. But there are enough belongings to fill a room. Trunks, hold-alls, bags and sacks containing kitchenware and household things. Some young men come and start unloading the truck.

Some women are washing utensils in a basin. Unsettling looks are thrown at us.

'All of you go upstairs. We will bring the luggage,' says a bystander who seems to have a sense of the goings-on.

We climb the stairs and enter a large hall. There are about fifty people in the hall. A woman is trying to light a stove. She spreads a piece of cloth in front of her husband, who is quietly sitting against the wall.

'You will have dinner with us tonight,' another woman tells us. 'In a little while. The rice is coming to a boil.'

Hunger pangs are driving my sister insane and all she wants is something cold to drink.

'I am thirsty. I want cold water.'

'Wait,' I tell her.

I start counting the people in the hall, but I lose count at fifty-seven.

From a cold winter dawn at home to a scorching night in the camp. It's been the longest day of my life.

Only one question remains: What's going to happen now?

Ratni Aunty springs into action, attempting to set up a corner for us. If only there was enough room to set up a corner. Somehow, she manages to create an enclosure.

At last, we sit and dinner is served to us. There is no second helping. The woman serving us dinner places some more rice and vegetables on Henna's plate.

'Tomorrow we will get curd and you can have that too,' she says.

'How and where will you treat us on your fifteenth birthday?' Choti Didi and Babli Didi tease me.

* * *

'When will you take me back home?' Baisaab asks his grandson.

'We will have to be here for a few days,' Kuka Bhaiya replies.

'Don't lie to him,' whispers Ratni Aunty.

'Then what?'

'I had told you, begged you. We should have left earlier. At least, we would have found a better place than this . . . But you never listen to your own mother . . .'

'Whose house is this? I want to go back home. My home . . .'

'Home . . . do you want to get killed? They are killing people there!'

'Nobody will kill me . . .'

'Take his cap off . . .'

'What for? He's not going to lie down and go to sleep. Let him wear it.'

'It is hot here.'

'I will have dinner at home . . .'

'Bhaiya, I am tired. Can I go to bed?' Henna asks me.

'Don't worry, my child, we will make some space for you to lie down,' Ratni Aunty says.

* * *

It's taken just a day to turn us into refugees. At sunrise, we were home, even though the world outside was burning.

'Migrants,' say the locals, looking at us as though we are aliens.

* * *

The First Night

'Bhaiya, I'm thirsty,' Henna whispers in my ear. 'Will you get me some water? It doesn't have to be cold.'

I get up, tiptoe over dozens of people and, in the darkness, go in search of water. I return empty-handed. There is not a drop anywhere. The only faucet down the corridor is dry. Even the basin is dry.

'Fresh water will be pumped in the morning,' says a woman lying down next to us. 'Wait for some more time. Dawn is only an hour away.'

'Bhaiya, what are these marks on my hands and feet? Wrap me in a sheet, please?' Henna mumbles in her sleep. She's too exhausted to even open her eyes. And she's terribly thirsty. Her lips are dry and cracked. She's hallucinating. Her face is red. It is the heat, coupled with mosquito and bug bites. It's hot as hell here.

I look at my watch again. The hour hand is at three. The minute hand is trembling, struggling to climb any further. Henna's thirst is unbearable. I get up and walk towards the makeshift kitchen at the other end of the hall. A shadow follows me. I lift the lids off the two earthen pots that I find there. The pots are empty but smelly.

Henna mumbles in her sleep, 'You are right, Bhaiya. Dawn is only an hour away. Will you get me a cola in the morning?'

Light filters in through the ventilator. She rests her head on my arm and falls asleep.

The Second Night

A centipede is crawling on her neck. It's headed straight for her ear. The woman is asleep. If the centipede enters her ear, it will lay an egg there. The egg will hatch and a centipede will be born inside. It won't come out. The woman will lose her hearing. She will die of pain. The centipede shouldn't get inside her ear. I'm afraid of centipedes. They are vengeful insects. They take revenge by crawling into your ears and laying eggs in them. It is 3 a.m. The shadow has multiplied. When will it stop hounding me? When will the sun rise? When will the cow moo? One more hour and the centipede will go away.

The Third Night

Strange sounds of touching and licking! Hushed whispers!

> She: 'Don't do that.'
> He: 'One last time.'
> She: 'No.'
> He: 'Please . . .'
> She: 'Stop.'
> He: 'I'm dying.'
> She: 'So am I.'
> He: 'I'm begging you . . .'
> She: 'No.'
> He: 'Why?'
> She: 'You are killing me.'
> He: 'How can I? I am your servant.'
> She: 'Spare me . . . There are people around . . .'
> He: 'No one will notice.'
> She: 'The little girl is awake.'
> He: 'Let me place my hand there.'
> She: 'Do what you wish. I hope I die tonight.'

I insert my fingers into Henna's ears. She should not hear any of this.

The two of them carry on endlessly until the woman falls silent.

The Fourth Night

I sense the woman's touch. She gives me a kiss, leaving an earthy smell on my cheek. She seems to be dreaming at last. Her dreams are my reality. My dreams are her reality. Time changes hands. I miss the old man. I wonder where he is. What must they have done to him? His spit stains are all over the mattress. His laughter and weeping still echo off the walls. His reflection is still trapped in the broken mirror. His absence is more horrifying than his presence. It has turned me into his equal.

What the day gives, the night takes. The night is a stone grinder. It grinds everything that passes through it—even dreams. I long for the night to bring me the light of a distant star. The moon is watching everything. I wonder what she sees and hears.

The Fifth Night

Rain is lashing against the roof. Water trickles off the walls of the barn. It enters the hall and brings the smell of dung. The cow hasn't mooed tonight. The shadow has started to tremble. I want to drink rainwater just like I wanted to eat snow the night I came here. But I'm not thirsty tonight. One more dream before the light breaks.

The Sixth Night

The old man is sobbing.

'Your wife is dying,' the grandson blurts into his ear.

'What?' cries the hard-of-hearing old man.

'Your wife is being beaten. She won't survive the night. Look over there, how she cries like a child!'

The old man gives out a feeble cry. 'Please stop! Don't do this to her. What has she done to you to deserve such treatment? Have mercy! Please, I beg you. Stop . . .'

'She's still crying. She's in pain.'

'No, no, please . . . Don't do this. Oh God! Please do something . . .'

I want the act to stop. I pretend to be asleep. I bury my head deep inside the rugged blanket. My mother's shawl is my pillow. The hour and minute hands on my watch haven't moved since I last looked. Time stretches on. Outside, a buffalo moos. No, the buffalos and cows are not outside. This is their house. They are downstairs in the hall. They don't like the sight of us. After all, this has been their home for years. The old man closes his eyes. His head is resting against the wall. A tear has stained his sunken cheek. A smile has come to settle on his cracked lips. The rash on his nape has turned ashen. He's quiet at last.

The Seventh Night

The old man is back. He's no ordinary man. He's a retired police constable, who until a few days ago, was the lion of his neighbourhood. Powerful and free, he is now at the mercy of his grandson, who, during the day, thinks the man is a burden, but loves him at night. He cries and caresses his sores. He rubs talcum powder on his body. He throws his arms around him and makes him drink water from his hand as if he were his child.

'You are my son and I am your father,' he says.

The old householder sits pensively with a frown frozen on his face. A beautiful woman is prostrate on the floor. She covers her head and buries her face in a bundle of clothes tied together, doubling up as a pillow. She doesn't want to see anything. She moves closer to the man's feet and plants remorseful kisses on them. 'Teach me how to be happy,' she pleads. 'Teach me how to bear the pain. Teach me how to conquer fear.'

Dear Pa,

I'm writing to you because I'm not able to talk to you. Don't read this letter now. Read it when I am gone. Someone keeps looking at me all the time. When I am washing my clothes at the canal. When I am fetching water from the well. When I am asleep. When I am putting on clothes. When I am alone in the hall. Maybe the watcher is just an apparition. Maybe the shadow has come off the wall to take me away. Maybe I am hallucinating. But the gaze marks on my body are real. How do I make the marks vanish?

Night after night, it's the same dream. I can't utter what I see and hear. It's a curse. When will the dream end?

Tomorrow, one more day will be put to death. Yet, no one will mourn the passing of days. Yama will come for me to feast on my bones. What will I offer when I have nothing left to offer?

My yesterday is my tomorrow. What if it doesn't return?

I will stop now. The night is endless. The sky is lava. A boat is sailing up in the sky. There are no sails. There's no boatman. A little boy is searching for a place to sit. He gives me his only smile.

Yours always,
S

2

At Least We Have a Place to Hide

Day One

A pall of thick smoke has engulfed the hall. Henna has been thirsty the whole night. We have spent the night sleeping in snatches. Some of the Koul family's household belongings are in the trunks. Ratni Aunty begins setting things up. Bedding, a bundle of clothes and some utensils.

I explain the two compartments of the bag to Henna. 'This is your compartment and this is mine. Your clothes and things are in this compartment and my things are in this one. Here are your toothbrush, soap, cream, towel, water bottle . . .'

I don't reveal that the soap, cream and towel are to be shared.

'I want my own things and my own bag,' Henna insists, throwing a tantrum. She has always wanted to have her own things. But I know her tantrums are short-lived.

Henna is nine. Six years younger than me.

Now that the sun is up, I survey the building. This place is a buffalo shed. There are cows and buffaloes on the ground floor. There is a large hall full of hay.

Is this where we're supposed to live? The entire place is smelly. I remember the day, years ago, when I asked Pa if we could keep cows in the new house we were going to build that year in Ompora, a posh neighbourhood on the outskirts of Srinagar. And Pa had agreed. I had then made plans to get a cow and a calf from Pampore.

Kuka Bhaiya works for a pharmaceutical company. He misses his Yezdi motorbike. He left many things behind. Among those things was his bike, too. 'I will go back soon to get the rest of the things,' he says.

Everyone has practically left all their belongings behind. Babli Didi taught me Hindi. But now there is neither adequate space nor time for Hindi lessons, although she ensures I devote some time to studies every day. Chaman Uncle is full of love. He offers Henna his share of food and so does everyone else. Such is their love for her. She is everyone's darling here. She was everyone's darling in our neighbourhood in Srinagar, too.

'Keep aside some morsels of rice and vegetables, especially for the stray dogs in the compound,' says Uncle.

An old man is constantly looking at the ceiling, wondering what to do next.

'What is the point of getting up?' he thinks. 'What is to be done with the day?'

What are Ma and Pa doing right now? How are they? How is everything at home? Should we have stayed behind and not rushed off? Should we have waited for one more day? We would not have landed up here at this place. This place that has no drinking water. This place that belongs to cows and buffaloes. This place that is not ours.

Perhaps I will be able to return after a few days. Henna and I can't continue living here. We will board a bus back to Srinagar in a few days.

The voices of children and the moos of cows waft in from the backyard downstairs.

A woman from the adjacent room starts talking to me.

'What is your name? Where are you from? Is she your real sister? Her eyes and skin colour are like those of a foreigner.'

A child is playing with a wooden toy. The woman's father-in-law hums a prayer and breaks down, unable to recollect it.

'Thank God the governor saved us. He is our saviour. Otherwise, we would have ended up like Roshan Lal,' blabbers a man.

'You seem to be from the city,' the woman says. 'Where is your family? Are they alright?'

'Don't look so sad. You are safe now.'

'We are ruined. What shall we do now?' wails another woman.

The Pandit families have set up at least a dozen makeshift kitchens in the hall. There is also a common kitchen for new arrivals. Even now, people keep coming here looking for room in this building. But there is none, though some people believe that space can be created if we are a bit more ingenious and accommodating.

'We can't take in any more people now,' a man tells a group of men who keep bringing in new arrivals. 'Not even an ant! What will it take for you to understand this simple thing? Don't bring any more people here or else we will . . .'

'Where do I take them? The ground floor has some room, right?'

'You mean next to the buffaloes?'

'The hay room? The landlord is happy for us to bring some more people to be adjusted in the hay room. He is giving us a discount.'

'Look around! Look at us! What do you see? Do you see any space?'

'We have to put our children on our laps.'

The argument is endless.

'Both parties are right . . .' mumbles an old man. 'But let them sort it out amicably. I must not intervene in the affairs of the young people. They live in a world of their own.'

Another family starts placing their luggage down the hall next to other people's belongings. Odd things emerge from baskets and tin cans. Electric fittings, bulbs, lanterns, keys, clogs, idols, photos, ornaments, a stone mortar, a pestle, a radio, a winnowing basket, a broom, hand fans made of willow stems, brass vessels and some strings.

'Come, I will show you the way to the toilet,' says one person.

'There is only one latrine–bathroom for the entire building. It would be best if you could wait until the afternoon . . . Let the elders go first, as they need to go out and get on with their day. And the women need to do their puja and then begin cooking. There is another bathroom downstairs in the backyard, but it is not as clean as this one. But it's okay. It is only a matter of a few days . . . We will have to get hold of a sweeper . . . the regular sweeper hasn't shown up for days . . . Until then, we will take turns cleaning the latrine ourselves . . . Tell your sister to cover her nose when she steps inside. Ask her to be quick when she has to go to the toilet. Don't be long. Use water judiciously. You will have no more than two bottles per day. There is no regular water supply here. We have to pay for the tankers . . . You can go to the canal to take a bath, but be careful. Three kids are already missing. Maybe they drowned . . . Stay away from the strays . . .'

There is a guava tree in the courtyard, but it hasn't borne any fruit yet. It's the first time I've seen a guava tree.

Two men are talking.

'We can't let any new families in now. There is no room left.'

'We will die in this heat.'

'But . . . what if we . . . ? Let's try and make some room on the ground floor.'

'That's for the buffaloes.'

'I think we can create some extra space.'

'At least there is a basin full of water.'

'Would you drink that water?'

'Not for drinking, but for washing purposes.'

'It's better to go to the canal! The water is cold and fresh.'

'Have you noticed how men gather there to ogle at our women?'

'Ogling is the least of our worries.'

'But still, you know what they did to . . .'

* * *

A newborn, wrapped in a sheet, is crying incessantly. The child's parents are distraught. The mother seems to have forgotten everything. She can't take her eyes off her baby. She clings to the baby as if it were all she had. She sings a lullaby—a song of home.

We're going to take you home.
Are you ready to go home? O prince of Pampore.
Your grandma and grandpa have been waiting.

She places the infant on an old man's lap. A smile flashes on the newborn's lips. The old man's lips quiver. A new lease on life to a man whose journey is coming to an end. His 100 years are almost up! Grandson and grandpa have the same smile and the same blood. Their histories converge here, but their destinies will part in the time to come.

'What will we give our children?' asks the father.

'These are the times when our children will have to give us a reason to live,' the infant's grandpa mumbles.

Three other women are pregnant. They have the same look on their faces. They talk to one another while attending to their daily affairs. What will they do when the day comes? I don't want to be around when . . . But what if?

Some Days Later

More families have arrived. Some men are talking in hushed tones. The same refrain.

'How is the situation in Kashmir? Any more killings?'

'No. Not in our neighbourhood. All the Pandits have left. No one is left behind . . .'

'Did you bring along everything?'

'Almost everything!'

'I saw Shadi Lal and his wife in the temple last evening. They were alone. They don't know where their sons are. They have nothing with them.'

'Where are they staying?'

'They got into a similar camp near the Raghunath temple, but they can't adjust there. So, they spend their days in the temple and go to the camp only to sleep at night.'

'This will not last forever. We will return home soon.'

Many elders have been abandoned by their sons. They have been left to fend for themselves. They are alone and helpless. They have nowhere to go. They have nothing except hope. The hope that their sons will return. There is only one wish on their lips: 'Our children will come back for us and take us with them.'

Baisaab has no means to shave. He can't locate his shaving kit.

'Maybe it is hidden among the other things,' Aunty reassures him.

'Why fret over a shaving kit? The kit should be the least of his worries,' she mutters to herself. The truth is not to be disclosed.

'I will find it for you,' Aunty says to him.

Kuka Bhaiya takes me along to explore the place—the vegetable market, the grocery stores, the dairy and the water tankers supplying drinking water. We go from one area to another, from one camp to another. There are people everywhere. It's as though a mela is taking place here, with a gathering of people from all over Kashmir.

In the hall, children are running around playing hide-and-seek and other games. Their mothers and fathers are constantly yelling at them for creating a din.

'This is not a picnic, you brats . . .'

'Do they have any idea what's going on?'

'We are better off with their ignorance. Let them be. They are kids, after all . . .'

An old woman sits still the whole day with beads in her hands. She counts the trunks to know which family has the most household items. There are families who came with just one or two pieces of luggage and others who arrived empty-handed.

'The end is here,' a man says.

'Stop this nonsense. Have faith!' the old woman shouts.

'Faith in what?'

'God, who else? Be a man. Stand up on your feet and stop whining . . .'

'She is right,' another man says, adding, 'you must do something.'

'He is such a useless man,' the old woman says. 'We've lost everything—our house, our shop and our orchard. We are finished. And here is this maharaja, sitting here all day, doing nothing, thinking that his servants will come and serve him. Go and do something worthwhile, Mr Maharaja. Find something useful to do. Be a man.'

'What do you want me to do? Is there anything worthwhile left for me to do?'

Another woman starts humming.

At least we haven't been evicted . . .
At least we have this bread to share . . .
At least we haven't been made to part . . .
This will be over soon . . .
At least we are still . . .

'Are you mocking me?' asks her husband, sitting in a corner.

'You and your "at leasts". That's all you do the whole day. Recite verses . . .'

'These are my verses. I am a poet. What do you want me to do? Dance to your tunes?'

'Help me chop vegetables . . . The least you could do is arrange for some rations instead of wallowing in poetry . . . Go to the ration ghat [shop] now . . . We have mouths to feed . . .'

'There is no ration ghat here. Ration ghats are in Kashmir. Here, we have the relief office.'

'Go to the relief office then. Get us some more relief.'

'The 6 kilos of rice allotted to us for the month are over?'

'I am having to feed the ones who are yet to register at the relief office to be eligible for the monthly relief. Where will the poor folks go?'

'Because they couldn't bring along their documents . . . ?'

The argument doesn't end. One thing is certain: we don't exist without our documents. We are nothing. Documents mean food and shelter.

'How would they have gotten documents? Their houses were torched. They have nothing.'

Who are these people? Where have they come from? What's going to become of them? I think Ma and Pa are better off. At least they are home.

A little girl plays tirelessly the whole day and creates a din in the hall. Her brother sits in a corner. He seems mentally disturbed and keeps making strange voices continuously.

'Be patient. We will leave soon and go to a better place,' the girl's mother says to her.

'When will your *soon* come, Ma?' the girl asks.

To me, she will always be the *soon* girl.

* * *

Three Months Earlier
Residency Road
Jammu

Pa and I reach Jammu from Delhi where we spent a few days. We go to the tourist reception centre to buy two tickets to Srinagar. At the ticket counter, we are told that the national highway is closed due to bad weather and landslides. 'The highway is being cleared. Wait until tomorrow.'

'Could you make an advance booking for us? On the first bus out of here to Srinagar tomorrow . . .'

'All the seats in A-Class buses are booked.'

'We are okay travelling B-Class.'

'Even the B-Class is sold out. You will have to wait.'

We will have to spend a few more days here.

In a restaurant, Pandits are speaking in hushed whispers. Outside on the road, they are saying strange things. 'Things are taking a turn for the worse in Kashmir. It is better to leave and go to Jammu for a while, until the situation normalizes . . .'

Something is not right.

We go to a restaurant, where Pa bumps into a friend who's rushing through his lunch.

'My wife and I are not going back,' he says. 'You mustn't either. Call your family here. Ask them to board a bus and come here . . .'

'The highway is closed. We are going back as soon as the highway opens.'

'You will be committing the biggest mistake of your life if you go back now. Don't you know what's going on there?'

It begins raining. I am sick of this place. I pray for the highway to open so that we can take the first bus out of here.

After a couple of days, we manage to get two seats on a bus home to Srinagar. Srinagar is a different place when we get there. It seems as though a war is about to erupt.

But I am happy to be home. I vow never to leave home again.

* * *

I am happy yesterday is gone. It was the worst day ever.

The days are all alike here. We go through the same routine every day—the same rut. Wake up, go in search of water, wait for our turn to use the latrine–bathroom, wash our clothes, guard the clothes drying out in the sun, eat, while away our time, wait for evening to fall, wait for dinner, sleep . . .

'These youths here are . . .' Kuka Bhaiya says irately, 'They think we are pests and will assault their sisters. While it is the other way around. Be careful of the boys and men. They have their eyes on our girls and women. They come to ogle and tease. They won't spare anyone, not even you. Some come on bikes and others in minibuses.'

'Why don't we complain to the police?'

'Nobody is going to bat an eyelid, let alone register our complaints.'

Pandemonium erupts nearby as a chaotic traffic jam makes it impossible for a funeral procession to proceed further. The men start hurling swear words at one another. Minibuses honk incessantly. The bus conductors have taken matters into their own hands and are directing passers-by and traffic towards the lanes. Traffic policemen are nowhere in sight. Hawkers start yelling.

Several Days Later

I should not have had the sugarcane juice from the roadside vendor. I've never had it before in my life. But what choice did I have? The heat has been driving me insane. I sometimes feel like jumping off the Tawi bridge into the river. I am sick now. I throw up by the roadside. My stomach aches. I am going to die. I lie next to a drain.

It is the ice. The infected water. Flies settled on dung and excreta, hopping from one food item to another. Viruses and bacteria. The intolerable humidity. I will never buy anything from the roadside vendors again. My precious money has gone to waste. I won't have any money left now. What am I to do?

I hear nothing from home. There is no word about Ma, Pa, Babi and Babuji. I have no idea how they are or where they are. There is nowhere to go and no one to inquire with. I can only hope that they are okay and safe. And that our neighbours will protect them in case . . .

R and I start exploring the different localities in the city. What else do we do? Choti Didi and Babli Didi look after Henna while I am gone. Sometimes, Kuka Bhaiya takes me along and buys us lunch at a dhaba. He treats me to butter chicken and naan. One day, he buys two bottles of chilled beer and I taste beer for the first time. The days are hot. I am not used to such weather. I enjoy the taste of chilled beer.

R wants to become an engineer. 'I want to go to an engineering college,' he says. 'What about you?'

I think of an answer, but I don't know yet. What I do know is that I am not good at mathematics and science subjects, such as physics, chemistry and biology. I've never been good at these subjects! Taking the Class Ten board examination was an ordeal. I wasn't certain of clearing any of the subjects except English.

My interest in studying is dwindling. I hate taking exams. I don't know if I'm good at anything.

R lives in a rented place across the road, opposite the Shiv Temple. That place is also a camp for several displaced Pandits. The camps are where we live between two meals a day. Where nothing happens except waiting.

When food is served in the evenings, we eat slowly. We don't want the meal to end but it does in no time. We remain hungry, but there is no second helping. We eat small morsels, not big ones. Why small morsels? Because the portions on our plates are small. What is the point? We eat slowly until we are full. We are never full. But we tell ourselves that we are full and can't eat another morsel. We trick ourselves into believing things that are not true. It has taken me weeks to do so. It is cruel, but what choice do I have? Henna isn't convinced, but she is used to it now. She dreams of a day when she's finally back home, with Ma placing a plateful of food in front of her and Babi feeding her with her hands, but she can't eat anymore because she is full.

There are evenings when all I want is some more rice. That's all. Nothing else. I don't even mind having less curry. But there are no leftovers. Rice shouldn't be such a luxury, should it? It shouldn't even be something to ask for . . . But how do I . . . ?

Tonight, I dream of home again.

It is a bright afternoon. The sun is out after two months. It is the gentlest of the suns. You can stare at it for hours. It allows you to look at it.

The snow is melting and the patches of grass are back. Children are playing in Pajnu's playground as if there was no yesterday and there will be no tomorrow. I don't want this moment to ever fade. Time should stop. After completing their chores, mothers rush to windowsills to look at their sons and daughters play. They are smiling. There is food in the kitchen. Ma has cooked mutton. There is rice and apple jam too. No one will sleep hungry tonight.

* * *

Baisaab is dreaming once again. But he's lost his childlike smile. A frown plays on his lips. I whisper into his ear, 'I dreamed a dream in which you were happy after a long, long time. You were so happy that you started crying.'

'I want to die a happy man . . . I don't want to die . . . Take me home please . . . Do something . . . They won't take me home, but I have faith in you . . . I know you love me more than anyone else . . . No one loves me more than you do . . . I have some money in my pocket . . . For the fare . . . Go and

buy two tickets . . . Go right away before I die . . . Take me
home . . . I don't want to die here . . .'
    Oh God! Put an end to his horrible nightmare.
    'I have no place here. Pray for my death. May it happen
tomorrow. Why wait! I should go tonight itself . . .'

* * *

Days mean nothing more than aimless wanderings. Everything
seems futile. Sometimes, all I wish for is to go back home,
sleep in my room and never wake up! I wish for a meal cooked
by Ma and Babi. I wish all this were a bad dream and that
I would wake up soon and all this would be forgotten like a
bad dream. It seems like a bad dream. What else is it?
    Days are also full of hectic yet heroic parleys, encounters
and adventures. Going from one place to another in search
of better accommodations. Maybe a one-room set or a two-
room set. If only I had some money. Kuka Bhaiya is doing his
best to make ends meet. After all, he's the sole breadwinner.
His grandfather's pension needs to be sorted out.
    We live in an alien city now. All of us are lost souls here.
People don't even recognize each other. Something terrible is
happening to each of us.
    I see houses and the families living in them. They have
gardens. They have safe and loving homes to go back to in the
evenings. I see strange looks in the eyes of local Dogra kids
my age who are staring at us displaced Pandit kids. They even
attend school. This area is named after Mahatma Gandhi. It's
the poshest neighbourhood in Jammu. I can't bring Henna
here for if she sees the ice cream parlours here, she will throw
a tantrum.
    R lives with his parents. It's a blessing to have your parents
around you at the camp. He's lucky to have them. At least he

has a good reason to return to the camp once we are done loitering during the day. His mom cooks for him. He invites me to his camp for dinner.

'Mom wants to see you,' he says. 'I keep telling her about you. She says she knows your father, Professor Gigoo, from her college days in Anantnag. She wants to know if I am speaking the truth or not. That you really are here and that I am not spinning a yarn. "Bring him over for food," she told me . . .'

I am reminded of the time when I would invite friends and classmates over for parties at our home in Kashmir. Birthday parties were fun. Ma baked the most delicious chocolate cakes. Will those days ever return?

'This city is not for me,' says R. 'I will go mad. So will my dad and mom. I see Mom crying when she thinks no one is looking. I am helpless. Why did this happen to us? What did we do to deserve this? I want us to go back home.'

R finds solace even in my false assurance, such is his desperation. He is at a stage where even a touch could make him cry. But he doesn't cry. He struggles to remain calm and brave.

R reveals they might shift to another camp. 'A better place,' he says. 'Where there is a fresh supply of water for at least a couple of hours every day.' I agree. We are all fed up with having to live without adequate water. Even drinking water is being rationed out to two bottles per person per day.

R takes me to his place. There, I see an old man quietly sitting in a corner, asking the same question over and over: 'Is it lunchtime?' No one answers him. R says everyone is fed up with him because it's not that he's even hungry.

'He is irritable,' R says. 'Perhaps he misses his family. You should watch him shout at everyone at night. He does not sleep for hours and keeps cursing us. No one knows where he is from. He was seen wandering near the marketplace until some passers-by brought him here. No one has any clue about his family or their whereabouts. He first spent days and nights in a shed near a temple. He had not bathed for days. When he was brought to this camp, he pleaded for food.'

The camp has a foul stench. The kitchen sink is littered with unwashed utensils. The women have collected drinking water in large and small vessels. 'Are you going to stay here?' someone asks me, thinking I am a new arrival in need of accommodation.

R's mom has made the most sumptuous of dinners. I am too shy to tell her that I want to bring Henna too, and stay for the night. This place is not as cramped as ours. It doesn't smell as bad as ours. It smells of food. Perhaps I am biased. The grass is always greener on the other side. Kuka Bhaiya, Choti Didi and Babli Didi worry about me if I am out of sight even for a moment.

'You are our responsibility until your father and mother are here to take you back. They trusted us and handed the two of you over to us.'

I get to know some facts about the two buildings. One of the two-storeyed buildings is owned by a wealthy trader who used a part of it to store hay for his buffaloes. When he saw Pandits from Kashmir descend upon the town in thousands, he rented out the building.

The women spend the days sorting out the things they have salvaged. They count the items, dust them and arrange them carefully in the trunks. This has now become a regular activity while the men are out. Women show one another their belongings and narrate how they came to acquire them and under what circumstances the possessions were salvaged. Some of the things are family heirlooms, having been handed over from generation to generation, from mother-in-law to daughter-in-law and from grandfather to father to son. Some women boast of their possessions but refuse to take them out of the trunks and boxes, saying that there is no need to unpack since it is only a matter of a few days before they return home.

The old man possesses nothing except a bundle of clothes. A few shirts and a couple of pairs of trousers. That's all. He says that his sons will come for him soon. Sometimes he speaks of his riches. 'What is the hurry?' he says when asked how long his children will keep him waiting. 'They must be looking for me. They will come for me when it is time to go home. They can't live without me.'

R whispers to me that he has seen the old man sob silently.

* * *

People bring news that the results of the Class Ten board examination held last year are being announced on the radio and have also been published in all the local newspapers.

I pass with a first-division rank. Many of my classmates are distinction holders. Two of them—Archana Koul and Amit Koul—have secured the first and the second positions. Their photographs are in the newspapers. Their future is bright, as they will get admission to any good school. But I don't know where they or my other friends and classmates are. I have no idea which camp or place they are in.

I am eager to bump into my best friends, at least. Every day I pray that I get to see them on some road here or in some camp nearby. If I am to search for them in Jammu, I will have to go from one camp to another or from one house to another. Rahul, Anil, Sunil and Neetu—my best friends. We had promised to stay together through thick and thin under all circumstances, go to college together, dream the same dreams and remain united in our resolve to never let anyone separate us.

They must be somewhere in the city. In some camp or a house their parents might have rented. The good old days of our togetherness in school and outside school seem like a fantasy now—something that never happened, a figment of imagination.

'You will get to meet your classmates,' says Kuka Bhaiya. 'They must be somewhere here. Almost everyone is here. There is nobody back there in Kashmir except your parents . . .'

Days later, when I receive the mark sheet, my fears come true. I have the lowest marks in English (Part A)—twenty-eight out of eighty-five. This is what that Muslim invigilator wanted. He wanted me to fail in the subject I loved the most.

* * *

I am now trying to get used to living like this. There has been no word from Ma and Pa so far. But at last, my prayers are answered. Pa's colleague brings reassuring news.

'Your dad is in Udhampur. He's staying with the Aimas, who have rented a house there. He doesn't want you to worry. He doesn't want to come to Jammu yet. Udhampur is better, he says. You know how unreasonably adamant he can get at times . . .'

I decide to see him, so I board a bus to Udhampur the next day. My only mistake is miscalculating the travel time from Jammu to Udhampur. The journey takes me almost half a day as the bus keeps stopping every fifteen minutes to take on more passengers. I reach Udhampur in the afternoon and manage to locate the house that the Aimas have rented. Udhampur is a breezy town. I see the mountains again. Snow is still shining on the peaks. Beyond the mountains is Kashmir.

At last, I am united with Pa. I get to spend a couple of hours with him.

'We shifted to Indira Nagar last month,' says Pa. 'To Dr Dewani's place, since it was vacant. They are in Delhi. Go back to Jammu this evening. I will bring Babi, Babuji and your mother here soon. I have seen a two-room set that seems good for us. The best so far after searching the entire town. We will take it for now. Will pay an advance so that we don't lose it. The landlords are a good joint family. Their daughters are studying at the Degree College. They respect me.'

Aima Aunty feeds me lunch and packs some food for my return journey, though she insists that I stay for the night. 'Why don't you bring Henna here and you both can stay here until your dad brings your mom and grandparents here?' It's a good idea, but I know the Kouls will worry. Moreover, they have been taking good care of us, sacrificing their own comfort for the sake of our small comforts. This isn't the first time they've done this. They have been taking care of us ever since we were born.

'You both are ours,' they say. Babi has also said the same thing many times. 'You both are theirs.'

Kuka Bhaiya says I am his only brother. He says he can't live without me. Babli Didi and Choti Didi say the same thing about Henna.

* * *

Baisaab has stopped talking. All my attempts at getting him to speak and be cheerful are in vain. But there are times he gives Henna and me a smile, as if he knows we need it the most. When nobody else is looking. It is the smile of a child. He has lost some more teeth and stopped complaining of pain. He doesn't even say that he wants to be taken home anymore.

Some Days Later

Baisaab is missing. He may have run away or lost his way back to the camp. I hope he is safe, wherever he is. But I can't keep bad thoughts at bay. What if he is . . .

* * *

June 1990

My maternal grandfather, Pushkar Nath Dhar, whom I call Papa, shows up and manages to locate us in the camp. He is furious, seeing my sister and me in such a condition, but controls his temper. At first, he doesn't say a word. His stare does all the talking and scolding. Then, he isn't able to hold back any longer . . .

'Do you realize for how long I have been trying to find both of you?' he fumes. 'What it has taken me to reach here? I searched everywhere. I almost gave up hope, going from one camp to another. Finding a needle in a haystack may be easier, but finding you has been the most difficult thing I've had to do in my entire life. I can locate lost aeroplanes in the sky, but you two . . . (Papa is the air traffic controller at Palam Airport, Delhi). Why didn't you ring me? Why didn't you come to Delhi straightaway? You're not a child anymore. You're supposed to know things. You could have taken a bus, train or taxi to Delhi. I should be taking care of you! Unlike others, you have a choice, don't you? Don't you realize that you have a home in Delhi? Look at your sister. Look what has become of her . . .'

I have no answers. He is in tears. I decide not to tell him everything we have been through all these days. After some time, he calms down. 'You are not to blame. Your parents are. They are irresponsible. They should have called me to pick the two of you up!'

The next morning, we are to board a train to Delhi.

Kuka Bhaiya, Choti Didi, Babli Didi, Ratni Aunty and Uncle are sad. They don't want us to leave. But they know it is for our own good. I've never seen them so sad. Not even when we were going through the worst of days. The last few months have changed a lot of things. We have grown closer like never before. Closer than we were to one another when we were in Kashmir. There, we had two huge houses sharing the same compound wall. But there was no such thing as a wall between us! Rooms and rooms everywhere. Two big courtyards. We shared everything. Here, we have nothing. Not even the 10ft x 10ft space in this big hall. This, too, is not ours.

Ratni Aunty and Chaman Uncle are looking at us as if they are being asked to part with their own children.

Henna starts crying when she finds out that we are to leave them behind and go to Delhi.

'You will get a chilled Coca-Cola every day there,' Choti Didi tells her.

Henna cries, 'I don't want Coca-Cola. I want to be with you.' She doesn't let go of Choti Didi's hand as she tries her best not to cry.

'We will meet again. We will be together again,' says Babli Didi.

Kuka Bhaiya whispers into my ear, 'Don't forget me.'

Aunty packs our bags and gives us a hug. We didn't cry the day we left Kashmir. We didn't even cry while parting with Ma, Pa, Babuji and Babi. None of us cried. But today, there are only tears. Nothing else. What has happened to us? The camp has changed us.

The next evening, we reach the Mayapuri flat in New Delhi, where Nani, my uncle, aunt and cousins greet us. Henna is still sad.

Papa has kept a crate of Coca-Cola for Henna. He opens the door of the refrigerator and shows Henna chilled Coca-Cola bottles. 'These are for you,' he says. 'You can have as many as you want . . .'

For the first time in months, Henna's old Coca-Cola smile is back.

Papa sends word for my parents to leave Kashmir immediately. They promise to heed his advice, but they keep him waiting.

He complains to me: 'Don't they read the papers and listen to the news there? They should leave that wretched place. It is hell out there. It's no longer safe for us Hindus anymore. It never was. Everyone has left. They are the only Pandits there now. I have been telling them to come here. If only they would listen . . .'

I am desperate to see Pa, Ma, Babi and Babuji. They must leave Kashmir and go to Udhampur so that Henna and I can join them there. Pa sends a message that he's doing his best to make this possible.

Days pass. I am helpless. I don't know what to do.

* * *

July–August 1990
Delhi–Shimla

Papa reaches Delhi one morning. The next evening, we are to take a bus to Solan to meet his friend, B.L. Dhar. Then we are to go to Shimla to apply for admission to one of the boarding schools there. His friend in Solan has suggested Bishop Cotton School in Shimla. 'It isn't easy to secure admission there, but they may understand the situation and take Siddhartha,' his friend has said.

'We will spend a night at Solan and then go to Shimla. Dhar will put in a word for us . . .'

We reach Shimla and go from one boarding school to another, narrating our story. The gates of Bishop Cotton School are shut. 'Don't even try; there's no point,' someone says to Pa. 'Your son stands no chance. This school is for the children of industrialists, politicians and celebrities.'

Pa doesn't give up. While talking about what we are going through, we become conscious. Are they able to frame the picture in their minds? Will they ever be able to imagine? Maybe they don't believe a word of what we are saying.

'I am sure someone will understand and consider taking a chance on you,' Pa says. He looks tired, but he keeps going. 'We must not give up.'

We submit applications at every school, but we have no certain address to write in the forms. We give the address of Papa's flat in Delhi.

Excuses are thrown at us.

'We are sorry our school has no seats left.'

'Admissions are closed for this academic session. You are late.'

'Your son doesn't meet the admission criteria.'

'Your son doesn't have the marks required for admission to our school.'

'We only consider distinction holders.'

Rejection after rejection . . . I am tired of roaming around here and there. There's no hope.

'We will try schools in Delhi now,' says Pa. 'Maybe we will get lucky there.'

After days of futile pleading with schools in Shimla, we are left with no option but to return to Delhi. All our pleas go in vain.

We are back in Delhi.

In Delhi, we roam from one school to another, presenting our case once again. We visit both big and small schools, hoping to be heard. We apply everywhere but receive the same old responses: 'We are sorry. But we wish you good luck elsewhere.'

Someone gives us another idea. 'Try the schools in Chandigarh . . . Keep trying . . . Be willing to travel down south . . .'

We arrive in Chandigarh early one morning. We go to the Panchayat Bhawan, take a bath, get dressed and reach Sector 10. We knock at the gates of DAV College Chandigarh.

'Which way to the college principal's office?' asks Pa.

Desperation is our constant companion now. We have nothing to lose. There is little time to waste.

We introduce ourselves and present our case.

'You mustn't be shy. Present your case politely,' says Pa.

'You are our last hope, Mr Principal. This college is our last hope . . .' pleads Pa. The principal appears to be a compassionate man. He asks us to sit down and tell him everything.

After listening to the story, he says, 'If you can convince the head of the department of admissions and even one lecturer, I will have no problem admitting your son. You will find them in the staff room at this time. Go right now and tell them everything you have told me . . .'

Pa narrates the story in the staff room. The head of admissions doesn't seem to be convinced at first. 'You are a professor yourself, you will understand the rules . . .' says the man. 'We closed admissions months ago. We wish we could do something.'

'If you want to say no, say it to my son, not to me. Look into his eyes and refuse him. We will go away immediately.'

The man pauses, looks at me and then asks us to follow him. I do exactly what Pa has asked me to do. The man takes us to the admissions office and instructs the staff to allot me a seat reserved for special cases and children of the faculty.

'I am making an exception for your son,' he says to Pa. 'He better meet our expectations.'

'You won't regret it,' says Pa. 'He won't let you down. He won't let the college down.'

Pa thanks everyone in the staff room and the office.

'From one professor to another. You are from our fraternity, after all,' says the dean.

Pa leaves for Srinagar soon after buying me the things I need. Some new clothes, bedding, buckets and stationery.

I am now on my own until . . .

* * *

7 August 1990
Room Number 90,
New Hostel,
DAV College Chandigarh

My dear Papa,

The human heart is a very strange thing. The moment we parted from each other was no ordinary moment for me. I don't know why that little thing inside my chest became my enemy. It gave me some frightful feelings. To be frank, tears came rolling down my cheeks.

In my room, I sat lonely, trying to understand life, but the nectar was nowhere. I didn't go so deep into the well of my thoughts but only struggled through the calm ocean of loneliness. Soon after your departure, a million thoughts engulfed me, but the voice of my knowledge led me to an oasis in a desert. My soul, no doubt, did tremble for some hours, but certain kind thoughts, namely, courage, will, etc., showered their fragrance to embalm it. Then I turned to my diary. I wrote about the day and everything else I keep thinking about.

Afterwards, I experienced a soothing feeling, but my mind was still puzzled. I started talking to myself like a lunatic. I was deprived of company. It seems to me as if life has snatched from me something too precious and too dear. But I am not desperate.

I still remember: 'Where the mind is without fear and the head is held high . . .'

Then suddenly, to my astonishment, a wave of intense feelings came over me, taking my scary thoughts away and leaving behind some beautiful thoughts about enlightenment. I am not frightened now. I've got the right opportunity to peep into my inner self and get to know my weaknesses and my strength to face situations all alone. The time has come for me to seek the right path that leads to the right goal.

Among the people, beneath the naked sky, upon the thorns, I try to go ahead, carrying the lamp of my life on my palm, to join those who have succeeded in giving their lives meaning. My attitude towards life must also be like that. I want to blend my thinking with theirs. I want a tryst with myself to know what I have to do now.

Anyway, this work will go on. I will strive very hard.

I joined the classes today. I find the English professor very impressive. Her name is S. Kapoor and she has a PhD in English. Her way of teaching is tremendously precise. The other teachers are also exceptionally good. I've developed friendships with a few students in my class.

I've got the bank work done. I also got an identity card from the library. I've found the hostel-dwellers to be good. Some are polite and some are indifferent to what happens.

Your words are etched in my mind. I will always walk the path of truth. I think truth is the supreme of all religions. The sanctity of this word lies inside a man. We must alter ourselves in order to spread love in the world, but that change must be guided by certain virtues, namely, truth, goodness and beauty.

Concerning college, I find everything going on nicely, except for one thing. The mathematics professor is not such a good teacher. He is a young person, perhaps inexperienced. I will have to seriously consider this matter. I've bought the books that I need. You needn't worry.

Get everyone at home shifted to Jammu as soon as possible. If I get some holidays, I will go to Delhi. I'm perfectly alright here. If you get a chance, do come and see me here. And please don't smoke.

I will continue writing to you regularly. Please drop me a letter. Note my address:

Siddhartha Gigoo
Roll Number 2849 (Class Ten+1)
Room Number 90, New Hostel,
DAV College, Sector 10,
Chandigarh

Yours ever,
Love,
Siddhartha

* * *

16 August 1990
Room Number 36,
New Hostel,
DAV College Chandigarh

My dear Papa,

In my previous letter, I laid before you my every thought. Now, keeping you abreast of the times, I reveal my feelings, impressions and experiences to you.

You will be relieved and happy to know that a week ago, I shifted from room number 90 to room number 36 in the same hostel. A gentleman came to me and suggested that I share room number 36 with him since I was alone. This nice gentleman is Mohit Khokaran, a Class Ten+2 student from Kasauli. He is good company. When the right time comes, I will lay before you a picture of his nature and the thoughts that usually arise in his mind. Let me understand these things myself first. All that I have gained is company and someone to talk to. At last, loneliness has left me.

I went to Delhi on 10 August. The Punjab Bandh paved the way for a couple of holidays and then we had holidays on 15 August and Janmashtami including Sunday, which totalled five holidays. So everyone in the hostel went home. I returned yesterday. Where else will I go?

Nanaji bought me a night suit, a kurta–pajama set, a t-shirt and some vests. Babi gave me Rs 100. I also talked to Mummy and Babuji on the telephone. Haven't you brought them to Jammu yet? Please do it immediately.

I will go to Panchkula to meet Dr Anil Raina in a day or two. I hope he is back from England.

I attend my classes regularly. I felt feverish earlier today, but I took a tablet and I'm alright now. I think I need tuitions in mathematics. I've written two new poems. I am continuing my writing practice.

I've become accustomed to the kind of food served here. Once a week, I have lunch at a coffee house near our hostel. It is reasonably priced and very affordable too, for the benefit of the students. Masala dosa costs Rs 3.50 and tea costs Rs 1.25 and so on.

Now, I will certainly acclimatize myself to living in this hot climate. The sweltering heat of the plains makes me feel horrible. Sometimes I go out for a walk in the market with my friends. There are many of them around our room.

Ganjoo Sahab of Greater Kailash has handed me a letter introducing me to one of his closest relatives in Sector 8 here, Mr Raj Kumar Bhan. I will go there. Ganjoo Sahab told me that Mr Bhan could help me if needed. Perhaps Mummy knows him.

Mamaji has also given me the address of one of his friends. He's at Ferozepur and working in the Hawkins factory. Anyway, I'm content with my situation. My friend Anil also studies at DAV School, Delhi, and not at Delhi Public School. I met him in Delhi. He came to see me. They are in a camp nowadays and in a bad position. His father is very desperate. Time is responsible for all this.

I'm very worried about you people. If possible, write to me about yourself. How are you doing in Jammu? I don't think you must be happy. Did you reach Jammu safely that day? I'm longing to hear from Mummy. I miss Babi and Babuji very much. I miss Henna and you. I hope we meet soon. Drop me a letter soon.

Love,
Yours ever,
Siddhartha

* * *

26 August 1990
Chandigarh

My dear Papa,

It was a moment of great joy and pleasure for me to go through the kind and soothing words in your affectionate and adorable letters. To be honest, I found myself in a state of tremendous contentment and satisfaction after reading something from someone who is so close and dear to my heart.

I understood from the letters that you must be in a state of uneasiness. I understand that we are in great difficulty. But life is incomplete without such hard times. I can only tell you that one must face such hardships with courage and the will to do things. Time will set everything right.

Our financial condition must be bad, I know. I do realize that we are becoming poorer and poorer.

Papa, our main purpose in fleeing from Kashmir was to be away from death. But can anyone run away from death? I can't understand why people are killing people. Man is not brutal, but mankind is brutal. If I try to think in such terms, I happen to see many mysterious faces among mankind. Many thoughts pass through my mind. The prevailing circumstances are such that man is attempting to conquer mankind. I fear whether they are well aware of the beauty they can create in their lives. But realization has been curbed by the power of man. Men are indulging in various activities that are very cruel and inhumane.

The concept of nation should be brought to an end. There must be no differences between one another, no boundaries and limitations. The relationship between people should be one of love, truth and eternal goodness.

Only then can mankind reach the zenith of survival and sustenance. The duty of man should be to protect man. But this is too good to be true.

I went to Punjab University. There, I met Uncle Anil Raina. He and Aunty took me with them to Panchkula. I stayed there for a couple of days. I found the family to be very kind and loving. Uncle Anil's parents are there as well. They took good care of me. If possible, you must drop him a letter.

Recently, I came across a number of experiences. The college is on an indefinite strike. The students are protesting against the reservations made in favour of the scheduled castes and tribes. I also joined the protest a day ago.[*] The other day, some of them took to mischief and resorted to violence. The police took action against them to maintain order. The students used disrespectful slogans and misused language. They abused the government by using impolite language. I feel bad about this practice.

Dr B.L. Dhar visited me a couple of days ago. We exchanged greetings.

Life is going well. I will have to arrange a tutor for mathematics. In that case, I would need some money after a fortnight. I will inform you then. My bank account number is D-7855, ledger number 25.

Newspaper headlines about Kashmir horrify me nowadays. You must bring everyone to Jammu immediately after arranging accommodation. I'm worried about you. Do keep in touch.

Yours always,
Siddhartha

* * *

---

[*] I did not understand the matter comprehensively at the time.

Evening
31 October 1990
Udhampur

I am in Udhampur to receive Pa, Ma, Babi and Babuji who, at last, are about to reach Udhampur later in the evening. I am waiting near the house that Pa has rented. Bobby Aima, my childhood friend, is there too. Bobby is Aima Uncle's son. Aima Uncle and Pa have been friends and colleagues for years. The Aimas live in a rented house in the housing colony near the traffic check post (TCP).

The truck arrives at 5 p.m. and Babi, Babuji, Pa and Ma get off. We begin unloading the truck. Babi holds me in a tight embrace. 'I will make you puris,' she says, kissing me. 'Find me the stove and the bottle of oil. They are in a trunk. I have the dough ready.'

'There will be enough time to make puris later,' I say to her. 'Let us first get all the things out of the truck.'

'I saw you in my dream,' whispers Babi into my ear. 'Last night . . .'

I am dying to hear all about the dream. Babi's favourite greeting is, 'I saw you in my dream.' Then she narrates the dream for hours—what I was doing in it . . . what she was doing . . . where we were . . . what everyone else was up to . . .

We have a new address:

c/o Chatriwaale
House Number 101
Ward Number 4
Chabutra
Udhampur, J&K State

After seven months, food tastes like home.

I can take a bath without worrying about someone
knocking on the bathroom or running out of water.

I want to know everything that happened at home after
Henna and I were sent away. It is a miracle that Ma, Pa, Babi
and Babuji have survived. Anything could have happened.
The only news from Kashmir has been about the killings of
Pandits who refused to flee.

'What happened after you sent Henna and me away with
Ratni Aunty and family?'

'Some Pandits who didn't want to leave Kashmir shifted to
Indira Nagar next to the Badami Bagh cantonment in Srinagar,'
says Pa. 'After we sent Henna and you away in March 1990,
we too contemplated shifting to Indira Nagar. It was a safer
neighbourhood given the presence of the armed forces in the
cantonment nearby. Some families took shelter in the temples
in Indira Nagar. It was safer there than elsewhere in Kashmir.
We left home for Indira Nagar the day our neighbour, Prithvi
Nath Tiku, was killed. That day, it became clear that we had
to leave. Tiku's killing was the last nail in the coffin, a clear
warning to us, the lone Pandit family in Khankah-i-Sokhta,
that we were next if we refused to leave. Moreover, we had
disregarded many warnings and feelers earlier. Prithvi Nath
didn't deserve to die. He was a noble soul and a saintly man.
But you know how things have been ever since December.
Living in Kashmir is a death sentence, people said. Babuji was
completely shattered the day we left home to go to Indira
Nagar. We were lucky to move into Saiba Dewani's vacant
house there. He and his family had left for Delhi some months
earlier. After being transferred from the Government Degree
College, Anantnag, I joined Amar Singh College in Srinagar
and even taught some classes. Mohammad Abdullah Challoo,
a close friend, came one day and took me with him to the
boulevard on his scooter. Near Nehru Park, Central Reserve

Police Force (CRPF) personnel stopped us and asked us to show our identity cards to them. When one of them saw my identity card, he gave me an intrigued look. He didn't seem to understand my relationship with Challoo. I wanted to go back to our house and salvage my grandfather's and my remaining books, my collection of stones, the latticed windows, the portrait of my great-grandfather painted by S.N. Dhar and many other things. I wasn't allowed to go back. One Pandit, Bansi Lal Bazaz, a clerk in the accountant general's office, left Indira Nagar on his bicycle. He was on the way to his house in Habba Kadal. When he reached Habba Kadal, he was shot by militants . . .'

'What about the other things? Baiji's books, Uncle Gasha's paintings, your paintings and other collectibles?' I ask my father. He shakes his head, saying, 'All pillaged, gone!'

He then narrates the saddest story.

'I had hoped I could go back to our house from Indira Nagar and salvage them. But I was late by a few days. The day I managed to go back home from Indira Nagar, the books and everything else in our house were gone. Nothing remained. Not even a needle! I asked everyone in the neighbourhood. Everyone blamed the security forces. It is the army's doing; it is their handiwork. They are looters. They did it to us too. They keep coming to loot us.'

Those books were my great-grandfather's. Some were very rare books in Latin and Greek. About theology, philosophy and history. An entire library is gone. Gasha's paintings too. Sad!

'Look at the bright side,' Pa continues, 'we didn't lose other things I managed to take along when we moved to Indira Nagar. We could have lost everything. I know people who lost everything. Some of my friends and colleagues. Their houses were looted completely. A friend's old Sharada

manuscripts.* About 40,000 in all. All looted. Nothing can
ever be recovered now . . .'

* * *

Ma has her questions ready: 'How are your studies going on?
Are you getting used to the hostel life in Chandigarh? How
many days will you stay here? When are you planning to go
back to Chandigarh? You must leave soon. No need to worry
about us now. We are going to be fine. Don't compromise
on your studies. Don't miss your classes. Study hard. Your
destiny now lies outside the state. Keep writing to us. Come
here only during the holidays . . .'

* * *

'Panditji, we are nothing in comparison to you and your
scholarship,' says a Dogra neighbour to Pa. 'We are your real
brothers. After all, we are Hindus. You can trust us. We have
so much to learn from you. The Muslims, after all, showed
their true colours. They are not to be trusted.'

I explore the new place: the walls, the courtyard, the
terrace and the staircase leading to the two rooms. A lone
shelf awaits things to be placed on it.

---

* The Sharada script is a native script of Kashmir named after the goddess
Śāradā or Saraswati, the goddess of learning and the main Hindu deity of the
Sharada Peeth. The script was used between the eighth and twelfth centuries
to write Sanskrit and Kashmiri. Many Kashmiri Pandits were in possession of
Sharada manuscripts—handed over from one generation to another.

3

You Are Directed to Leave the Valley in Thirty-Six Hours

Pa's Journal

A Day in 1989
Residency Road, Srinagar

At India Coffee House, 'intellectuals' gather to discuss everything. Often, a political event is 'invented' and endlessly debated. There was a bomb blast in the bathroom of the India Coffee House.* Clearly, a plot to prevent people from going there. The blast at such a place was aimed at spreading fear among those who speak fearlessly. The India Coffee House was a symbol of harmony, freedom and free speech in Srinagar.

---

* The blast became a precursor to the closing of India Coffee House on Residency Road in Srinagar in the summer of 1990. The place, once iconic and popular among the intelligentsia in Srinagar, has remained closed until this day. There are no online references for this, but I am sure archives of print newspapers from Kashmir will have reports. In those days, blasts across Kashmir were an everyday affair.

Discussions are going on about the blast.

'This is the work of Pakistan.'

'This is the doing of Indian intelligence agencies.'

'The CIA is active in Kashmir.'

'The KGB is doing all this.'

'India is a strong country.'

'Pakistan is no less.'

'What is the Indian occupational force doing here?'

Highly imaginative theories are propounded. India, Pakistan, the US, the USSR, etc., are discussed. Pandits say that the 'Indian army is here to protect us (Pandits) and Kashmir'. Others laugh at this bomb blast of 'no significance'. I am among the laughers.

Another Day in 1989

The words on the signboards are written in green paint. Some years ago, it was the three colours of the Indian national flag. Cinema halls have been closed down. The shops that lend or sell film cassettes are also closed. People have been asked not to play cards. I saw a Pandit child in tears who asked his parents, 'Will they take away my pack of cards?'

Another Day in 1989

In the evening, my wife, who teaches in a private school, tells me, 'A few students of Classes Nine and Ten have not been coming to school for many days. Today, I asked my students where they were. A student said that one of them had "crossed". I didn't understand what he meant. Outside the classroom, he told me that the other student had crossed the border. I still didn't understand.'

I tell her, 'Your students are naughty.' And I laugh.

Wife tells me, 'A lovely child studying in kindergarten said to me, "We make firecrackers in our home. Abba has told me not to tell anyone."'

I laugh heartily.

Another Day in 1989

Wife tells me, 'Today, some students fainted in the classrooms. They were admitted to SMHS Hospital for treatment. When some of the women teachers went there to inquire after them, we were asked not to enter the ward. But we entered the ward and saw our students. I don't know what the matter is. The police came to the school and inspected the classrooms. Someone said he smelled gunpowder. School has been closed for one week. The school management is worried.'

This sets me thinking for the first time. What is all this?

March 1990
Eid Gah, Safa Kadal, Srinagar, Kashmir

I am in Eid Gah, a ten-minute walk from my house. So many Muslims are here. A man from Spain tells me, 'I am a convert to Islam. It is the best religion in the world. Why don't you embrace Islam?'

What is going on here? I find Muslims from other countries here. Muslims from other states of India are also here. What do these people want? I understand nothing.

And I don't care.

Eid Celebration in Eid Gah, Srinagar

I go there with my daughter, Henna. Suddenly, there is panic. People start running. There is total confusion. I lift my daughter, place her on my shoulders and run like the others. They say even the chief minister left quickly. I am panting and reach home breathless. What was the matter? I can't even guess. Nobody knows.

A Day in the 1970s
Hotel Ahdoos, Srinagar

Today, I was having tea with my friends. They are well-read and well-informed. They are discussing the politics of Kashmir. One person—an engineer—says, 'Kashmir is the best place for guerrilla warfare. We have to fight for freedom from India.'

Basheer responds with, 'Kashmir belongs neither to bloody India nor to bloody Pakistan. Kashmir is only ours . . . I mean it belongs to us Kashmiris.'

A Day in the 1980s

I watch Moustapha Akkad's *Lion of the Desert*. It is about Omar Mukhtar, the Libyan tribal leader who fought the Italian army. People are distributing posters and leaflets asking everyone to watch this movie. Suddenly, hundreds and thousands throng to Regal cinema hall. People say, 'We watch this movie because Omar Mukhtar in the movie resembles Sheikh Mohammad Abdullah. Both had been teachers. One laid down his life for his country; the other betrayed his people.'

November 1989

I am walking through Hari Singh High Street. I hear the sound of a gunshot. People run away. I see a dead body on the road. Somebody has been killed. I walk up to the bus stand and board a bus that takes me home.

The next day, I get to know that the person killed in Hari Singh Street was Neel Kanth Ganjoo, a retired judge.

January 1990

I am in Delhi for a few days. The newspaper is very disturbing. I read and re-read the news.

Some Days Later

Wife, son, daughter and I leave Delhi for Jammu. We reach Jammu on 31 January in the morning. On Residency Road, Tej Krishen tells me, 'Call your parents to this place. Don't go there with your children.' I ask, 'What happened?' He replies, 'Nothing happened. But I can't describe the night between 19 January and 20 January. It was simply horrific.' Moti Lal says the same thing.

What?

31 January 1990

We are on our way to Srinagar. Pandits in taxis and trucks are going to Jammu. There is a young Pandit lady in the bus. We reach the tourist reception centre in Srinagar by 7 p.m. A policeman doesn't let anyone leave the premises. A State Road Transport Corporation bus arrives and everyone boards it. There is one policeman with a rifle in it. Security! He asks the passengers the names of the localities they are going to. We reach Safa Kadal in Downtown Srinagar.

31 January 1990
10 p.m.

When Babi sees us, she asks, 'Why did you come to this place?' We have dinner and then talk. Father is calm. He doesn't say anything. A few people shout from the mosque through the microphone and ask the people to enter the mosque. It continues until late in the night.

The atmosphere is very bad. Muslim neighbours—men and women—ask my wife where she was, why she has come back, etc. 'You know that I go to Delhi every winter.'

'Yes. But why did you return early this time?'

Interrogation on the road! The same person asks the same questions to my wife, daughter, son and me separately, and weighs the answers.

A Day in February 1990

Shaha, the old Muslim woman in our neighbourhood, tells me on the road, 'What nonsense this is! We are fed up.' A Muslim gentleman joins us. Shaha shouts, 'We are prepared to die one by one for independence.'

Searches and searches. Deaths. Killings. It is horrible. A Muslim neighbour tells me in confidence, 'I am afraid of my own son. Strangers have become his friends. I have never seen them before.'

Pandits whisper to one another: 'There will be an army crackdown. Run away.'

A Pandit organization, through the columns of an Urdu daily, asks the Jammu Kashmir Liberation Front (JKLF),[*]

---

[*] A militant and separatist organization that waged war against India in Kashmir in 1989.

'What are we supposed to do in these conditions? Please tell us in ten days.'

There is no reply. One Pandit is killed near Habba Kadal. Pandits think that this is the reply.

Everybody says, 'We must leave by the 5th of March.'

'When are you leaving?' This is the refrain of the Pandit conversation. There is terror in the minds of all Kashmiri Pandits, who are locally called 'Bhattas'. Every morning, mother says, 'That family has left for Jammu. Their house is locked. When do we go?'

She knows nothing about Jammu. Father has heard that there is a place called Jammu.

In the evening, the Radio Kashmir newsreader says that Lassa Kaul, director of Doordarshan Kendra, Srinagar, has been killed outside his home in Bemina. He is a friend.

I reach his place in Bemina the next morning. Many people, mostly Muslims, are there. His young, brown-haired daughter is hysterical. I accompany the funeral procession from his place to the crematorium in Karan Nagar. Hundreds of Muslims are carrying placards that read:

'*Lassa Kaul ka qatil koun*? Jagmohan.' (Who is the killer of Lassa Kaul? Jagmohan.)*

The central minister for information and broadcasting arrives surrounded by security personnel. One man is carrying a wreath. The people shout, 'Nobody should go near him.' The minister places the wreath on the pyre, joins his palms and leaves. He senses the atmosphere in one second.

I had known Lassa Kaul, a real Kashmiri, for many years. One day while walking on the Bund, he talked to

---

* This is a slogan that my father recalls vividly.

me about his officers in Delhi, Jagmohan, the threats that he got and said, 'I am thinking of leaving this place now.'

Another Day in February 1990

Shiban Dhar, a neighbour and friend, is terrified and wants to go to Jammu with his wife and son. He has arranged a horse-drawn cart. We board the cart by 5 a.m. The CRPF jawans see us seated in the cart. They laugh and ask us, 'Pandits, leaving for Jammu?'

We say nothing.

The driver asks us, 'Pandit Sahib, why are Pandits going to Jammu?'

I am horrified at the scene unfolding at the tourist reception centre. I see thousands of Pandits board the buses there. There is a long queue at the ticket-booking counter. I go near the small opening and see an old classmate inside. I shout his name. He directs the peon of the office to open the door for me. I enter the room. There are three people there. One man accepts the money, another person hands over the ticket to the Pandit standing in the queue and the third person writes the amount in a register. All three of them are nervous. They are shaking and trembling. My old classmate, a Muslim, asks me nervously, 'Are you also going to Jammu? What do you know? Please tell me. Will we be killed when all of you leave this place?'

'I am not going anywhere. My neighbour and friend is going. I want tickets for the family.' The tickets are handed over to me. I see terror and death in the six eyes. The other two people don't speak.

I watch the horrible scenes. What is all this? I had never imagined this. Where are these Pandits going? I am very angry. I see coolies setting the luggage on the roofs of the buses. I leave the place with a broken heart.

March 1990

At the crack of dawn, Siddhartha and Henna leave this place with the Koul family. We don't know where they will go, but we hope they find a place to stay in Jammu.

A Day in February 1990

Nazir Gash (a well-read shopkeeper and friend) comes to my place with a copy of an Urdu daily and reads: 'Pandits are directed to leave the Valley in thirty-six hours.' Another clipping from an Urdu daily: 'The Kashmiri Pandit is a poisonous snake.' I accompany Nazir to his shop in Safa Kadal. A young man shouts, 'Some men haven't come to their senses yet.' Nazir Gash enters his home and I turn back.

A Night in February 1990

Wife and I hear some sounds. We peep through a chink. A family is dumping arms into the earth. We don't sleep. Wife asks, 'What now?' I reply, 'Silence.'

Daytime

I am walking in the lane adjacent to my house. A young boy is coming from the opposite direction. He has a beautiful black-and-red pistol in his hand. I turn my head and ignore him.

Night

'Who is walking in the lane?' Wife and I look outside. Two young men are standing near the gate of our house. They share a cigarette. They walk a few steps and then come back. The two young men walk to and fro. An hour has passed.

Morning

I am standing near the gate of our house. I see three young men walking fast. I hear one man saying to the other two, 'This is the professor.' Their shoes tell me that they are militants. Our next-door neighbour has also heard these words. She comes to our place, and reports to my mother and my wife. I tell her, 'Don't worry.'

10 May 1990

The bus I am seated in is on its way to the Government Degree College for Boys, Anantnag. At Bijbehara, an old student, a Muslim, sees me, politely greets me and says, '*Aadaab araz, mahara.*'* I remember this man. He was a very nice student who respected me during his college days. All the passengers seated in the bus turn towards me with looks that seem to say, 'all Pandits have gone and you are still here'. I feel uncomfortable, but I am not scared. I enter the college. I see students loitering. Others are sitting on the turf. Nobody talks to me.

---

* This was a traditional greeting. Whenever Muslims greeted Pandits, they said, '*Aadaab araz, mahara*'.

Muslims die at the hands of security personnel. Pandits die at the hands of militants. When a Pandit is killed, a rumour is spread: 'He was an informant.' When militants kill a Muslim, the same rumour is spread: 'He was an informant. An identity card was found in his pocket.' Every evening, we hear that someone or the other has been killed.

One evening, Fazi, our neighbour, says in a very low voice, 'Uma Shori, Uma Shori, don't drink water. Poison has been mixed in it.' There is gloom in the family. Some people continue to shout from the mosque during the night.

There is firing from many guns in the lane adjacent to our house. We sit in the corridor.

I am in a minibus that is going to Safa Kadal. In Karan Nagar, there is a dead body on the road. Nobody says anything. When we reach Kak Sarai, the conductor of the vehicle gets down and shouts, 'Hum kya chahtay?' (What do we want?) 'Azadi!' people shout back.

Aslam, a neighbour, looks at me, smiles, shakes his head and moves his lips. I move my lips too.

The news reaches us that a security personnel has killed the son of Takai, a neighbour. There is terror when the dead body is brought and kept in the compound of our next-door Muslim neighbour. One woman shouts, 'May the seeds of Pandits perish!' I dare not move out of my house. When Maulana Farooq is killed, the same woman shouts, 'May God destroy the seeds of Pandits!'

Hassan, a good friend, comes to my home. We are having tea in the living room. He picks up a biscuit and tells me: 'I swear by this . . . tell me if you have any sort of connection with the CBI . . . I will save you.'

I am silent but unafraid.

Ghulam Nabi, a dear friend, tells me: 'Some people were asking me about you. They have seen you walking near Safa Kadal and having tea at a tea shop.'

I am silent but unafraid.

17 May 1990

Soom Nath Saproo, a neighbour, has been kidnapped. Neighbours—Shias and Sunnis—leave their homes to talk to the various organizations about him. Mohammad Shafi tells me, 'I am going to get our brother Soom Nath back.' There is no news of him on 17 and 18 May. He is home on the morning of 19 May. Muslims and Pandits go to his place. I find Soom Nath dazed. He doesn't speak. He is sitting like a statue.

Hafiz, who had confided in Soom Nath about the possibility of his kidnapping a few days ago, has been kidnapped. He is freed in the evening. I visit Hafiz. While turning the pages of *India Today* magazine, Hafiz tells me, 'In the future, I will not tell anybody anything.' I ask him, 'What do you suggest for me and my family?' He replies, 'I don't know.'

Silence of tension and mistrust!

20 June 1990
Around 8.00 p.m.

Chand Saproo's little son used to play with my little daughter in our home. I hold the little boy's left hand, for I have to hand him over to Chand Saproo. We walk through the lane and reach the road. More than twenty Muslim neighbours are sitting on the road. When we step on the road, they abruptly keep quiet. All of them know me and love me. But this time they look at me in silence. I experience the feeling of terror for the first time in my life. Even now, I shiver when I recall that moment.

21 June 1990
Morning

People are running in the lane. I am standing near the gate of my house. I ask a running neighbour, 'What is the matter?' He replies, 'Pritha Tiku has been killed.' I tell my mother, father and wife that Prithvi Nath Tiku has been killed. They are terrified. They stop me from going to Tiku's place. There is total rebellion now. They want us to leave too. Wife tells me, 'Why don't you understand? We have two children. Babuji is old.'

'Give me a minute to think,' I tell them. In that one minute, I decide to leave. We pack our things. Father is weeping.

22 June 1990
11 a.m.

I ask Hafiz to arrange a truck for us. He says, 'Go home. A minibus will come to you in twenty minutes, but don't talk to me on the road henceforth.'

A minibus driver comes with a young boy. We stuff the vehicle with beds, bedding, utensils, etc. The minibus reaches Indira Nagar, Srinagar, where my cousin, who is in Delhi, has his house. I find hundreds of Pandits in Indira Nagar. I go back home to pack the remaining luggage. When my wife sees me, she is very tense and says that in my absence, a young man was asking for me. She says that she has never seen the young man before. We put other things in the minibus very quickly. One almirah full of old books belonging to my grandfather remains untouched. I will come some day and carry them. These are rare books that my grandfather had bought in Italy, Turkey and other countries. The other books are mine.

Through the window, Mohi-ud-Din's daughter-in-law tells me, 'Forgive us. Go wherever you want to go. May God protect you!' She is weeping.

4

The Man without a Reflection

November 1990
Chabutra, Udhampur

Babuji's first day as a 'migrant' in rented accommodation—in a place he hasn't even heard of—was a day he thought would never come. He has never been away from home, not even for a day. He hasn't been anywhere else. He's been an early riser since his childhood. He hasn't slept at all. He's a 4 a.m. riser even now. He wants to shave but can't locate his shaving kit. Babi has kept it safe. She takes the kit out of a trunk and hands it over to him. But there is one problem. The large mirror with a wooden frame is missing.

'It is at home—remember, we couldn't carry it with us when we went to Indira Nagar,' Babi tells him. 'But never mind, get yourself a new mirror from the market.'

The point Babuji tries to make by shaking his head is that it wasn't just a shaving mirror—it was his father's mirror. There is no shaving without that mirror.

'I am a man without a reflection,' Babuji laughs, trying to accept the fact that he has no choice but to make do without the mirror.

Babi discovers a Shiva temple in the neighbourhood. She decides to set up a small shelf in the room. There are no idols to be placed on the shelf. Just an almanac and a portrait of some gods and goddesses!

Days Later

Pa decorates all the walls, including the ones in the toilet, with wall hangings and paintings. Going to the toilet continues to be an ordeal. Ma goes through a tough time. We must close our nostrils and breathe through our mouths when we are inside. We must also close our eyes. Otherwise, we will vomit and die because of the bad smell. We have to swallow shame. We can't even ask anyone to come over to our place. We can't invite the neighbours or Pa's friends over for a cup of tea. What if they want to use the toilet? But many of them are in the same boat—some of them don't even have toilets, so they have to go out every day to search for a place where they can defecate without being seen by anyone.

'Women have stopped complaining—theirs is an unimaginable plight when it comes to such matters,' says Pa's friend, Pandita, who is a school teacher. He keeps dropping by quite often. Sometimes to use our toilet and sometimes to keep his sanity intact.

'I don't even know what to do. Sometimes, I go to the public toilet at the bus stop and sometimes I go to tea shops nearby and use the toilets meant for the customers, but my wife . . . Where does she go? I don't even know. She has to beg the neighbours every day. Sometimes they agree and sometimes they don't. Some camp-dwellers in the Garhi camp have decided to construct a couple of toilets in their camp using their own money . . .'

The day the sweeper doesn't show up is the worst of days. We have to clean the toilet ourselves. If we don't, then you can't even go near it.

I remember our house being renovated the previous year. Pa spent a fortune—almost all his savings—on it. He also bought a small plot of land in Ompora, hoping to build a new house the following year. Crushed dreams! But he doesn't bring the topic up now! The plot of land is atop a plateau! Gorgeous views, especially of the mountains and the sunset—a painting!

All finished now! Maybe not, thinks Babi. 'We will get to go back . . . We will go back . . . Don't you think so? What makes you think we won't? Don't be mad . . . Have patience and keep hope aflame in your hearts . . . Hope is our everything now . . . The only thing we have . . . The only thing that will keep us alive . . . This phase won't last more than a few months . . . The madness will end . . . By winter, we will be back home . . . Just in time to welcome the snow . . .'

That explains Babi's steadfast unwillingness to open two of the trunks and take things out of them.

Why unpack when we will be home soon?

Days pass. Babi keeps waiting. So does Babuji. So do the rest of us—Henna, Ma, Pa and I.

Our landlord, Mohan, owns an electronic shop in the market in Dabbad. I call him Dixon because the shop is called Dixon Electronics. Mohan's wife is concerned about us. She keeps asking us if we need anything.

'This is your home now,' she says to Ma. 'We are your family. Feel free to use our toilet . . .'

'We won't trouble you,' Ma says. But she's reassured by Mrs Dixon's empathy.

* * *

December 1990
Kashmiri Pandit Migrant Registration Centre
Dhar Road
Udhampur

Thousands of Pandits are lined up outside the registration centre on Dhar Road. Many are getting registered and others have lined up to collect relief—the monthly allowance of Rs 500 and some kilos of rice and sugar. People from the villages who have lost their only means of livelihood, their orchards and farms, are queued up in front of the registration centre. They are complaining to the authorities and the officers.

To get registered, you need a ration card. For the first time, we are made to realize the importance of documents such as the ration card.

Outside the registration centre, an old man and his wife wait for their turn to get registered as migrants. The queue is long and every moment is long and dreary. The registration process is fraught with perils. The woman talks aloud to herself. She mumbles some inanities and shows signs of fatigue and disorientation. Others in the queue make gestures at one another.

A bystander asks the old man if his children are around.

'We are all by ourselves here,' the man says indignantly.

'No, no, they are very much around . . .' clarifies the woman, wistfully. She breaks down. 'We are with . . .'

The form asks: Permanent Address.

'What is to be written here?'

'Address in Kashmir. Our home address.'

While returning, we walk past a deserted football stadium just across the highway.

'This is the camp,' says Pa's friend, who teaches in the school set up at the camp.

'You must send your son and daughter away from this place. They mustn't stay here. Send them off to Delhi or some other city in India. They should do their schooling in Delhi. You should not have brought them back from Delhi in the first place. They are better off there than here.'

I don't quite agree with the man, who is my father's friend, though I know he is a well-wisher and means well.

Reluctantly, Pa registers us as 'migrants'. We are given a ration card. Babi and Babuji are now eligible for the monthly relief. Little do I realize that the ration card will seal our fate as migrants for life. Migrants forever.

One day, Pa and Ma take Babi to Jammu to visit some of her relatives.

'Can you cook fish and rice for dinner today?' Babuji requests. It's been ages since we've had rice and fish.

Some days later, I am back in Chandigarh to resume college. But I am restless. Nothing interests me. I want to run away. I can't bear anything any longer. I don't know what to do or where to go. I have no purpose to keep me going. Morbid thoughts enter my mind. I want to end everything.

* * *

DAV College Chandigarh

Early one morning, I leave my hostel, run to the Chandigarh bus terminus, buy a bus ticket to Jammu and board a Punjab Roadways bus to Jammu. I tell no one about my departure.

Not even my roommate, Mohit. Not even Sudeep. I don't even take some of my possessions along. I reach Jammu in the afternoon and by evening, I am in Udhampur.

Babi and Ma are surprised to see me. So are Babuji and Pa. 'Why are you here so soon? Is your college closed for holidays?' They think I am back because the college might be closed. I don't want to hide the truth. But I can't tell them everything.

'I am back for good. I am not going back.'

'What?' Ma is horrified. At first, she thinks I am joking or pulling a prank. I do my best to reassure her that I will be okay. That I am better off staying with them than anywhere else.

'You want to be here? And do what? You are giving up so easily? You know what it took to get you admitted to college? You know more than I do, don't you? Look around you. What do you see here?'

She goes on and on. She's very upset and furious. She cries, sensing that I am serious, but she is confident that my madness is temporary and that she will convince me to go back. I stand my ground even though I feel terrible.

'You have everything there. You have a room in the hostel. You have a future. You can't leave all that for this. Think rationally. You aren't thinking straight right now. Let's talk tomorrow. Tomorrow, you will go back. No arguments!'

The argument continues for days. Ma keeps the topic alive.

'This college admitted you when all the other schools and colleges had no place for you. Your father went to great lengths to convince them to take you in. He would never have done that if the situation were different.'

'Don't worry, Ma. What's the worst that could happen? At best, I will . . . But at least, I will be here with all of you. I will do something . . .'

'He can join the camp school,' says Pa.

'The camp school?'

'Yes!'

'You both have gone mad.'

Babuji and Babi are happy that I am back.

'Henna is attending the Kendriya Vidyalaya near the Chinar cantonment. And you're thinking of the camp school for him? Do you even know what it means? Do you know what a camp school is like? Have you even seen it?'

Every day, Ma brings up the topic.

'When are you going back?' She is desperate now. I can't bear her tears. But I am helpless too. I don't want to go back. I fear going back. If I go back, I will most certainly fail. I will die out of shame. Here, at least, even if I fail, I will live. I don't want to die.

I don't tell them any of this.

At last, Ma relents! But there are days she coaxes me to change my mind.

'For my sake, please. I will never ask anything more of you in life. Just this! Go back to Chandigarh and finish college. I beg you! If you don't want to see me dead, go back to college. Not everybody gets such a golden opportunity . . .'

Ma is worried because she doesn't know what to tell the relatives who will come here just to taunt her. How will she face them when they find out that I am still here and have opted to join the camp school? They will blame her for my mistakes. And they will mock her for her son's bad upbringing. 'We knew he would do this. He's always been weak in his studies and has always been an escapist. What will he do in life now?'

'The camp school is for the children of villagers. They are the only ones studying there. You won't find anyone else from Srinagar.'

I can't imagine the shame! The vicarious pleasure on the faces of relatives when they see me in the camp school. They have been mocking Ma for years now.

'Oh, look at him! He doesn't even have proper . . .'

* * *

Pa gets me admitted to the camp school. The school is in the camp for displaced Kashmiri Pandits. An abandoned football ground that looks like a barren wasteland houses the vast camp. The camp consists of several hundred twelve-foot-by-twelve-foot canvas tents in rows. Some tents are slightly bigger than others. One after another, with barely any breathing space between tents. Each tent has one joint family living inside. If you step inside a tent, you will have to bend; otherwise, your head will touch the canvas. There is barely any room for two people inside. But the reality is horrible. You will see eight to ten people inside each tent. Most tents are occupied by joint families.

The address:

Camp for displaced Kashmiri Pandits (migrants)
Dumail, Dhar Road, near traffic check post (TCP)
Udhampur, Jammu Province

(This address of the camp is important because the camp doesn't exist now. In 2004, the camp-dwellers were allotted ORTs in Jammu. Many others were allotted two-room flats in camps that were set up by the government in Jammu and Jagti, near Nagrota in 2012.)

Raj Cinema Hall is the nearest prominent landmark. The building is in bad shape. Housing Colony, another prominent landmark, is a five-minute walk from the camp. It is an upcoming colony where houses are being built. The colony looks swanky with parks and proper drainage and arrangement of plots. The TCP is another prominent place. It is on the Udhampur–Srinagar national highway. Vehicles are searched here before being allowed to pass and go further towards Kashmir. There are a lot of dhabas and food stalls on both sides of the road. The ones doing brisk business are favoured by truck and bus drivers.

In the camp are five tents, which are used to hold classes for the displaced students who have nowhere else to study. These are tent classrooms. This is the camp school. There is barely any furniture inside the tent classrooms. Just a few old blackboards that are in terrible condition and a few plastic chairs for the teachers. Perhaps they were meant to be discarded but were given to this camp school instead.

Almost all students who study at the camp school live in the camp itself. Everyone is from different villages in Kashmir. Some are so remote that I haven't even heard of them.

'We were twenty families in our village,' says a classmate. 'The rest were Muslims. Now all twenty are here.' He points to a row of tents. 'There,' he says. 'The entire village is here. Just one fourth of a row.' I count the tents.

'This is a temporary arrangement,' the headmaster says to Pa. 'We are agitating to get us a proper building. We are demanding that we be given the government school premises to hold classes. It might take some time, but we won't give up easily. Why did your son run away from the DAV College Chandigarh?'

* * *

Ma doesn't give up. She now insists that I try for admission to some other school, if I don't want to go back to Chandigarh.

* * *

8 December 1990

We reach Aligarh! Pa presents the case to one of the deans of Aligarh Muslim University. The dean listens to every word Pa says attentively and says yes instantly. 'Don't worry. I am admitting your son and I will also give him a room in the hostel here.'

We are instructed to pay the fees and fill out some of the paperwork at the office the following day. We will complete the rest of the formalities over the next few days. A room is allotted to me in the Allama Iqbal Hall. I will be expected to wear a sherwani inside the campus. I must adhere to the rules. We decide to buy the uniform and stationery the next day.

Pa and I eat in the canteen. He's relieved.

We decide to spend the night in a cheap guest house.

At night, we hear screams. The caretaker comes rushing to our room.

'You are Hindus, right? Leave immediately or else you will be killed . . .'

Communal riots have erupted overnight. Muslims and Hindus are killing each other. Hindus living in hotels and guest houses are at risk.

We peep through the window. People are running with swords. A building next to the hotel is on fire. People are coming out, screaming and crying. There is blood on the swords.

'But where will we go at this hour?'

The caretaker takes us to a secret chamber to hide in until dawn.

'Stay vigilant tonight. Leave before the sun comes out. Don't be late. Go to the bus terminus at 4 a.m. and board the first bus to Delhi. Don't come back.'

At 5 a.m., we board a bus to Delhi.

The newspapers present horrifying accounts of the previous night, with headlines along the lines of:

> *At least 100 killed in Hindu–Muslim riots in Aligarh*
> *Rioting spills over at Aligarh Muslim University. Several*
> *Hindu students flee hostels*[3]

We are back to square one. Pa books train tickets.

'We will go back tomorrow,' he says.

Some Days Later

I resume classes at the camp school. Ma reluctantly accepts this.

'We tried everything, but . . .' says Pa to her. 'At least we are back safe and sound . . .'

Pa starts teaching at the college that has been set up in the camp. Pa's friend, Professor B.L. Zutshi, the president of the displaced teachers' association, recounts everything that the displaced teachers have been doing to ensure continuity in education for the displaced students. He, along with the displaced teachers' association, has been fighting a battle with the government to ensure that neither the displaced students nor the teachers suffer on account of the displacement. They have been going from pillar to post to get the government to do something and take adequate measures to ensure that at least the bare minimum of educational infrastructure is provided.

It is because of them that a few months earlier, in July 1990, camp colleges, camp schools, a camp university, a camp regional engineering college and camp BEd colleges (Gandhi Memorial College of Education and Vishwabharti College of Education) were established. But the reality is grim. There is no proper infrastructure. All these institutes are still linked to the Kashmir division, thereby causing paralysis in terms of the disbursement of funds and the support required to run them.

The association has also been approaching the National Human Rights Commission (NHRC) to apprise them of the situation that prevails in the displaced community.

'Give us basic amenities to ensure education,' they plead. They approach the cabinet ministers and the prime minister. 'Help us,' they say. Letter after letter containing proof of the problems faced by the students is submitted to the government.

'The future of these students and youngsters is at stake. The future of the community is at stake . . .'

How will the salaried class pay income tax in such a scenario?

At last, the Government of India issues 'the income tax deferment letter' for the financial year 1990–91.

* * *

31 December 1990

It is New Year's Eve. 'If winter has set in, why isn't it snowing yet?' asks Babuji. 'It always snows on New Year's Eve.'

We are all waiting, but it seems this town doesn't receive snow. The nearest place with snowfall is Kud. We could go there once it starts snowing. It's an hour's journey by bus.

* * *

January 1991

I spend some evenings at the shop of our landlord, Mohan. He plays movies on the video cassette recorder. He offers me whisky again. I have been politely refusing so far, but he is insistent this time.

'It's cold. Have one drink. You will feel warm. We will go home once the movie ends.'

It is my first time. I have one peg, then another and another.

'The last—one for the road,' Mohan says. Then he decides to teach me how to ride a scooter. Kick, gears, clutch, break, steering, horn and rear-view mirror. It seems easy at first. I try to balance with him sitting at the back and teaching me how to change gears while he holds the handle. We crash against a wall. I see bruises and blood. Ma cries when she sees me drunk and drenched in blood.

Bobby and Deepak think that I drink almost every evening. They blame me because they think I enjoy drinking rum and whisky. They are wrong. I am unable to say no to Mohan. Bobby thinks I lack reason and willpower. He isn't entirely wrong. But I am not brave enough to admit my follies. Not yet, at least. I want to be like him. He is studious. I lack discipline and focus. We have been friends since childhood. Our parents are friends, too.

Deepak's father is a manager at the army Canteen Stores Department (CSD). Our fathers are friends. They introduce Deepak and me to each other. Deepak studies at the army school. He asks me about my school.

'It's a long story,' I say to him. 'I will tell you everything . . .'

The three of us hang out together. People call us the 'Three Musketeers'. In the mornings, we go to the district library near Dabbad Park to read newspapers. There, I chance upon a dusty and cobwebbed rack stacked with Russian novels. Gogol and Dostoevsky on a shelf partly eaten up by termites. We hatch a plan for a grand heist. After a week's planning, we break in and steal a dozen books.

A month passes. We have stopped going to the library. Deepak's friend, Jaspreet, whose father is a colonel in the army, takes us to the Chinar library in the Northern Command Headquarters, which is 10 km from the Udhampur bus adda. Partly out of curiosity and partly to escape the ennui of our daily routine, we survey the area where civilian trespassing is prohibited.

One evening, when Deepak and I are ambling next to a tennis court near the general officer commanding-in-chief's residence, two security guards catch us with cigarettes dangling from our mouths and take us to a shed nearby. It takes us some time to realize that it is an interrogation centre. Unconvinced by our pleas of innocence—that we are students who inadvertently sauntered into the area— they interrogate us for hours. Finally, Deepak's father is summoned and apprised of the situation. He understands everything. After all, he knows the system well. He talks to a colonel who, in turn, talks to a brigadier who then gets us released on the assurance that we will never be seen there again.

The Link Road, connecting the highway to the Chabutra Bazaar, becomes a haunt where, at twilight, the three of us see strange things—almost like hallucinations. A grand plan to write a novel is hatched there. An elderly spice merchant at Lambi Gali recounts tales about the Dogras and the war of 1965. We sit in Dabbad Park and listen to the woes of the displaced Pandits living in a camp set up in the football ground. One day, looking at buses going to Srinagar, we come across Roxy Bar and enter with empty pockets. The unimaginable happens. All three of us get drunk and talk our way out.

At a chai shop in the Dabbad market, Raju is born, who then becomes the character of our column 'Looking

Glass' published in the *Daily Excelsior*, a prominent local newspaper. At Vatika, the college garden, we recite poems and hope someone hears them too.

Among other things, the three musketeers discover love and longing.

(The search for the three girls, who never got to know that three loafers secretly fancied them all the time, is still on.)

* * *

A Day in the Summer of 1989
Tuition Teacher's House
Karan Nagar, Srinagar, Kashmir

I am at Sir's place. He is teaching us mathematics. His method of teaching is unique. He has placed sheets of carbon paper between blank sheets—almost twenty of them. Two sheets containing his notes for each one of us. The last sheet is a bit difficult to read, but the student who gets the last sheet will figure out a way to read the notes and transcribe Sir's writing. We have been coming here for months now—in the run up to the Class Ten Board examination, which looms over us like a volcano about to erupt.

There is this terror associated with the matriculation examination. 'Only if you pass with distinction will you do anything worthwhile in life,' says everyone. Distinction means scoring 90 per cent and above. An almost impossible proposition for me. I will be lucky if I score 70 per cent. Even 60 per cent seems doable. Mathematics and science are my worst nightmares. Even these tuitions are not helping. Sir is hopeful that I will do well.

'Your son will pass,' he tells my father. 'I will make sure he scores decent marks.'

I think my docility is deceptive. Sir has the impression that I follow and understand everything that he teaches. He gives us surprise tests. To his surprise and mine, I solve some sums. That's because I have memorized the answers.

What will I do if I fail? What will happen to me? I won't be promoted to Class Eleven. One more year in Class Ten. What if I never pass?

Sunil thinks otherwise. 'Don't overthink,' he says. 'Even if you score less marks, you will go to Class Eleven.'

Some Days Later

I am at Sir's place again. He is engrossed in the lesson. Differentiation and integration. The most important concepts in mathematics.

'Learn them well,' he says, 'and you can learn and understand anything in life . . .'

There is commotion downstairs. Sir's servant rushes up the stairs. A sound of things falling off shelves is heard. The servant scream, 'Don't, please don't . . . Sir is not home . . .'

He tries to bolt the door, but it is forced open. Two youngsters barge in. Strangers, but familiar faces. One looks like a college student and the other is my age. I have seen both somewhere. Oh my God! Is he . . .

The black nozzle of a gun is partly visible to us.

The young man starts addressing Sir:

'From tomorrow, you won't coach these good-for-nothing fellows. Only boys whom I refer to you. You won't charge any money from them,' he goes on and on. 'There is no need to panic. We have instructed other Pandit teachers as well. They will comply. So will you . . . Or else . . .'

His eyes survey everything. The other boy scrutinizes us as if we are the culprits of some gruesome crime.

'You, you, you and you,' his look conveys.

They leave.

Sir's servant falls to the floor, apologizing as if were his fault.

'I am sorry. I tried my best to tell them there was no one at home. He showed me his gun and I got very scared . . .'

Sir gets up and indicates that we are to leave immediately. We follow Sir's orders. The look on his face is one of horror, but he conceals his fear. His hands are shaking. He rushes to an adjacent room. We leave.

On our way back home, Sunil and I try to make sense of the incident.

'You know who he was!' Sunil exclaims. 'Arif knows him . . . His cousin . . . He's the area commander . . . Just returned from POK . . . After training . . . His brother is also in Class Ten, but he has other plans . . .'

What do you think will happen?

I am at Sir's place again, but the entire house is deserted. It is a four-storeyed house in Karan Nagar, one of the poshest localities in Srinagar. There are days I wish our house were here too. I love the neighbourhood. Many of my friends live here, including Anil and Justice Ganjoo's granddaughter. A new cake shop has opened in the vicinity. Neelam Cinema is not far from Sir's house.

Sunil says he has been waiting for me all this time. 'There won't be any more tuitions now,' he says. 'Read this note.'

'Dear students,

I had to leave at short notice. Please carry on with your studies and use all my notes to practise the sums.'

'Where has Sir gone?'

'Some say he has gone to Canada?'

'His son is settled there,' says his servant. 'He will be back soon.'

* * *

Ma comes back early from school. She's terrified. Something must have happened. But she's not telling me. I narrate the entire incident to Pa and Ma.

The next day, Pa tells me that many of his colleagues had 'visitors' too. And they were told the same thing: 'Stop charging money for tuitions. Teach only Muslim students. Or else . . .'

They said the same thing to Kashmiri Pandit doctors and shopkeepers: that Pandit doctors must not charge fees from Muslims; Pandit shopkeepers must not charge Muslims for goods sold to them; and Pandits must pay if they are to live in Kashmir.

What about you, Pa?

'Nothing so far . . .'

'They won't say this to him because he doesn't accept money and has never accepted money for tuitions,' Ma says sarcastically. 'So, he's safe. By the way, our school might close for a few days.'

* * *

Ma is preparing to go to school.

'But you had said . . .'

I overhear Pa and Ma talking in their room.

Pa: 'Who was he?'
Ma: 'I don't know.'
Pa: 'A student?'
Ma: 'Looked like.'

Pa: 'Ignore him.'

Ma: 'But he kept following me . . . I didn't know what to do . . .'

Pa: 'Then?'

Ma: 'Then he stopped.'

Pa: 'Don't go to school tomorrow.'

Ma: 'What did he want?'

Pa: 'Nothing.'

Ma: 'But what have I done? Did he mean to . . .'

* * *

March 1991
Udhampur

I read Sudeep's last letter to me. The last line:

Don't send me letters from now on. If you respect me, don't ever get in touch with me. Forget me. Forget everything. If you respect me, burn all my letters.

Sudeep

The next morning, I burn all the letters. I read the last two letters one last time before burning them.

Dear Siddhartha,

I read in *The Tribune* about the camps in Jammu and Udhampur. I got to know how Kashmiri Pandits are living in miserable conditions in these camps. Why didn't you tell me all this when you were here? Such injustice! Are you also going through this misery? Are you also in a camp?

Why can't you come back to Chandigarh! Mohit has been looking for you. He is waiting for you. So am I.

Sudeep

* * *

Dear Siddhartha,

The Anti-Mandal Commission protests have ended. Our college has resumed now. So has your college. There is no disturbance. What are you doing there? Which school do you go to? Waiting for your letter.

Sudeep

* * *

Summer of 1992
Udhampur

The tuition teacher's daughter waits for me at the bus stop. She waits for me almost every day here. And then she takes me to her place—a two-room set down the hill. The house is next to a spring where women wash clothes, and fill buckets and cans with water to carry back to their homes. There are two separate bathing areas for men and women. The water in the spring is cold.

I am in Class Twelve and preparing for the board exams. I have no fear of failure now. Somehow, I don't care if I pass or fail, though I am certain of not doing well in mathematics. My tuition teacher doesn't think so—he still has faith in me. Much like the other tuition teachers do.

It's been raining for the past few days. Sir's daughter carries an umbrella for me when it is raining. She looks at me, walking in the strangest manner and smiles. 'Look at you!' her look says.

'How do you manage to keep your feet clean even while walking through these muddy puddles?'

After the lessons, we sit down to eat and she sees me off again. Sir treats me differently because of the respect he has for my father. He and Aunty always insist that I stay back for lunch after lessons. I am the only student who is asked to stay back for lunch or some snacks.

I live with the fear that she might stop waiting for me if I say no. She's the only company I have. She is in Class Nine.

She has the unmistakable gait of a village girl. Her accent is different. She speaks in a sweet manner.

'Is this why you are late? Because you walk slowly?' she asks.

'It was raining.'

'No wonder your feet are spotless and you manage to keep your feet away from the mud. Who taught you this?'

'My grandpa.'

'Next time it rains, wear shoes instead of flip-flops.'

'How do you manage to do this?'

I look at her feet. She's also wearing flip-flops. She has also managed to keep her feet spotless despite the muddy path.

Some Days Later

Another rainy day. She's walking me back to the main road when it starts raining. She asks me what I plan to do in the immediate future. Whether I will opt for engineering or something else. She asks if I will leave Udhampur like the rest of the students who are about to begin college life. She says she loves mathematics and wants to do a master's in the subject. 'I want to become a high school teacher like my father and teach in his school in Kashmir.'

I tell her about my fear of mathematics. She says she would love to teach me. 'I will show you how easy mathematics is. You can do the sums with your eyes closed.'

'I will wait for that day.'

'That day will not come . . .'

'What makes you say so?'

'Because you will leave this place like others from Srinagar and never come back?'

'Why do you think so?'

'Because you can leave. Like everyone who belongs to Srinagar. We will always be here, so that when it is time to go back, we will be the first ones ready and closest to our homes . . .'

* * *

October–November 1989
Srinagar

Day One of the Class Ten board examination—English (Part A). Piece of cake, I think. I haven't slept the whole night. I feel confident. I know the entire syllabus by heart. English is my favourite subject. I can answer the exams with my eyes closed. The examination centre is a twenty-minute walk from home. The school has a large playground where we play cricket in the summer.

Hundreds of students are waiting in the playground for the exam to begin. The gates will open at 9 a.m. and we will be allowed inside. The exam will begin at 9.30 a.m.

The bell rings and we rush in. We locate the rooms assigned to us as per our roll numbers.

Several of my classmates are in the same room as me. Amit and Ajay are sitting next to me. Arif and Showkat are seated in the next row. The invigilator hands over the question paper to us. And then the sheets that we are to use for the questions that require descriptive answers.

At first, the invigilator gives the impression of being a kind and compassionate person. Minutes later, he interrupts me. 'Help some of your Muslim friends too,' he says, pointing at some students who are sitting in an adjacent row. 'They need your help. You are a good student.'

'What do you want me to do?'

'Here,' he says, handing me someone else's answer sheet. 'This question. Write the right answer.'

An hour later, I ask him for a supplementary sheet of paper. He keeps me waiting. The bell announces the end of time. Still no paper. I plead. He collects all the answer sheets and leaves the room.

Some Days Later

English (Part B) paper. A student has placed a machine gun on the desk. Another student has placed a pistol. Their answer sheets are given to other students. I am taken to an adjacent room and asked to give the exams, but the answer booklet isn't mine. It bears someone else's name and roll number.

In the evening, I inform my father. He speaks to his Muslim colleague, who is associated with the Board of Secondary Education.

Some Days Later

Mathematics paper. The invigilator asks me to hand him my answer booklet. 'Don't worry, you will have it back soon,' he whispers. 'I am your dad's friend.'

* * *

Henna stops going to school—Vishwa Bharti, Rainawari. There has been a blast near her school. People are saying that it is a sign. Some children narrowly escape death.

'The next blast will take place inside the school premises,' is the warning, 'unless the Pandit administration accepts the conditions . . .'

* * *

31 December 1989
Morning

Encounters erupt in Downtown Srinagar almost every other day. Encounters between militants and security forces. Every morning, we wake up to blasts and the sound of gunshots. A strange euphoria has the neighbourhood in its grip, as if people's wishes are about to come true. As if their prayers are about to be answered.

Habib arrives on time to clean the courtyard. He behaves as if nothing has happened. On his face is the same old look—the look of contentment.

Amjoo comes home to carry Babuji's tiffin to the lab. He hasn't missed a day. Babi serves him food.

Babuji hasn't gone to the lab. He has never missed a day, but for the first time in his life, he is not in the lab. His lab is everything to him. He is dying to go to the lab.

Amjoo leaves, indicating that he will be back the next day.

'I must open the shop today. My patients must be waiting,' Babuji mumbles.

Babi asks him to stay silent and not behave like an obstinate child. 'Do you want to get killed?'

'Nothing will happen to me.'

'You aren't their "Doctor Sahab" anymore. Look, what they did to Shamboo Nath . . .'

Babuji shakes his head to indicate that he will always be their 'Doctor Sahab'.

'I have been their "Doctor Sahab" for forty years. I will be their "Doctor Sahab" until my last breath.'

Afternoon

'I am going to the shop and will come back in an hour,' says Babuji. He starts wiping the dust off his bicycle.

'You are going to get me ruined,' Babi tells him. 'Do whatever you want to do.'

Evening

Babuji tunes in to the news at 7.30 p.m.

'This is Ali Mohammad Lone from Radio Kashmir and you will now listen to the news at seven-thirty . . .'

The news is discouraging. It seems as if a war is waging outside.

'The situation is tense but under control,' announces the newsreader.

'In an encounter in Kavdor today, militants killed twenty CRPF jawans and five policemen. They hurled grenades and rocket launchers at bunkers in Raj Bagh and Lal Chowk.

But the security forces gave a fitting reply to the militants by thwarting their attempts to infiltrate into the Valley. In a retaliatory fire, security forces killed eighty militants . . .'

For twenty minutes, the newsreader goes on and on about the law-and-order situation, desperately trying to paint a rosy picture of the government, the administration and their heroic deeds.

'Despite all this, everything is under control and about to be set right,' he says repeatedly.

The last five minutes are devoted to positive news.

'Preparations are in full swing to welcome the first snowfall in Kashmir . . . People are storing coal and firewood . . . Dal Lake has frozen and some people were seen playing football on the ice that has formed on the surface . . . A man drove a jeep on Dal Lake, creating a world record . . . The chief minister has appealed to the people to stay calm and have faith in the administration . . . The curfew will be relaxed for four hours tomorrow so that common people can step out of their houses to go to mosques for namaz and to the markets to purchase essential supplies . . . People are advised to stay alert and indoors during curfew and when shoot-on-sight orders are issued.'

Night

A slogan rends the sky. It is the same slogan that sent shivers down our spine last night.

'Merge, leave or perish!'

They really want us dead.

* * *

The Camp
Udhampur
Summer of 1992

People will never stop dying here. God, please don't take someone away today. One more dead body is taken to the Devika cremation ghat. Ten men are part of the funeral procession. All camp-dwellers.

The way to the camp college is via the cremation ghat at the Devika River.[*]

Seeing Pa break down while shaving, Babi goes into a fit. She scolds me. 'You should not keep quiet. Drive some sense into your father's head; otherwise, he will go into depression and not come out . . .'

Pa cries every day. Ma comforts him, but she's helpless. Pa seems beyond comforting. Babi scolds him at first, then comforts him too. Babuji is calm. Pa seems to be on the verge of a nervous breakdown. But there are moments when he is cheerful and philosophical, especially when his friends visit. They discuss books, ideas, philosophy, myths, history, literature, religion, current affairs and politics.

Pa takes me to Professor Malmohi's place. He lives in a rented two-room set near Dixon Electronics. When we enter the room, he's dressed like a mystic in a long white tunic made of cotton. He sings.

'This is his own verse,' Pa says, adding, 'he is a great man and the best professor of Urdu literature! He knows more than all of us. None of us can match his scholarship and wisdom . . .'

---

[*] According to the *Nīlamata Purāna*, the Devika River is a manifestation of the Goddess Parvati.

We keep going to meet Professor Malmohi almost every evening. His days are horrible, but he comes alive at night. One of his sons is schizophrenic.

Deepak's relative also has two sons who are both schizophrenic. One cousin has disappeared. He is nowhere to be found. His parents don't know what to do. They must learn to accept their fate. Just as we must learn to accept ours.

Every evening at 7.30 p.m., Babuji tunes in to Radio Kashmir for the news broadcast.

'This is Mohammad Shafi Bhat from Radio Kashmir and you will now listen to the news at seven-thirty . . .'

The same news. No two broadcasts are different. The only difference is numbers and dates. Everything else is the same.

'The situation is tense but under control,' announces the newsreader. 'In an encounter in Lal Chowk today, mujahids killed eleven CRPF jawans and thirteen policemen. They hurled grenades and rocket launchers at bunkers in Safa Kadal and Nowhatta. The security forces tried to thwart fresh attempts by mujahids to infiltrate the Valley. In a retaliatory fire, security forces killed 200 mujahids . . .'

Over and over, the newsreader goes on. Repeating the same news items except for one: instead of the chief minister, it is the governor who is in charge now. The administration under the governor did this and that . . .

The last five minutes of the news broadcast are once again devoted to good and happy news, full of hope. Just that it is not winter but summer.

'The Mughal Gardens are in full bloom . . . Tourists were seen frolicking in Gulmarg and Pahalgam . . . The governor has appealed to the people to stay calm and have faith in the administration . . . The curfew will be relaxed for one hour tomorrow morning so that common people can step out to go to mosques and purchase essential supplies . . . People are advised to stay alert and indoors during curfew and when shoot-on-sight orders are issued.'

Babuji switches the radio off and sighs. A long sigh!

'The situation in Kashmir seems to be improving . . . A few more days and then . . .' He turns to Babi and summarizes the news.

'And then what?' asks Babi? 'We will go back home . . . You and your wishful thinking . . .'

Babi is practical. Babuji is hopeful. Pa is sceptical.

* * *

March 1993
An Evening
Jammu Railway Station

Thousands of Kashmiri Pandits, along with their sons and daughters who have cleared their Class Twelve board exams, are waiting for trains to Delhi. From Delhi, they will go to Maharashtra, where the children will get admitted to engineering colleges and polytechnic institutes. There is only one name on everyone's lips—Balasaheb Thackeray. 'He is our saviour,' people are chanting. 'All this has become possible because of him, otherwise our children would have been doomed.'

I meet some of my classmates from Srinagar for the first time in three years. They are on their way to Delhi, Maharashtra, Karnataka and Andhra Pradesh.

'Which college are you getting admitted to?' asks Ajay, who I know from Jammu.

I have no answer.

'What about you?'

'I have got a seat in an engineering college in Nagpur.'

'What about others?'

'Sandeep got into computer science. You know she's always been studious. Abhay got into electrical engineering. Some are going to Karnataka. You should have come to Jammu. There still is time. What is in Udhampur? It is a village . . .'

My only reason for travelling from Udhampur to Jammu is to buy music cassettes and window shop. There is a musical instrument shop where I like to spend time looking at various musical instruments. If only I could afford a violin or a mandolin.

Overcome by a sense of futility, I decide never to come to Jammu Railway Station in the future. I don't even want to visit Jammu again. There is no point in leaving Udhampur.

* * *

June 1994
Typing and Shorthand Training Institute (Next to Kak Opticians)
Dhar Road, Udhampur

I have started learning typing and shorthand. Don't ask me why. Shorthand is boring and difficult, but I am trying to get used to typing. Ma is happy now. 'At least you will obtain technical skills and someone will hire you as a secretary or a stenographer . . .'

Ma is now a teacher at Happy Model School. She wants me to land a respectable job too. She is not happy that I chose to leave DAV College Chandigarh and stay back with them at Udhampur, and that I didn't even work hard enough to opt for technical education at a polytechnic institute or something similar.

I appear for entrance exams for government jobs, starting with officer-level positions. But I soon realize how ill-prepared I am. I don't make the cut. I keep failing. Next, I apply for clerical positions, hoping to land a job as a bank clerk, a Life Insurance Corporation (LIC) agent or a postman in District Doda or Reasi, but I fail to clear even one of these simple and easy exams.

I want to run away, but where do I go? I am not even smart or lucky enough to become a postman in Bhaderwah, Doda, where there is only one post office. Bhaderwah is like the Kashmir of Jammu Province. The people of Udhampur call it *Chota* (Mini) Kashmir.

'What will you do now?' neighbours and relatives ask me.

Someone advises me to apply for the job of a lower-division clerk in the government dispensary in a neighbouring village.

'You could do file work, couldn't you?' he suggests. I appear for the test. A simple test. I am hopeful, but when the list of successful candidates comes out, my name is not on it.

I face rejection after rejection and disappointment after disappointment. I am a let-down.

Many relatives come to our place to express their concern over my successive failures. One of them brings a hand-drawn chart. 'My worst fears have come true,' she says, pointing to an illustration drawn on the sheet of paper in her hand.

'Look, *Shani* (Saturn) has entered his zodiac sign,' she says to Ma and Babi.

Saturn has always been my favourite planet. What have I done to bring its wrath upon myself?

'It is all powerful and won't let good things happen for the next seven-and-a half years,' the woman says to me. 'For seven-and-a-half years, you will go through turmoil and see the worst of times. Nothing can be done now. This phase is called *Sade Sati*, and you must navigate it very carefully and with utmost caution. You will have to struggle, but you should remain brave . . .' she goes on and on, painting a bleak picture of the years to come.

Babi gives me a worried look, as if I am doomed for good.

I look at the chart. The illustration. The planetary positions. Saturn is making a quiet entry. Why is he in such a hurry? Why now? Why would he want to ruin me?

Seven-and-a-half years is an entire youth. 'What if this chart is . . .'

'Don't you dare question the wisdom and foresight of the guru who has been kind enough to prepare your horoscope at my insistence . . . He's the most reputed guru in our community . . . He doesn't even have the time for ministers, bureaucrats and judges who come knocking at his door to know more about their destinies . . .'

'There must be a way out,' I say to her. She says she will consult the astrologer again and request a remedy for my situation.

She is back after some days. 'I bring good news. There is no way out of this phase, but you will be spared great misfortune if you do exactly what Guruji has prescribed.'

She reads out the tasks that I must do for 999 days. I am to wear a black vest. I must not eat anything on certain days. I must recite a mantra 100 times a day for a year. I must pray. And I must have faith. Profound, unwavering faith. Not even for a moment should I lose my faith.

I evaluate my options. It is 1994. By the time *Sade Sati* ends in seven-and-a-half years, it will be 2002. If I ignore the guru's advice, I run the risk of wasting my youth. But what if nothing happens even if I do wear a black vest, recite the mantra, pray, serve the poor, lick the wounds of lepers and skip one meal a day?

Once again, my life is a big 'what if'.

'There is no way out of this,' everyone says. 'Saturn is going to rule you now and not let good things come your way.'

Seven-and-a-half long and dark years are ahead of me. By the time Saturn exits and leaves me alone, my youth will be wasted and over. I will be a finished man. I won't even have the will to live. I will be left with nothing to live for.

Has Saturn only chosen me or are there others in his stranglehold? What could I have done to bring this upon myself? Saturn will cast an evil spell and I will be doomed. All I will see is darkness. Nothing will make sense. There won't be any meaning to my life. I will lose everything. I will never have anything.

I am left with no choice but to wait it out. Every morning, I recite the mantra 100 times. I sit with my eyes closed, invoke Saturn as though he were the lord of my life and plead. I plead guilty. I promise to atone for all my wrongdoings. I promise to lead a life of piety and virtue. All I do is make promises.

'O Saturn, please be kind and benevolent. I will do everything you say. I will not demand anything.'

* * *

'Mathematics and sciences will give you an edge over others,' Ma keeps saying. 'They are important for jobs. Philosophy won't fetch you a job.'

Ma is right. I am not able to think properly. Babuji and Pa are happy that I have chosen the arts stream. It is easier. At least I will score good marks. At least I will get a degree. I don't want to fail.

'Typing and shorthand will be additional skills,' says Ma. 'Don't lose interest in them now.'

The typing instructor, who is also the shop owner, gives me the first lesson. 'This is a typewriter. This is the paper grip. This is the roller ball. This is the margin tab. This is the ribbon and this is the ribbon spool. This is the lever. These are the keys. This key is next to that key. This is how you load paper into the carriage. This is how you set the margins. Don't worry about the rest. I will teach you everything.'

Mine is going to be a short-term course. Just to last the summer.

The first lesson: Posture. Hands. Finger placement. Keys. Eyes.

I type the letters: Q W E R T Y

Top left to right keys.

'No,' chides Sir. 'Don't do anything on your own. Just follow my orders.'

I type a full page, which takes me an hour: THE QUICK BROWN FOX JUMPS OVER THE LAZY DOG.

It takes me a few minutes just to locate certain keys.

'By the end of this month,' says Sir, 'I expect you to be able to type a page in no more than three minutes. Eighty words a minute. Nothing less will do.'

Every day, the quick brown fox jumps over the lazy dog. I have no idea why. Soon, I am sick of the brown fox jumping over the lazy dog. I want to see some other animals now. A bear or a lion perhaps.

A month later, I type my own poems, stories and diary entries. But the next day, I realize my silly mistakes.

'Not so slow,' says Sir, noticing me doze off. 'You won't learn a thing. Speed is everything in typing.'

'Not so fast,' he says next, watching me go haywire. 'You will commit a lot of mistakes. Perfection is everything in typing.'

But it is so hot today. I can't keep my eyes open. I want to sleep.

'Your father's money is precious. Don't let it go to waste. Or else I won't accept a rupee from him . . .'

Bobby says it is better to learn computers rather than typing. He takes me to a newly opened computer training institute in the market. But their fees are too high.

'You know, you must aim for a salary of at least Rs 6000 per month. It will happen only if you know how to operate a computer . . .'

'A salary of Rs 6000 a month?'

At Masterji's place, a student who is learning the flute says he plans to set up a paneer business. 'You want to join me? You should. There is no business better than the paneer business. We will supply paneer to the whole of Katra and the Mata Vaishno Devi shrine. Forget Rs 6000. We will earn Rs 20,000 per month. Imagine! You can still play your flute. And in a few years, we will make Rs 1 lakh per month. Then you can afford a place in the Housing Colony. Think about it.'

* * *

Pa's colleague from Jammu is paying us a visit.

'When did you come over?' he says.

'From where, Uncle?'

'From Maharashtra, where you study engineering?'

'I am not studying engineering in Maharashtra.'

'Then where? Andhra? Karnataka?'

'No, Uncle.'

'Then?'

'I am here!'

'You are still here? Doing what?'

'I am studying for my bachelor's in arts.'

'From where?'

'I am a private student.'

'A private student?'

Uncle shakes his head and looks at Pa as though to say: 'What have you done?' He then says, 'You will ruin him. What will he do in life? His life is finished. Send him to Maharashtra immediately. You still have time. Get him admitted to a technical course.'

Ma's expression—looking at Pa and me—seems to say: 'See, I told you so! And you thought I was wrong. One day you will regret it!'

Uncle is not the first person to have said so. Nearly all of Pa's colleagues who live in Jammu say the same thing. Their children are studying engineering in Maharashtra, Andhra Pradesh and Karnataka.

'It is important, Arvind,' Uncle first says to Pa. Then he addresses me, 'It is for your own good, Siddhartha. And for the good of your parents. You've got to look after them when they grow old. You need to have a good job to buy a house for your mom and dad. Don't you see? It is very important. Do you realize what we are going through? We will never get back what we lost. Forget Kashmir. Work towards settling outside this state, getting a good job in the corporate sector, saving money and buying a house somewhere . . .'

'He wants to become a writer . . .' Pa says. 'He writes poetry. *Daily Excelsior* publishes his columns every month.'

'All these hobbies are nice, but you should know that we owe a lot to Balasaheb Thackeray,' Uncle says. 'He welcomed us with open arms when no one else did. Not even our own government. He has directed all engineering colleges to admit students like you without any capitation fee. Balasaheb has also gotten the colleges to reserve hundreds of seats for us. You don't even need to take an entrance test. You must not waste this golden opportunity. Avail of the benefits and secure your future . . .'

Uncle is right. So are Pa and Ma. I am not sure of myself. I don't want to be around when such a topic is discussed.

* * *

'We need another Buddha to awaken us and save us from ruin,' says Arjan Dev Majboor. He is Pa's friend and visits us almost every week.

He recites some lines from 'Another Buddha', a poem he's writing.

'You must write, son,' he says to me. 'Poetry is the only way forward for us in these times. It is our only home when we have no home.'

He can't stop talking about his home in Zainapur, a village in Anantnag. The village is named after the medieval king Zain-ul-Abidin, who used to visit a Sufi living in the village. Zainapur is known for its countless springs. Wherever you look, you will see springs. And now here, our eyes thirst for one glimpse of a drop of water.

Majboor Uncle likes spending time at our place. He recites poem after poem. They are all about Kashmir and its beauty. He sings of mountains and lakes and gardens and flowers and springs and waterfalls and the seasons.

The two friends exchange views while sipping tea. I just listen.

'Is the beauty of the mountains and lakes and gardens and flowers more bewitching than the beauty of fall?' Pa asks. 'One must experience falls and humiliation. We were pushed into the mud. Let us learn to live in mud . . .'

'I tell my children, grandchildren and other members of my family that they will know my worth when I am gone, when I am dead,' Majboor Uncle says.

Later, Pa says, 'From Kashmir, he came with a bottle filled with the water of the Vitasta* and kept it on a shelf in the drawing room. He shows the bottle to all who come to his place in Udhampur . . .'

Pa's friends P.K. Goja, P.L. Goja, Bushan Lal Kaul (known as Dr Bushan Lal) and Vijay Zutshi meet at each other's places and spend hours together. They talk about almost everything. They sometimes share a bottle of whisky.

After some time, they crack jokes, share humorous anecdotes and laugh the whole night. This is Pa's first long laugh in two years. The six friends laugh at one another. They laugh at their fate. They laugh at the present moment. They simply laugh and promise to meet again the next morning at someone else's place. But they are aware of the uncertain nature of their condition. The uncertain promises they make to each other—to meet every day, share their griefs and joys and end all days by laughing, no matter what. The only thing worth learning is how to laugh like these six mad men, who have nothing else to give to the world except this great art— the art of laughing in all situations.

'Now we will meet at so-and-so's cremation or tenth day ritual; this is the only certainty,' laughs Goja Uncle. His sense of humour keeps the friends sane. Zutshi Uncle is an artist. He shows me drawings. Roots, uprooted tree trunks, ruins, a topsy-turvy world—I have never seen such drawings. They should be seen by everyone. Every drawing is a story. And I find myself in each one of them.

---

* A Rigvedic name given to River Jhelum.

5

The Link Road Daydreamers

Summer, 1993
Link Road, Udhampur

Deepak, Bobby and I are at Link Road once again. People call us 'The Link Road Daydreamers'. Others call us the 'Three Musketeers'. We have never missed a morning, an afternoon or an evening. We meet thrice a day, every single day. We are inseparable. It is an uncanny record of sorts. Our summer days are spent sauntering along the Link Road. Singh Cafeteria is our haunt. Evenings are given to hallucinations and dreams. Mornings bring with them a dull and drab reality.

I look at the familiar house, its windows, door and terrace. I sing songs of love and longing. I see you again. If only you looked at me. I am singing your song and dreaming that I am in it. If only you had stayed. But I know this moment will go away. And with it will go the feeling that it has indeed gone away. And from that moment onwards, you will never leave. The thought of leaving will never even occur to you. You will stay until the end of eternity. Even though I won't be there, I know none of this is going to happen. Everything that I have will once again be taken away. Everything. Even this moment. The thought and the dream of you. And finally, you!

Day after day, we oscillate between light and darkness. Our lives are nothing but rote. No day is different. Our todays resemble our yesterdays and our tomorrows are the same as our todays.

We see boys and girls from the camp squandering their youth. But it isn't their fault. What else will they do? They come and go while squalid days and nights trample them, leading to atrophy. This is not how childhood or youth should be.

Nobody visits us in the camp. Nobody cares. Where is the government? Where are the ministers? Where are the artists, the filmmakers and the champions of human rights in our country? Where are the great men and women of our nation? Where are those who we thought were heroes and whom we worshipped? Don't they know what we are being made to go through? The terrible things happening to us here in the camp? The truth is that they don't want to know. No one wants to know. Heroes turned out to be indifferent to our plight. We were wrong. We are betrayed by our own dreams and aspirations and by our own thoughts.

The newspapers don't even mention our existence, let alone our plight. It's as if we don't even exist. We are the nowhere people. We are the non-existent people. Not even shadows. Not even worthy of note.

For the last few days, there has been talk about a fashion show taking place in the Chinar Complex in Udhampur, at the Northern Command Headquarters. The fashion show has been organized by a cultural association of the Indian Army. The purpose of the fashion show is to raise awareness about the sacrifices of the Indian Army towards protecting the sovereignty of the nation and saving Kashmir from falling. The newspapers are full of photographs of models and celebrities participating in the fashion show. Hundreds of media people are covering the beauty pageant just 5 km away from the migrant camp in Udhampur, but not a single photojournalist or reporter is interested in dropping by the camp to document what is going on here.

It is a case of 'beauty' versus 'ugliness'. We can't even go there because we are camp-dwellers.

What will it take for the press and celebrities to take note of the camp and its miserable conditions? How about organizing a beauty pageant on the camp premises? If we can pull it off, maybe people will take note and we can present our case to the world.

Deepak, Bobby and I start dreaming of organizing a fashion show in the camp. What else can we do? We will get the children and teenagers in the camp to participate. We will get someone to train them. It won't be a fashion show like the one taking place in the Chinar Complex, but it will be a beauty pageant with a difference. People should get to see real beauty in its rawest and purest form. Naked, throbbing and trembling, but pregnant with life.

Imagine such a pageant in the camp! It will make world news. It will set an example for all refugees who find themselves in a similar situation as ours. Abandoned, sidelined, ignored, forgotten and made to live on the fringes.

This may sound like a dream. But dreams can come true. But we don't want this to be yet another Link Road dream.

Outside the camp and by the roadside, a few camp-dwellers have set up small handcarts to sell vegetables and other things. Things you normally need in the camp. Things that help you survive. You should look at the things atop these handcarts. Soap, incense sticks, kohl, talcum powder, ointments, better-quality rice and sugar, sheets, buckets, spices and earthen pots, along with bamboo poles that are used to hold a tent together. Some people who can't afford handcarts have placed these things for sale on plastic sheets on the ground.

Camp-dwellers are selling these things to fellow camp-dwellers while their children attend the camp school.

* * *

The science students at the camp school have been demanding access to a laboratory. Arts students demand access to a library. I am fortunate to have the books that Pa salvaged. But no other student has books.

The science students read about experiments, but they don't know how to perform practical experiments without a laboratory. However, their pleas fall on deaf ears.

This is what the camp-dwellers say to two people who have come to interview them: 'During the monsoons, which last from July until September, we have rain and hail almost every day. It is stormy at night. Tents cave in one after another at night. In the mornings, when the storm abates and the rain stops, people put the tents back up all over again. You can imagine how we've had to learn how to do this. There is nobody to go to when our tents collapse. No one comes to help. There is no mechanism to lodge a complaint or grievance. The canvas of these tents is torn and tattered. Not even the ragpickers and recyclers touch them. Such is the condition. Fit to be discarded . . .'

In fact, the tents allotted to the displaced Pandits are the ones that have been discarded by the department of tourism. Not even the *kabadi wallah* (scrap dealer) will take them. Even if you pay to get rid of them. Such is their condition. Some old tents were donated by the armed forces—not the unused ones but those that were rotting in their warehouses. Whatever is of no use to the authorities and the government is donated to us. This is how you kill two birds with one stone. Maybe not two, but three birds with one stone. First, get rid of unwanted, worthless and good-for-nothing things such as canvas tents and storage tanks. Second, give the impression that our needs are being taken care of and third, earn good karma and the goodwill of people.

'Don't give us anything else,' says a camp-dweller named Rakesh Kumar Bhat. 'All we ask for is new tents, at least. So that we have proper shelter over our heads. Back home, we had three-storeyed houses. Here, the only six-storeyed thing we possess is grief. We are trapped in this camp of grief. Look at my wife. She had a paralytic stroke. She can't even walk to the toilet and clean herself. I have to carry her several times during the day and night. The toilet next to our tent is a den of infection and disease. We live in stench all the time. Even the stray dogs stay away from here. You can't even lure the dogs with food that you place outside the tent. They detest coming here. This place is not even fit for gutter worms, let alone animals and humans. I wish time had fast-forwarded thirty years and all this was behind us. We haven't slept a wink in the past three years. Sleep eludes us in these tents. Will no one listen to our woes? Will no one come to help us and take us someplace else?'

* * *

This place—the camp—must be studied by psychologists, architects, designers, doctors and engineers. For instance, architects should take a look at the layout and arrangement of tents. They should examine the space from the perspective of space management. How much space does a family of six or eight need to live for a day, a month or a year? It will aid in their research.

Psychologists and behavioural scientists should study the silence of the men and women who seem to have lost their voices. It's not that they don't have anything to say, but their silence could be an expression of something far more complex. Something that can never be conveyed. It is the study of this language of silence that will contribute to the understanding of humans who go through hell. It will aid in devising coping mechanisms. How must one cope? Is coping even possible? What impact will it have on future generations?

Engineers should study the drainage and sewage systems and the sanitary conditions. Or maybe the absence of them in this camp. People have dug drains themselves so that they can flush dirty water out of the tents. Some people know how to create a slope in the floor for the water to flow out. People are learning how to do these things. You will find amateur engineers, doctors and psychologists here.

If you don't know how to fix a tent, you will meet people who will not only teach you how to repair a tent but also how to create space even when there is none.

Since the government hasn't set up a single clinic or health centre, some camp-dwellers have had to acquire rudimentary knowledge of the medicines that one is supposed to take for skin diseases, gastroenteric infections, fevers, blood pressure fluctuations, body aches, bone and joint disorders, insect bites and other ailments.

If you are terribly sad or depressed, you will come across people who know how to cheer you up. They are the best psychologists you will ever come across in life. They're always smiling, no matter what.

If you look at it this way, you will see the best minds living here. You will see innovators and magicians. You will see people who can perform miracles. And every day I see miracles. To be able to survive here for more than a day is a miracle. And look at us. Nothing is happening to us. We are doing fine. What could be worse than what we're going through now? We have learned how to defeat death and stay alive.

We are nobody's vote bank. We are on our own.

* * *

Ironically, hope is what took me down the road of despair. And impossible desires led me to Link Road. What should I do? Sometimes, I have dreadful thoughts. I can't keep them at bay. I desire things I don't deserve. My mind is full of sinful thoughts.

What if I die loveless? What if love deserts me when I need it the most, when I am still young? What if my youth fades without tasting love? What if no one falls in love with me? I long for someone's touch. Is it too much to ask for?

I go to the Devika river to bathe, thinking that my soul will be cleansed. How do I wash the stains off my soul? And then I remember the story.

Young monk: 'Master, what is the greatest sin?'
Master: 'Not sinning at least once in life is the greatest sin.'

Every time Deepak and I hurtle towards insanity, Bobby stands in the way like a rock, preventing his two friends from committing foolish and senseless acts. Such is our desperation, our longing and our pain.

The only thing that heals pain is pain itself.

* * *

A Day
DAV School, Lambi Gali, Udhampur

'Wrong,' says Swamiji to us, in response to a question I ask. He is winding up the day's lesson. Deepak and I have enrolled in a three-month lecture series on the Bhagavad Gita. A yogi has come from Uttar Pradesh to teach lessons at the DAV School every evening. He wears saffron-coloured clothes and speaks chaste Hindi and Sanskrit.

Towards the end of his lessons, he encourages the attendees to ask questions. The two of us are the youngest participants. The rest are locals who are in their fifties and sixties.

'Swamiji, is it true that the only thing that heals pain is pain itself?' is my question.

It is from a famous Urdu couplet, which I am not sure if Swamiji knows of. To my surprise, he does know. He smiles and shakes his head.

'You ask a good question. Let us hope that you will keep asking such questions and that my lectures on the Gita will help you find the right answers. If you learn how to serve others, they will cease to be others. You will see yourself in them. If you give up some of your comforts to help those who need them more than you do . . . then you will always be . . .'

Swamiji recites shlokas, lucidly explaining each one of them and interspersing the explanations with stories from the Upanishads, the Ramayana and the Mahabharata. Stories about the world, birth, life, body, mind, soul, desire, attachment, compassion, duty, worship, service, beauty, truth, goodness, consciousness, renunciation and death. And what constitutes each one of them.

'Hope, love, freedom, time and life are things to donate to those who don't have them,' he says.

We end the lecture by reciting a prayer:

Whatever you do in life,
you must always read Keshava's Gita,
for you will find answers to all questions
in this book of books,
this song of songs . . .

Silence prevails. Something stirs within. A fleeting feeling of experiencing infinitude. And then, suddenly, the same old sinking feeling returns once again.

What will we do tomorrow? Where shall we go? What will happen to us? How will we find peace? How will we find happiness?

Swamiji flashes us a smile, as if he's privy to our dilemmas and vicissitudes.

'Go on, ask any doubt,' Swamiji's smile conveys. An 'It-is-okay-if-you-still-have-a-silly-question' look. It feels as if something is being handed over to me. Something that is of immense use. Like cash to buy things—food, books, music cassettes, a cooler, a fridge.

He places his right hand on our heads and wishes us eternal happiness.

We go to our usual chai shop to make sense of it all. We derive our own meanings from these lessons to stave off negative thoughts. But madness has gripped us, and we feel drawn towards it. Mine is a life of recklessness. I have become a vagabond. I don't take anything seriously. I no longer know what I want from life.

Darkness descends and we return to the camp. We return to desolate mornings and desperate evenings. To our elders, whose fate is to struggle and to put up a brave front to stave off madness. The nights bring hallucinations and the days give birth to fantasies.

The next day, we head out into the new world with eyes closed and heads shaved.

I dream that a girl I have fallen in love with is making love to my dead body. I dream dreams that must never be dreamed.

I want to become a bangle seller. That's all I want.

* * *

Another Day

Dixon is in tears when he comes home one day. His younger brother is getting married in a few months. We will have to vacate the place. He doesn't want us to leave. Nor does his wife. This is their property, but they are helpless. In the heart of their hearts, they would rather have us around than their brother. But where will his brother live once he brings home his bride?

'When you look for a new place, make sure there's a proper toilet with a commode,' says Ma.

Pa and I begin searching for a two-room set in other parts of the town. No luck for days. There are rooms, but none with proper toilets and bathrooms. Then there are barns. Then there are rooms without proper ventilation. Neither doors nor windows. Rooms without walls. Rooms without roofs. Rooms yet to be constructed. Rooms that aren't even rooms.

At last, down the hill, in Barrian, a two-room set in a newly constructed house is available for rent. One must go halfway down the hill. The toilet and bathroom are decent. There is a tap in the toilet. The room has only a small ventilator and one window, but that's okay. The kitchen is decent too. The landlord, Darshan Kumar, is posted in a remote village. His wife and infant child live there.

Everything seems good initially, but we soon discover the only problem—there is no regular water supply. It's a ploy to demand more rent. 'Need more water? Pay more rent.' We have no choice. This doesn't end. Thankfully, there is a spring down the hill. At first, we think it would be easy to get water from there. But then, such things are easier said than done. We have little idea what is in store for us.

We start going to the spring to collect water and ferrying it back to our rooms. Every day, twice a day. In the sun and in the rain. It becomes a habit. For survival. But it is an ordeal.

The landlady looks at us with pity in her eyes. But she too is helpless before her husband.

Someday we will find a place with water and shade.

'Wishful thinking,' says a neighbour. 'We must swallow this poison. We are doomed. A cursed lot. Maybe this curse has befallen us. Or maybe we have been cursed by . . .'

He comes to our place almost every day and leaves reluctantly. There's a reason why he doesn't want to go back to his place. He shares his woes with us. He finds Pa's company comforting. Talking to Babuji gives him solace. Babi's words give him strength. Moreover, the place where he lives is not fit for humans. It's a hovel. The man's tears have dried up. His mother and wife seem to be holding up well. They don't have even a minute to spare. Always busy with chores. The man is lucky! Strong women at home are a good thing. He needs them, but he doesn't even know that he's alive and sane because of them. They argue about certain things. Important things and unimportant things. Domestic things. These are the only things that matter now. And sometimes they speak loudly. It takes me some time to understand why they do this. Speaking loudly helps. It gives them purpose. It keeps their minds healthy.

The man is a nervous wreck.

'Look at my wife, my mother, my father, my two children and me,' he says. 'I don't know what will happen to us.'

* * *

Our landlady comes screaming. She barges into our room with her infant daughter in her arms. 'Help me! Help me! There's a snake in my kitchen.'

I grab a bottle of phenyl and a stick and go after the snake. I pour phenyl on the snake. It is the best survival tactic I know. The snake is rendered unconscious. The only thing I have learned here is how to deal with snakes. The rainy season is the worst. I am an expert at catching snakes. I know how to grab hold of them and relocate them back to the snake hills down the hill.

The landlady cries. Tears of joy. The expression on her face betrays regret and guilt.

'If you need anything, please let me know,' she says. 'From now on, you won't have to face any problem with respect to water. You won't have to go down the hill. You will have all the water that is supplied to us . . .'

She keeps making promises. We will have to see what happens when her husband comes home in a few days. He comes almost every two or three weeks. He is not a bad man. He's just someone who has never had tenants, so he doesn't know how to treat them. He derives pleasure from doing certain things, such as stopping the water supply when we need it the most.

'Water is not everything,' he says when we confront him.

Compared to other landlords, however, he is a saint. There are other Dogra landlords whose selfishness is matchless. They completely shut off the water supply so that you are forced to leave their house and they can demand higher rent. And there is always someone willing to pay more.

* * *

'Do whatever you like, but don't cry like that. Don't make any noise,' A Dogra landlords scream. 'Or else be ready to leave this house.'

The Dogras are not like us. They don't like the sound of crying and weeping. They don't like the way we weep. We can't even cry now. We can't even mourn our dead.

They want to throw us out of here too.

'You have come to eat our jobs, you Pandits . . .'

All they want is more rent. They throw their barns and lofts open. Uninhabitable places. We have no choice but to seek shelter there. It doesn't matter if we don't have toilets or bathrooms. All we want are four walls and a roof to protect us.

We live in fear. Fear is worse than death, but it is better to be alive than dead.

No, it is better to be dead than to live like this.

There, the Muslims hounded and persecuted us. Here, the Dogras harass us. They think we will eat their jobs, grab their land and houses, and run away with their women.

Some women in the camp cry. Awful things are going on in the camp. The local Dogra boys and men . . . they come and stare. Ugly stares. And then they do the unthinkable. They come in minibuses and force hapless women and girls to go with them. This happens almost every day. They have gotten used to this. They do it openly and brazenly. In buses and outside schools and colleges. Someday, I will gather the courage to confront them. Someday, they will have to apologize to us. The women are helpless.

* * *

Some boys take me to a place that seems to be a school. I am introduced to the teachers there. In the courtyard, many boys are undergoing drills of all sorts. The men give me a booklet titled *Vishva Hindu Parishad*.

'Read it and understand,' they say.

Every day, I go to the place in the evenings. I join the classes. Pa finds out. Deepak and Bobby spill the beans. 'No,' they say. 'Don't go there. You have better things to do.'

* * *

I travel to Jammu to buy audio cassettes of Mehdi Hassan's ghazals, Pandit Shivkumar Sharma's santoor and Pandit Hariprasad Chaurasia's flute. Music is all I have now. My whole life depends on it.

Pandit Shivkumar Sharma's music transports me back to Kashmir. 'Come home; the seasons are waiting,' Kashmir keeps calling to me.

His music is the cry of my soul. The cry of desperation.

6

The Two Ghats of Time

A Day in the Autumn of 1992

Ma, Pa, Henna, Babuji, Babi and I board a bus to Krimchi, a village that is an hour's drive from Udhampur. It's been three years since we spent a day outdoors—in a garden, by a lake or in the lap of nature, where peace and tranquility are said to reside. Our lives in Kashmir were full of outings and picnics. With every change of season, we would visit different places. We would travel to the holy springs of Verinag, the meadows in Gulmarg and Pahalgam, the hanging gardens in Nishat and Shalimar, the almond grove in Badamwari, the saffron fields of Pampore, the orchards in Ladhoo and Khrew and the waterfalls in Aharbal. We would spend days sitting in gardens under the shade of a Chinar. We would have happy dreams of visiting other places the following year. We considered ourselves to be the luckiest people alive, for our happiness and contentment was boundless. Sometimes, we'd wonder if it were all true. Such was our life in Kashmir. Full of beauty, joy and time. Time moved slowly there.

But now, here, away from our home and in exile, many of the things we had followed for years have come to an end and many other things still alive are ending.

In Krimchi, we come across ancient temples. All that remains now are the ruins, which are surrounded by gardens. Babi spreads a rug and we sit quietly, just the way we used to sit in the Shalimar Bagh in Srinagar. There is silence. We are the only people here. Birds are chirping. Pigeons peek through tiny crevices in the ruins. Every stone seems to narrate a story.

'We should come here every once in a while,' Babi says. 'This place is an ideal picnic spot. Don't you feel as if you are back in Avantipur? Near the Sun temple. We should also go to Mansar Lake. I have heard that it is the Dal Lake of Udhampur . . .'

Babi goes on and on about the importance of making excursions at least once a month. She seems to have acquired a lot of knowledge about the picnic spots in and around Udhampur. But I sense it is not as much about picnics for her as it is about travelling and discovering new places. She's always been fond of visiting new places by herself. Taking the untrodden path, as it were.

She's right. We must come here at least once a month. And we must discover new places. Being out and about is what will keep us from losing our sanity.

One day, we will sit in Chasm-e-Shahi and drink the sweet water again. One day, we will go to Pari Mahal and speak with the fairies again. We will go to Swami Lakshmanjoo's ashram in Ishbar and pray that none of this happens again.

I look at Babuji. He seems lost in a reverie. So is everyone else. Our lives are now split between the two ghats of time—there and here.

* * *

There is a family in our neighbourhood. The woman has developed a strange disorder. She doesn't allow anyone to touch her. It is an affliction that no one understands. Some think she is a saint or the reincarnation of a saint. She has stopped touching others and the things of others. She doesn't want to wash other people's clothes or utensils, but she somehow does such things with absolute detachment. She believes everything is impure. Everything but her.

Babi's sister says Lord Shiva keeps appearing in her dreams to talk to her about the universe. She has scant interest in other things now. Even pressing things that require her attention. Such as family affairs and sustenance. But somehow, she manages to complete her domestic chores and feed her husband and children. Mentally, though, she is elsewhere. She has started to believe that she's not an ordinary person because Lord Shiva has blessed her by appearing in her dreams.

* * *

A Night in the Summer of 1993

Two men are on the prowl in the street outside. They begin knocking at the door and the window. At first, the knocks are gentle, but soon the knocking becomes violent. They start calling out names. Softly and then vehemently, as though they are enacting a play.

'Panditji, come out . . . Panditji, come out . . .' They go on and on.

Ma is terrified. Pa tries to calm her down. 'They are drunks; they will go away soon . . .'

But they don't go.

Minutes pass. It is now 10 p.m. The voices get louder and louder. Outside in the street—more name-calling, more vulgarity. Inside the room—more fear, more trembling.

They break the windowpane. Oh, the dread! It's the same dread we experienced in Kashmir, but here, it is unexpected.

'Why don't they go away?' Ma whispers. She shuts her ears. 'Do something . . .'

Pa starts screaming to scare the intruders away.

'I'm going to come out and kill you,' he says in an angry tone. 'Son, get me the big knife . . .'

The two men start laughing, almost calling out the bluff.

'Yeah, yeah, come out and kill us . . .'

Two hours pass. The torture goes on.

Midnight. 2 a.m. The drunks keep at it.

They won't go away unless . . .

'What do they want?'

Pa's patience is at an end. He is restive now. He is fuming. He gets up, makes a ruckus, opens the door and starts screaming.

The two men flee.

Some Days Later

'We will have to find a better place to rent. This house is turning us all mad, one after another,' sobs Ma.

Every day, she hopes that Pa will be able to find a better place. But there is no luck.

'I'm trying,' Pa says. 'I am going from one house to another to check if they are decent enough to rent . . .'

'If we continue to live here, we will not survive,' sobs Ma. 'How long will we live like this? We will go mad. All of us. Find us a better place. Look at yourself. Look at what has become of you, of Babi and Babuji. Look at their faces. This madness is worse than death . . .'

The daily hunt for water, going up and down the hill and carrying buckets of water, has taken a toll on Ma's health. Her back is affected. She doesn't even have a moment's rest. The purpose of her life has become to keep us alive. If she's not around, we will die.

At night, Ma retreats into a shell. The voices of the drunks outside the house keep us awake at night. The drunks keep coming night after night, knocking at the door, hurling abuses and calling out names.

'Panditji, come out . . . Panditji, come out . . .'

We are at the mercy of the local Dogras, who decide if we are to remain at peace or not. We are used to this routine now. This is our fate.

* * *

19 January 1991
Out of My Land

> *And then there is dark silence.*
> *One more day is put to death.*
> *The embankment is stained crimson.*
> *The sky is brushed vermilion.*
> *And the sacred hill*
> *Watches the scene*
> *In dim bewilderment—*
> *The village is set astir.*
> *Dawn witnesses a silent exodus,*
> *And dusk opens its long arms*
> *To silent deaths.*
> *I sleep in snatches.*
> *Dreaming nervy dreams.*
> *The sun is hard.*

The shade a thorn.
Alien blood oozes
Out of a familiar wound.
My tongue dangles
To lick the saffron dust.
The tune of my childhood
Is lost here,
But it saunters there
Among the distant ruins.
The echo detaches from the song
And seeks union.

* * *

A Day in the Monsoon of 1993

The desperation of the camp-dwellers waiting in front of the ration office near Raj Cinema is unsettling. Once again, hundreds of people start lining up very early in the morning, hoping that the food rations will be disbursed. They have been coming here for days. But there are no ration supplies in the office store. The jute sacks are empty. There isn't even a handful of rice or wheat. Some clerks say they are waiting for the supplies to arrive from Jammu.

'The Jammu truckers continue to be on strike,' they say. Others are blaming the authorities. No one knows the real story and nor is anyone willing to find out the truth and do something about the desperate situation.

It has been raining for days now and the weather is muggy. Almost everyone in the camp is sick. This is the season of infections. Men, women and children are down with fever, but nobody can afford rest. Everyone is up and about despite the fever. Moreover, to add to our woes, there is an outbreak of a strange skin disease. Rashes have erupted all over our bodies. Not an inch of our body is spared. Arms, legs, face, neck, back . . .

Doctors have no clue about the cause. They blame the conditions prevailing in the camp. 'You people are not used to such conditions; that's why you keep catching such infections,' they say.

None of the medicines work—ointment, antifungal or antibacterial. Our skin has begun to peel off now. But this isn't our only worry. For the camp-dwellers, it's a question of survival. Without a government-supplied ration, people are compelled to purchase food from shops, risking the depletion of their savings. Most camp-dwellers have no money of their own. Their only source of income is government relief, which is paltry to begin with.

Everyone is waiting for news about the availability of supplies at the ration office. But there has been no news for days. The officers are nowhere to be found. The clerks know nothing and offer false assurances. 'We are expecting the strike to end any day now,' they keep saying. 'You must learn to be patient . . .'

'This has become a stale excuse now!' scream the camp-dwellers. 'Think of a better excuse . . .'

'Lies, lies, lies . . . how many more lies will you utter . . .'

Whom do we turn to?

'We are doomed, we are doomed,' chants a man. His wife keeps chiding him for his behaviour. 'Stop it now; you have been saying this for three years. What will you achieve by exposing your weakness? Look at others; they are so strong and tough. You should learn from them . . .'

People come and go through the gates of the office in hordes. They ask the same question again and again, despite knowing there is little chance of having their concerns addressed.

'When will the supplies arrive? Is there a possibility of receiving the rations today?'

'Tomorrow?'

'How about the day after?'

Day Twenty

Camp-dwellers are still lined up. Many have been waiting since dawn. There has been some encouraging news about the departure of a ration truck from Jammu. The officials are relieved. They are preparing for the truck's arrival at the office.

A truck finally arrives. An expression of relief appears on everyone's faces. Mixed emotions. Anger, frustration, resignation, hope, despair and relief. Their faces beam at the sight of at least 100 jute sacks containing rice, wheat and sugar. People offer their blessings to the driver and the attendant. A man rushes to kiss the driver's hand.

Two labourers start unloading the truck. They carry sacks full of supplies—rice, wheat and sugar—to the store. After some hours, a clerk starts calling out the names.

Roshan Lal Bhat
Girdhari Lal Raina
Rattan Nath Pandita
Bansi Lal Koul
Mohan Rani Dhar
Omkar Nath Gigoo

The ration cards are stamped and relief is disbursed.

Day Twenty-Two

Rats have raided the store. They are all over the sacks of wheat, devouring it. Rainwater has seeped into the store. The whole place stinks. The stench is unbearable. There are more mud balls and black stones in rice sacks than rice itself. The sugar is yellow in colour. Ants are feasting on it.

This is not how food rations are meant to be stored, but everyone seems resigned to the situation. Anger is pointless—you can't do a thing. Who do you go to? Whom do you complain to? It's just widespread corruption and the death of morality. People are making money at our expense.

But nothing goes to waste. Babi quietly donates the monthly rations to mendicants and hermits at the banks of the Devika. 'At least they won't go hungry,' she says.

* * *

A Day in the Spring of 1986
Ration Ghat, Yarbal, Safa Kadal,
Srinagar

Babuji and Babi have taken me to Yarbal. It is our monthly trip to the ration ghat to buy rice and sugar. We are at the ghat and in front of us is the Jhelum, flowing quietly. Next to the ghat is Ram Mandir. Several big and small *dongas* (houseboats) are parked at the ghat. It is a quiet spring day. The snow has started to melt. Buds have started to sprout.

We are waiting for our turn. Finally, the ghat *munshi* (incharge) calls out for us: Omkar Nath Gigoo and Uma Shori Gigoo. The ghat munshi is known to Babi and Babuji. He sits cross-legged under an awning. In front of him is a houseboat-shaped wooden chest containing the money and people's ration booklets.

'Hurry up,' he says to people. 'We have got the best quality harvest from the fields of Islamabad. Go and take a look before it is all finished. Take a few extra handfuls today. Doctor Sahib, your mushk bud has arrived, finally.'

We step inside the big donga. A heavenly aroma greets us as we go near a pile of rice on the wooden floor. A delightful sight! 'This is mushk bud rice,' says Babi. 'You won't find it anywhere but Kashmir.'

A labourer carries one small sack of rice and places it in the carrier basket of Babuji's bicycle parked at the ghat.

'It will last us a month,' says Babi.

Some girls are playing hopscotch at the ghat. We spend some more time at the ghat before heading home. Babi decides to make a quick dash to the Ram Mandir. 'Both of you wait here. I won't be long,' she says.

* * *

The Summer of 1994

Pa brings good news. 'I have found a better place to live,' he says. 'The rent is affordable. It is a proper house. We will have the ground floor to ourselves. The kitchen is good and spacious. There are two bedrooms, a large living room, two bathrooms and a garden. Babuji and Babi will have a room to themselves. The rooms have good windows and proper ventilation.'

'What about water?' asks Ma.

'In abundance,' says Pa.

'And the landlords? Are they . . .?'

'Very kind. They are giving us access to the terrace too.'

'How long will they allow us to live there?'

'Don't worry about all this. At last, you will live in a better place . . .'

'How do you know . . .'

We move to the Bhatiyal house.

* * *

Udhampur is flanked by forests. Pa and I start going to the forest. It is a lovely place. Nearby, a stream flows. In it floats driftwood. We start gathering the pieces. 'Nature is the greatest sculptor,' says Pa. 'You should have an eye for the best pieces.'

Pa's collection has grown to about fifty pieces of driftwood.

The terrace of the house is now full of wood. Pa buys an entire wood carving set: mallet, chisels, gouges, veiners, knives and sandpaper. Next, he buys polish, paint and varnish and sets up a makeshift studio on the terrace.

One day, he comes home with the trunk of a fallen tree. Babi is horrified. 'What's happening to you?' she says.

'Look at the roots,' he says. 'What do you see?'

In her heart, Babi is happy that Pa is not crying anymore. And that he has stopped gazing awkwardly and blankly at the ceiling for hours and hours and that he has, at last, found something worthwhile to do, although it doesn't seem to be the best of things to do. She would rather have him tutor students, as she has seen him do in Kashmir. She wants him to resume going to college.

'How are they tolerating your absence? Don't they seek an explanation from you?'

'It is because the college principal is his friend,' scoffs Ma.

The sculptures start taking shape and form. An exile. Jesus Christ. The Dancer. Two dancers. Man and woman. The embrace. Roots. The Migrant.

'Where will you keep these things?' asks Babi. 'Where is the room for all this? This is not our house!'

But the Bhatiyals are not like Darshan Kumar. They are kind, loving, supportive and have a sense of humour.

'This is your house,' they say.

I no longer feel like running away from here.

On Henna's birthday, I gift her a baby rabbit. She names her Bunny-Bunny. Babuji is happy.

* * *

The Camp, Udhampur

A strange affliction has gripped the camp. People have started buying lottery tickets. Lottery vendors are all over the place in the evenings. They have set up stalls and are enticing us to buy lottery tickets. The local Dogras are doing their best to get us hooked on these lotteries.

Betting on a number and making money is the new obsession among the camp-dwellers.

First-timers like me are lured by those who claim to have cracked the code.

'You can double and triple your money. Your Rs 10 can become Rs 30 and Rs 100 can become Rs 300. Imagine! Don't worry; we will help you choose the right numbers.'

Some claim to have made Rs 500 in a day. Others are now tempted to throw their hats in the ring.

All I have in my pocket is a tenner. A battle is raging in my mind: Should I or shouldn't I? What if? But then . . . I should not . . . It's okay . . . Just this time . . .

'Don't overthink. Go buy a ticket,' says Ajay, a camp friend. He notices the dilemma on my face. 'It takes three or four tries and you will hit the jackpot . . .'

'What makes you think luck will favour me?'

'Hasn't it favoured you so far?'

'Have you ever won?'

'Many times . . .'

I buy a ticket for Rs 5. That's all I can afford now. The drawing of lots is announced in the evening. My money has gone to waste. I curse my luck. It wasn't my money. It was Pa's. I was supposed to spend it judiciously, but look what I did. I wish I could turn back the clock by just an hour so as not to commit the mistake. But you can't turn back the clock—not for this, at least. The deed is done. One never gets one's lost money back. It is gone forever, no matter what one does.

Nearby, a celebration erupts. Some people are tearing up their lottery tickets and others are dancing. The dust storm keeps its promise and swirls around hundreds of torn lottery tickets. It is raining lottery tickets now.

'Never again,' I scream. 'I will never waste my money on lotteries.'

'Don't say that . . . the lottery season will last the entire summer,' says Ajay. 'You must buy tickets every day. A day will come when you will win and make money. What is your lucky number?'

'How much have you made so far?'

An elderly man says, 'Some people are on the path to destruction, not even caring about what is really at stake. Their families watch helplessly as they burn the relief money. It's not their fault. It is nobody's fault. Such is this madness that has gripped everyone. It is a disease, but it is not incurable. Time will set things right. A day will come when this lottery obsession will be over.'

He looks at me and says, 'Stay away from the devil. Do not let this habit ruin you and your family. Your parents' money is far too precious. Save every paisa and every rupee. You never know when you will need it the most to save your life . . .'

* * *

August 1994
Udhampur

Deepak, Bobby and I board a bus to Patnitop. It will be our first trip to the highest point on the Jammu–Srinagar national highway. A home-like place. If we get lucky, we will see and touch snow for the first time in four years. The familiar smell of pinecones brings respite.

We explore the canopies and the slopes. While trekking, we are intercepted by some men in uniform. Mistaking us for infiltrators, they take us into a tent and start asking questions as if we are troublemakers.

'Why are you here? Who has sent you? What is your intent? What are you up to? Who are you?'

It becomes clear to me. We are being interrogated.

'We are Kashmiri Pandits,' we plead. 'We are students. We are here because we miss Kashmir and this place is closest to Kashmir.'

These men have a look of acute distrust on their faces.

'We are Hindus,' says Deepak to the officer who is observing the interrogation. 'Please let us go. We will leave immediately. We are sorry to be here. Our aim is not to create any trouble.'

We don't know what is going on in his mind. Doesn't he believe us? Does he really think we are concealing our real identities? Does he think we are terrorists? Do we look like . . .? Why does this keep happening to us?

'We are letting you go on one condition. You will never be seen here again,' says the officer.

The Next Morning

We are waiting at the Patnitop bus stop to board a bus back to Udhampur. From the left, we see a bus coming. The board says: Jammu to Srinagar.

Deepak and I exchange a glance. The next thing we realize is that we are on a bus en route to Srinagar.

'This is the wrong bus,' Bobby points out. 'We must get off.'

Deepak and I don't want to agree with him. We sit still, our hands tightly clasping the grills of the windows. Our gazes are fixed outside and at the valley in front of us.

'What are you both up to? Where do you think you are going?' Bobby keeps repeating.

'Where else? We will reach there in the evening and take the same bus back. At least, we will touch the soil there . . .'

'Both of you have gone mad,' Bobby says.

Reluctantly, we get off at Batote. The Chenab is flowing alongside. The current is dangerous. There are pear trees along the bank of the river.

We jump into the water to take a dip. Nearby, a gypsy family is watching us and laughing at our antics.

* * *

A man is sitting on a mound of earth in Dabbad Park. He comes every evening and sits all by himself. That's all he does. Next to him, two people are arguing about the current situation. 'The prime minister is responsible for our plight. May he be struck down by lightning! We were made to part with our hearths and homes under his watch. He did nothing. He is still doing nothing.'

'This parting is temporary,' says the man sitting on a mound of earth. 'We will go back soon. Time will come for us and carry us back to its other ghat . . .'

Our ancestors never used soap to wash their hands. Instead, they preferred soil and ashes from their courtyards and ovens—for them, the soil and the ashes were the most sacred and purifying things ever. In the camps, people longed for a fistful of soil and ashes from their courtyards and ovens.

7

The House of Snails

Home
Srinagar
Spring of 1985

Pa takes me to Eid Gah. We plan to get some turf beds for a patch in our courtyard. He knows the best spots in Eid Gah for turf, which we will then sow in the front yard of our house. Pa is creating a garden. 'The pansies will be in full bloom anytime now,' says Pa. 'And so will the morning glories.'

Some Days Later

We are in the Botanical Garden again, which is at the foothills of the Zabarwan and flanked by tall Chinars and poplars. It overlooks Dal Lake. One of the caretakers is Pa's friend. He instructs a gardener to assist us. The gardener tells me everything about the plants in the garden. I memorize the botanical names of some plants.

Ours is not the best garden in the neighbourhood, but we love it more than anything else. A lot of hard work has gone into creating it.

While digging the soil, Pa looks at me as if he's seeing me for the last time. A strange look flashes across his face. As if he has peeked into the future and sensed something ominous. 'You must come back to this place after you leave. Even if it takes years, but do come back and look for things that you are now going to bury in the soil. The seeds will have become trees by then. They will be waiting for you . . .'

'But why would I leave? Do you want me to?'

'When you go away to study at some college . . . Don't you want to study outside Kashmir or go abroad?'

'What about Kashmir University? I am thinking about going to SP College. The same college and university as you. Perhaps I will sit in the same class that you sat in.'

* * *

May 2022
Home
Delhi

It is a quiet Sunday. I am thinking about the last two years and the months of lockdown. I am whiling away the hours by scrolling through Facebook. A video grabs my attention. The holy pond in Nagbal, near Anantnag, Kashmir. It is springtime. The snow-clad peaks shimmer at a distance. A friend is broadcasting the pictures live.

* * *

1988–1989
Home, Kashmir
Winter

Pa takes me to the basement of our home. This isn't the first time I've been here. The basement is supported by large wooden pillars, which are now in bad shape. The wood is in a state of decay and the pillars are wobbly.

'Do you know we once had cows?' Pa says, handing me a broom and asking me to sweep the floor. 'I have not told you about them. This was years before you were born. Baijee, my grandfather, reared cows, apart from doing other things he excelled at . . .'

What happened to the cows then?

'After his death, we were not able to keep them. Not that having them was a hassle. But we went through difficult times . . .'

'Why can't we resume rearing cows? We could get hold of a couple of cows and a calf . . .'

Pa is of a different opinion. 'That is not a good idea. Look at the condition of this shed. If we delay repairs any further, the entire house will come crumbling down this winter when it snows.'

There are snail nests all over the floor. Some snails are crawling along the crevices and cracks in the rotting wooden pillars.

Pa explains: 'The floor of the kitchen above has started giving way. It is a risk. I have been meaning to get the pillars repaired, but they are beyond repair now. Renovating the entire house or maybe a part of it, is the only option we have. And I have been planning this for the past three years. It will cost at least Rs 5 or 6 lakh to carry out basic renovations of the basement and the first floor. All the rooms, including the toilet and bathroom, will have to be renovated. We need a proper toilet and bathroom with modern sanitary fittings such as a commode and flush tank, a water heating system like a hamam, a wash basin, a shower and drainage. We will get two bathrooms made. One in the courtyard and one attached to the living room.'

Ever since I can remember, we've had the old toilet in the courtyard. A sweeper comes once a day to clean it. On days when the sweeper doesn't show up, Babuji does the cleaning himself. The entire place reeks of a foul smell. In winter, we take turns covering the filth with snow. It's a hassle when it's freezing cold, but we are used to it now. In summer, we must carry our own water when we go to the toilet. There is no tap inside. But the most unnerving thing are the insects—spiders and centipedes all over the walls. If one of them falls on you while you are sitting over the pit, you are done for. There are days when you can hear screams coming out of the toilet.

The bathroom is next to the willow tree. It is unlike any of the bathrooms in the houses of some of our relatives who live in posh areas like Rajbagh, Jawahar Nagar and Indira Nagar. The tap is not connected to any water source. So water must be carried in a bucket to take a shower. This bathroom, too, is home to various insects. The spider on the wall is the largest spider I have ever seen in my entire life.

There are creepers all around the outer walls and the roof is made of wooden tiles that are very old and mossy now. Here, too, you will see snails all over the ceiling and the walls. This place makes for a superb hiding place. Through the window of Babuji's room, the bathroom looks like a small house. 'The House of Snails' is now the title of my painting. And the painting is on the wall of my room.

'If we decide to renovate the third floor as well, we will need an additional Rs 2 lakh,' says Pa. 'It is as good as building a new house. We will begin the work once the winter ends and spring arrives. I've already decided everything. A few more years and we'll have a new house in a posh neighbourhood. Everything will be modern. We'll buy a car too . . .'

Pa is very happy today. The thought of renovating our current home and having a new house in a posh area makes him happy.

'Can we also have a cowshed there? I really want to have our cows back. And a calf too.'

'Why not?' says Pa. 'But rearing cows and looking after a calf is not easy. It is hard work. And you might get fed up soon.'

Spring

The snow has started to melt. The sun makes a regular appearance now—almost every day. The carpenter and mason have been given instructions. Pa has told them what he wants. Flooring, staircase, basement, kitchen, bathroom, toilet and attic.

Every morning, we go to the Safa Kadal labour bazaar to hire labourers. The labourers are mostly Gujjars and Bakarwals.* They are strong men who can lift heavy sacks and rocks and work tirelessly day and night and in extreme cold. We negotiate prices every day, starting with Rs 25 per day. Sometimes, it is Rs 50 or Rs 100 depending on demand, availability, weather and many other factors.

---

* Gujjars and Bakarwals are tribal communities in Jammu and Kashmir. While many of them are pastoral nomads, some of them are engaged in manual labour.

Pa gives the contactor time until June. Spring will last three months. 'Come June, I want the house ready . . . with the courtyard and the drainage done . . . all new . . .'

It's such a beautiful sight to see the old pave the way for the new. The old maharaja bricks are being replaced by new bricks and tiles. Everything is going to be new. Neighbours and relatives come to share the joy and excitement.

'This has been long overdue,' says a Muslim neighbour. But then another Muslim neighbour who has been paying attention since Day One says something that makes us laugh.

'What is the point of all this renovation, Professor Sahib?'

'Why?'

'You know the word around the neighbourhood? Not me, but some people are saying . . .'

'What?'

'They are saying, "Don't stop Pandits from renovating their houses. All these newly built and renovated houses will be ours next year or the following year when they leave Kashmir en masse." . . .'

Babuji laughs. Ma and Babi are angry. Pa is amused.

'But some of us well-wishers don't agree. After all, we are brothers. We don't want you to waste your precious money and savings of a lifetime on renovation. What's the point of spending lakhs of rupees on a house when you are not going to live in it for the rest of your life?'

'What do you mean? What makes you say this?'

'You will have to leave in 1990. Like the birds that fly out of their nests and never come back . . .'

'They cooked up similar tales to scare Zutshi when he was building a house in Jawahar Nagar last year. He didn't stop,' whispers Pa.

The mason and the carpenter laugh too while taking turns at the hookah.

'Professor Sahab, yours will be the best-looking house in the whole of Khankah-i-Sokhta! Everyone will be envious, including the Paitghars and Nissars, even the Ansaris . . . Once your house is ready, we will celebrate . . .'

8

This Won't Last; We Will Go Back Soon

A Day in May 1990
Jammu

Zutshi and his wife are living in rented accommodation in Jammu. His house in Jawahar Nagar isn't done completely yet. He had to flee in the dead of night and with his departure, the construction halted. But he cleared the contractor's dues and even tipped the masons, carpenters and labourers before leaving. The only trouble is that he still talks about going back to complete the pending jobs.

'I want to get the study done before I die.'

'Have you gone mad?' his wife says.

'This won't last; we will go back soon . . .'

He cries. Building a house in Jawahar Nagar is his only dream in life. The next best thing is to move into the house and live happily with his wife and children.

I bump into him at Jewel Chowk. Other Pandits are there too. Pa's old gang from Srinagar. The Coffee House gang. It's the same story everywhere. The story of dream houses— some to be constructed, some under construction and some already constructed and waiting for families to conduct the *grahpravesh* (house-warming) and move in.

'Where is your dad?' they ask. 'Are they still there . . .'

'Yes, they are still in Srinagar.'

'And you and Henna? Where are both of you staying?'

'Talab Tillo.'

We spend some time by the roadside. I want to go to the Jewel restaurant, but I have no money.

Pa's colleagues are talking about the situation in Srinagar and their houses.

At least ten of them left their houses that were under construction in two posh neighbourhoods in Srinagar— Jawahar Nagar and Sant Nagar. Two of them want to go back to finish construction, even at the risk of their lives. The rest are trying to come to terms with the situation. The money that has gone into building these houses. Lakhs and lakhs—savings of a lifetime. Gone! One of them is left with no savings at all. He bought land with all the money he had been saving for over forty years. He spent his provident fund and retirement savings too. He even sold his wife's jewellery to build the house, only to desert it within days of completion. They weren't able to spend even one night in their new house. Now he has lost his speech. He has not spoken a word for over a month, ever since they fled Kashmir and landed in a camp in Jammu. They have nowhere to go now, even though they have a palatial house in Srinagar. His wife is concerned that something bad might happen to him. She's a strong woman, while he continues sinking by the day.

'Say something,' she begs. But he is quiet and in a state of shock.

Zutshi removes something from his bag. It is a name plate made of walnut wood. On it are engraved two words: The Nest.

'I was supposed to fix it on the main gate myself, but . . .' he says. 'What do you think? The Nest is a good name, right? Or should I think of a better name?'

Pa's friend, who has just arrived from Srinagar, whispers: 'Thousands of things belonging to Kashmiri Pandits are on sale in Kashmir. Clothes, utensils, bedding, furniture, books and other household things. Among other things are rare manuscripts, antiques, jewellery, family heirlooms, preserved for generations and handed over from one generation to the next. Everything is at a throwaway price, except antiques, jewellery and manuscripts . . .'

I shudder. What will happen to our things if, God forbid, we can't salvage them . . .

* * *

I have the same dream again. The dream I don't want to dream. It's a curse to keep having the dream. The house that Pa has built is caught in a storm. The earth beneath it is separating.

* * *

The Summer of 1986

Pa has brought me to Eid Gah! This is where he's going to teach me how to ride a bicycle. He says he will teach me on the ground to begin with and then take me to the road by the Tibetan refugee colony. We have brought along Babuji's old bicycle. I will learn on this bicycle and then buy my own with the money I've been saving for three years. The bicycle I desire is red in colour and it costs Rs 750 at the bicycle shop in Hari Singh High Street.

Pa explains while giving me a demonstration: 'This is how you sit. Your gaze should be forward. Don't look down. Hands on the brake. Feet firmly placed on the pedals. Sit erect but relaxed. Like this. Look at me. And then you start pedalling . . .'

A gentle push and then Pa starts running while pushing the bicycle. His hand is on the carrier. He doesn't stop running. After several minutes, I turn back to see that I've left him far behind. I am cycling on my own! I scream. I fall off the bicycle, not knowing how to stop correctly. But I am still screaming in excitement. Pa is happy.

'Next month, I will take you to Dal Lake to learn swimming. So what if Tyndale Biscoe School and Burn Hall School rejected you? You won't be any less than the students who study in these schools. I will make sure you learn all the things that are taught in these schools. I will make sure you learn cycling, swimming, horse riding, mountaineering, skiing, water skiing and everything else that is taught in these schools . . .'

A Few Days Later

I am the proud owner of a new bicycle, but it isn't red. 'The red bicycles will take a few months to arrive from Delhi,' the shop owner informs me. My new bicycle is turquoise in colour.

Fifteen days later, I cycle to Trisal Uncle's place in Fateh Kadal. I might as well give Henna and Sangeeta a ride back home if they wish.

* * *

February 1987
Gulmarg, Kashmir

Pa has enrolled me for a three-week beginners' skiing course at the Indian Institute of Skiing and Mountaineering, Gulmarg.

He accompanies me to Gulmarg to drop me off for the course, which begins in two days. Some of the administrative staff members at the institute are Pa's friends. Pa returns home the same evening.

'Don't worry, you will be taken care of,' he says. 'Besides, you must learn how to be on your own now. You are thirteen now.'

Pa knows how to keep his promises. I am excited at the prospect of being on my own for the next three weeks. I want to become a professional skier when I'm older.

* * *

Indian Institute of Skiing and Mountaineering
Gulmarg
Hotel Nedous
Room Number K.5

My dear Papa,

As soon as you left, the man gave me the ski equipment— skis, sticks, goggles, boots and gloves—and took me to the room. I got my quilt, pillows and the sleeping bag.

There are seven students, including me. I am the youngest. One is working in a bank, one is at ONGC. One is an Anglo–Indian. Those who were on the bus with us are here too. There are also some students from Ahmedabad and Mumbai and even a famous personality from the Bombay film world.

One room has a *bukhari* (traditional room heater), which keeps us warm. It was foolish of me to bring along two blankets. The bathroom is not so good. We get one or two buckets of water in the morning. We give our laundry to the washerman for washing. The food here is very good. We are served rice, porridge, cheese, peas, potatoes, cabbage, pulses, tea, biscuits and coffee.

Everyone speaks English here, including me. They all speak to me in English and I respond.

Strangely, there aren't any girls in our batch. There aren't any girls in the intermediate and advanced batches either. I see some girls skiing at the state-run institute. They are all in their school or college uniforms. The instructors are from Kashmir, Ladakh and Himachal Pradesh.

Photos of many film stars adorn the lobby, the corridor and the rooms of the hotel. The hotel overlooks the best slopes.

Your friend, the Kashmiri instructor married to an American woman, keeps a close eye on me. He keeps inquiring after me. 'Come to me if you need anything,' he says. He has instructed everyone to pay special attention to me given that I am the youngest and also his friend's son.

My favourite instructors are the brothers Randy and Sandy, and your friend, Gul Mustafa. They are terrific at ski jumping. The chief instructor is called Guruji. He isn't a Kashmiri. His son is a skier too.

Please come here soon with the camera. Now, I am off to play cards. Please don't mind.

My full regards to Babi and Babuji. Tell Babuji that I will write to him later.

Yours lovingly,
Siddhartha

* * *

Week Two

Guruji gives me personal attention. I am keen to graduate from snowplough to parallel, but I know it will take time.

Guruji takes me on the Gondola cable car, a five-minute ride from the base to the topmost point. I am eager to ski all the way down, as I want to overcome my fear.

'One last round and then we will go,' says Guruji. We hop on the cable car to go up.

As it starts moving, Guruji takes the ski poles from me and attaches them to the harness of the car.

'Take your gloves off,' he says and casually grabs my right hand to place it on his lap. I can feel my hand touching a strange thing. I'm overcome by a sudden rush of dread. It's a feeling of fear I've never experienced before. The cable car creaks and slows down. I silently pray for it to reach the top as quickly as possible. I am unable to speak a single word. Sensing my resistance, Guruji takes a bunch of photographs out of his pocket and shows them to me. I look at them in shock. They are photographs of naked men and women doing things I can never imagine.

'You're going to be a champion skier,' he says. 'I will teach you everything and give you extra lessons, but you must do as I say,' he says, without letting go of my hand.

The next day onwards, I resume lessons, acting like nothing happened.

Twenty-One Days Later

I win the silver medal.

One of my fellow batchmates, Y. Kaushik, invites me to Bombay and Assam. He comes home with me and stays for the night before taking the flight out of Srinagar the next day. He writes me letters from Assam.

* * *

February 1988
Srinagar–Gulmarg

There is talk of me being one of the skiers nominated to represent the state in a competition in Europe. But for that, I will have to stay back in Gulmarg and take the advanced-level courses. I don't wish to see Guruji's face ever again. But I don't want to miss this opportunity. My dream of becoming a famous skier is on the verge of coming true.

* * *

The Spring of 1985

Tyndale Biscoe School rejects me. Burn Hall School rejects me.

'Your son can't speak English,' the principals of these two schools tell Pa. 'If you want us to admit him despite his shortcomings, then he will have to repeat Class Four.'

Pa says no. 'You will not repeat Class Four. You will not lose a year. We will keep applying to other schools.' Tyndale Biscoe and Burn Hall are the best schools in Srinagar.

The National High School in Karan Nagar admits me. It's a school without a building. Ever since it caught fire a few years ago, little has been done to renovate it. We sit on tarpaulin sheets in half-burnt classrooms with ceilings that leak. When it rains, we unfurl our umbrellas. The school

takes us on picnics to Verinag, Yusmarg, Gulmarg and
Pahalgam. But it doesn't provide extracurricular activities
such as swimming, mountaineering or horseback riding.

'Your son requires tutoring,' say the mathematics, science
and Hindi teachers to Pa during a parent–teacher meeting.
'He is weak in these subjects and could fail without tuitions.'

Every morning, during the assembly, we sing the same
Urdu prayer:

> Lab pe aati hai dua ban ke tamanna meri
> Zindagi shamma ki surat ho, Khuda ya meri
> Ho mere dum se yun hi mere watan ki zeenat
> Jis tarah phool se hoti hai chaman ki zeenat
> Zindagi ho meri parwaane ki surat ya rab
> Ilm ki shamma se ho mujh ko muhabbat ya rab
> Ho mera kaam gareebon ki himaayat karna
> Dardmandon se, zayifon se muhabbat karna
> Mere Allah buraayi se bachaana mujh ko
> Nek jo raah ho uss raah pe chalaana mujh ko . . .

Babuji and Pa tell me that it is a famous prayer titled
'Bachche Ki Dua' (A Child's Prayer) and that it was written
by Muhammad Iqbal.

* * *

It won't be until many years later that I will find out that this
prayer is recited during school assemblies across Pakistan.

* * *

I am not happy with the house that I have been assigned
to in school. The name of the house is Budshah. I get to

know that Budshah was a king who ruled Kashmir in the fifteenth century. We are told about his valour and greatness. But I am more inclined towards Kalhana. I am sad about not being assigned to Kalhana House. Kalhana, the author of Rajatarangini (River of Kings), is a household name in Kashmir. An account of the history of Kashmir, Rajatarangini is one of the earliest documented histories to have been written in the world. All the bright students belong to Kalhana House. Everyone says it is the best of the four houses because it has the best students. The other two houses are named Suyya and Mahjoor. Suyya House is named after Suyya, an engineer and architect appointed as the prime minister of Kashmir by the great King Avantivarman, who ascended the throne of Kashmir in 855 CE, establishing the Utpala dynasty.[4] The fourth house, Mahjoor, is named after the poet Ghulam Ahmad Mahjoor, who lived in Kashmir until 1952.

'Budshah is a good house to belong to,' Pa comforts me, sensing my disappointment. 'You should not be sad. You will change your opinion once you get to know what he did for the Pandits of Kashmir five centuries ago . . .'

This is the story.[5]

Zain-ul-Abidin became the Sultan of Kashmir in 1420. He took over from his brother, Noor Khan. During the preceding years, their father Sultan Sikandar 'Butshikan' (destroyer of idols), descendant of Shah Mir, founder of the Shah Miri dynasty, had unleashed a reign of terror on Kashmiri Pandits by imposing *jizya* (poll tax), forcing them to convert to Islam and ravaging their temples. He had also established Sikandarpora on the ruins of the ancient temples he razed to the ground. To escape religious conversion, thousands of Pandits fled to Kishtwar and Bhaderwah in the Jammu region. Those who didn't leave or refused to be converted to Islam were burned alive at a place near Rainawari in Srinagar. Even today, the place is known as Bhatta Mazar (the graveyard of the Pandits).

Butshikan's son, Noor Khan, had continued his policy of intolerance towards Pandits. But when Zain-ul-Abidin succeeded to the throne, he changed the policy at the behest of Pandit Shri Bhat, a physician who cured him of a disease and influenced him to save Pandits from further persecution. Zain-ul-Abidin abolished the jizya and allowed the Pandits of Kashmir to rebuild their temples. He came to be known as 'Budshah', meaning a great king. His rule lasted about fifty years, during which the Pandits thrived.

My sadness vanishes. I am happy. Perhaps being part of the second-best house is a blessing in disguise.

* * *

Little do I realize that a few years later, in 1990, when we will be forced to leave Kashmir for the seventh time in history, we will pray for another Budshah to come and save us.

* * *

1986–1987

Pa takes me to the college where he teaches. Sri Pratap College is a great college and I dream of attending it after completing my schooling. While returning from college, he takes me to India Coffee House on Residency Road to meet his friends. Next, he takes me to Lambert Lane and Forest Lane to shop for clothes.

I start going to Trisal Uncle's house in Fateh Kadal for tuitions in mathematics and science. Uncle Amin's daughter,

Henna, is my best friend and so is Sangeeta, who lives in Habba Kadal.

Pa takes me to Hind Book Shop and Kashmir Book Shop on Residency Road and introduces me to the owners. We buy books and stationery: sketch books for painting and some cursive writing books.

* * *

A Day in the Spring of 1985
Tulmul, Kashmir

Babuji, Babi, Ma and I are in Tulmul. We are spending a few days at the Mata Kheer Bhawani temple. Pa is not a temple-goer and neither is Babuji, but his main purpose seems to be different from everyone else who has come to the temple to take part in the mela. He wants to meet someone in the village nearby. He says he's a Sufi who he has known for years. He has never talked about him before. Babuji rarely talks about his friends. He doesn't have any friends. The only people he knows apart from his patients are Habib, Ahmed, Saleema and a tailor in the neighbourhood. He's quite close to them. Sometimes he sits at Shamboo Nath's shop, though he doesn't seem to be fond of him. He also spends some time at Bohri Uncle's shop while returning home from his laboratory. I have seen him talk a lot with Bohri Uncle. Later, he goes to the pinwheel shop to buy me a pinwheel. But despite all this roaming and sitting at shopfronts, he is always back home on time. He is never late, not even by a minute.

From the temple at Tulmul, we undertake a walk. It takes us twenty minutes or so through the narrow pathways along a paddy field in the village to reach the house of Babuji's friend. It is a large village house. Various smells—of cow dung and hay and rice, pickle and red chillies—greet us. We go to the second floor of the house. It's a beautiful, sunny day. Kites are flying high in the sky. An old man with a long white beard is sitting stoically on a rug on the floor. On the floor is a fly trap. A boy is pouring a green, sugary concoction on the floor. Flies get attracted to it, thinking it is sugar syrup and die instantly upon tasting it. 'Flies are a nuisance here,' says the man. 'They drive me mad. This is the only solution. They don't feel a thing.'

The man looks like a mystic. Babuji and him spend the next hour or so chatting about inane things. I've never heard of the things that figure in their conversation. The man's family brings me snacks to munch on.

Later in the afternoon, Babi and Babuji sit in the cobbled courtyard of the temple and pose for a picture. They look like a bride and groom.

We visit Tulmul twice or thrice a year. On Zyeth Aetham,* Pandits arrive here from all parts of Kashmir to celebrate the birthday of Mata Kheer Bhawani and partake in the festivities.

This is the place where I learn how to walk through small gravel paths in paddy fields without making a mess and with no mud stains on my feet.

* * *

The Winter of 1986
Home

There is snow all around. School is shut for the winter. At first, it didn't snow for days. I kept waiting. There was talk of snow. Everyone kept talking about it and predicting when it

---

* An auspicious day for the Kashmiri Pandits that marks the birthday of Goddess Ragnya Devi.

would happen. 'It's going to snow tonight,' said some people in the neighbourhood. 'Not tonight; it will snow tomorrow,' said others as if they were weathermen.

Then it finally began to snow and now there is no sign of it stopping! There is nothing much to do. I am in my room, arranging things and writing my diary. The entries read the same.

'I did this . . . and I did that . . . I am going to do this . . . I am going to do that . . . Snow keeps falling . . . There is nowhere else to go . . . I miss going out . . . I miss the sun . . .'

I must figure out a way to write about the days differently, even if all days are alike and I end up doing the same things day after day.

How long will I be stuck in this room? I dislike not being able to go out and cycle. When will spring come?

'You should write,' says Pa. 'It is the best thing to do when you have nothing else to do and nowhere to go.'

'But what do I write about?'

'Why don't you write about your room?'

Pa knows how madly I am in love with my room and how obsessed I am with its upkeep and the order of things in it. So much so that I don't allow anyone else in. It has been given to me by Savita Aunty (Gasha's wife). It used to be her room, but now it is mine.

I am going to take this room with me when we build a new house.

* * *

March 1993
The Camp
Udhampur

I dream I am in my house. Around me are broken stairs laden with scrap, ashes, potshards, ancestral clogs and an old winnowing basket—Babi's precious belongings. A room has its windows half-closed, yet it is full of light. This is a room where time never goes away and where the evening has come to stay forever. This is the room of our ancestors. This is where they tell us stories about who they are.

The dream ends and I find myself stranded in a barren wasteland. The river has dried. The cranes are gone. Birds are flying away from here. Someone has sent his bulls to pull the buses carrying people.

'Set us free!' cry the people, desperate to scale the barricades and cross over to the other side where there is food, water and shade. Everyone's skin has blackened in the sun. If we stay here longer, we will burn to death.

'Take the ration cards and leave everything else behind,' says a voice. 'Enter through the gates only if you have proof of who you are and where you have come from.'

People are waiting for their turn to be identified. I, too, stand in the queue for identification. But I have nothing. I have no proof of who I am.

9

Waiting Will Keep Us Alive and Sane

December 1995
Room Number 13
Jhelum Hostel
Jawaharlal Nehru University, New Delhi

My dear Papa,

My hands tremble, my heart sinks and words seem hollow as I write this letter. Our dear rabbit, our own sweet Bunny-Bunny, is no more. No matter how much I try to deny this terribly shocking and painful news in my own thoughts, the ugly truth mockingly gapes at me and reminds me of man's sorrowful helplessness. Your words ring true in my mind: death is not a philosophy; it is merely painful. We humans are the worst of all the creatures God has created. We don't even know why we live or why we die. We should never dare to know. All knowledge is futile. Nothing in this tragic world is worth knowing. All craving is a foolish activity. We have been tricked, deceived and ridiculed by some sinister, mischievous and unknown power into believing that life is good and beautiful. We revel and rejoice at our own ability to see, hear, touch, feel, taste and understand the outside world. The gift of the five senses is nothing but a wicked curse upon all mankind.

The consciousness of life and death is man's ultimate power and it is this power that places him at the top of all creation. But this is what we must reject as the lowest form of knowledge. It is this consciousness that lures us to believe in all sorts of big entities—natural and supernatural, mundane and divine, permanent and transient, real and imaginary. It is this consciousness that gives birth to an unbending faith in existence, beauty and truth within us. It is this consciousness that determines our happiness and sadness. We are slaves to this consciousness, which has been injected into the human mind by some mysterious power that governs the scheme of things in the universe with all its animate and inanimate bodies. This consciousness is not ours. It is an alien spirit that appears to be man's own inner self. It is foolish to accept this consciousness as a source of hidden and forbidden knowledge. The realization that nothing can ever be known is good enough to live peacefully and in silence.

To accept oneself as a knower of higher truths, to claim supremacy over other creatures of this world, to call oneself a happy being, to go on living with sentiments like pride and honour, to mistake sleep for wakefulness, to keep striving for hollow concepts such as truth, goodness, beauty and knowledge, is nothing but falling prey to those hidden and invisible powers whose aim is not just to corrupt but also to seek entertainment while we, like helpless pawns, change places and move aimlessly on the chess board of life. Those supreme powers toy with us. We find ourselves trapped in a scary game in which we all end up dead.

We see those powers. But we do not *see* them. That is our tragedy. Nobody can offer us a solution or lead us out of this labyrinth. Perhaps the mystics could. They laugh with a deep, mystical and divine laughter. They laugh at God, at men, at death, at life and at everything. They will laugh at that dark night of the soul too. And they finally weep and weep and weep until their laughter and tears become one. What lies beyond that state is darkness or maybe it is light.

In that state, one can't tell darkness from light. What state is that?

I digress. Thoughts of death always give birth to digressions.

Whatever I've said so far could all be lies. I can't even trust my words. I have travelled far from the hour of grief that engulfed me at the beginning of this letter. All words are deaf, dumb and hollow. They are not what they are. They are neither true nor false. They must not be written. Banish them and we shall then be free.

I feel lonely and devastated and in this state of desolation, I've lost the strength and energy to even stand on my feet. The only recourse left is to knock my head against the wall and weep.

Have I lost Bunny forever? Amid these macabre thoughts of death, decomposition, earth and fire, I crave some shade where I can peel off my memory and cast it away.

Where has Bunny gone? I want to touch her, kiss her and keep her with me forever. I want to steal her away from the cruel winds of time. She never lived. How could she ever die? If she died at all, then she died young, virginal, pure and chaste, like a true child of God.

I am ashamed of myself and I feel extremely guilty that I could not even see her and be with her during those painful moments when life was oozing out of her warm body. You write that she was warm even when dead.

I will surely visit her grave when I come to Udhampur. Grief can't be reduced. It can only be forgotten. There's nothing to prove that we're awake or that we are what we are. It would not have made a difference even if we were to confirm or prove our own existence. It is all a joke. And ours is a sad history of purposelessness, meaninglessness and vain flight.

We must either keep these fears alive and burning in our hearts or we must end our lives. The only way out of suffering is forgetfulness and madness, which lead to God or, who knows, realms beyond God himself.

Death is life's only cure. It is a painful liberation. It is always better than life.

With pain in my heart,
Yours,
Siddhartha

* * *

**An Evening
Jawaharlal Nehru University
New Delhi**

Pandit Bhimsen Joshi is expected to arrive for a concert. Everyone is waiting for him. I've been given the responsibility of escorting him to the stage and making sure he is seated comfortably. I am to sit within his sight so he can gesture to me should he need anything. I have been designated his attendant for the evening. It is a dream come true for me. I will get to hold his hand, touch his feet and seek his blessings.

If I'm able to muster up the courage and if luck is on my side, I will tell him about myself. I'll tell him I'm a student of music, too, and that it is my dream to learn under him.

'Panditji is God,' everyone says.

I am reminded of the days when I would walk a long distance to learn music. Sometimes, I'd wait for hours on end for my guru to return home from his school, rest a while and then teach me. His was a 'one raga, one year' teaching philosophy. And my impatience almost killed me.

'You know, it could take a student of music up to forty years to play Raag Yaman and it would still be far from perfection. Satisfaction does not exist in the world of music,' he used to say. I always enjoyed waiting for him at his place. At the end of each lesson, he would ask me to accompany him to the market. I longed for him to talk about music during our walks and share some of his secrets, such as how to instantly create lilting melodies and play beautiful ragas.

Patience was my enemy in those days. I wanted to learn everything within a day's time.

People jostle around, waiting for Pandit Bhimsen Joshi's arrival. I am sitting in a corner, right in front of the dais. The hot day has made me weary. A motorcade arrives. People speak in hushed tones. 'Panditji is here . . .'

I rush towards the cars. The maestro steps out of his car and starts walking towards the podium bedecked with silken drapes and marigolds. I offer him my hand. His eyes are half-closed, but he seems to know the way, as if he's familiar with the place and has been coming here regularly.

He quickly takes his seat. His eyes are still half-closed. He is chewing a betel nut. I sit in the front row and make sure I am in his line of sight. Should he need anything, I am just at arm's length.

The tabla player begins to tune his tabla. A beautiful woman with long tresses, the daughter of a famous vocalist, starts plucking on the strings of the tanpura that she is holding as if it were a child.

Panditji clears his throat and begins the *aalaap*, drowning everyone in a vast ocean of beauty and harmony. I try identifying the raga. It's got to be an evening raga. But I am not able to recognize it. I have lost touch with music. I curse myself for not being able to pursue music along with my studies. Such a waste, for what is youth without music?

Being a student isn't always a good thing. One is usually aware of what one is subjected to. However, it takes years to simply listen in silence. And right now, I am listening to the moving rendition. All sadness has disappeared and so has happiness! There is no desire left in my heart. Panditji doesn't open his eyes throughout the performance—divine tranquility and quietude reign supreme.

Time appears to be resting on the dais as if it were one among us—a devotee, a learner.

* * *

7 February 1996
Jawaharlal Nehru University, New Delhi

Dear Papa,

I feel hollow. Everything seems so superfluous and unmentionable. A sense of unfulfillment, of not doing any fruitful or meaningful work, devastates me. The other students are so sure of what they should be doing, while I remain confused. Yet there is an urge that keeps me from sheer abandonment and regret.

I don't want to be a recluse, nor do I aspire to conform to the boring curriculum here. My pursuit remains the same: to write. Although I allowed academics to rob me of my desire to become a flautist, I will never allow it to interfere in my literary activities, knowing that both academics and genuine creative writing have little to do with each other. Especially when one is stranded in a place such as this one.

There is more to education than is present within these walls, with privileged students talking about issues they are unsure about themselves. Scanty knowledge about things has spoiled them.

Most of them, including me, are rootless.

Anyway, I'm not as bad as I was in my previous semester. Nothing has changed. It's just that I have started laughing at things and I occasionally brood over the funniness of life. I find it absurd to give shape to things.

I have ceased to brag about my knowledge of life. I am no longer a seeker or a person who thinks he's living the life he wants. I realize that if I live a life of comfort, I can't have any genuine human experiences.

I don't know how to earn a livelihood yet. My time at home with you proved very fruitful and enlightening. Your philosophy of truth is difficult because of its unique simplicity. If I were to pocket a stone every time I uttered a lie, I would, by sunset, collapse under the weight of stones.

I will go to New Palam Vihar in a few days. If possible, please complete the translation of Lal Ded's *vaakhs* (verses).

With unbounded love and regards to all!

Yours,
Siddhartha

* * *

June 1996
New Delhi

Anil has been my best friend since our school days in Kashmir. I lost touch with him in 1990, when we had to leave Kashmir without being able to inform each other.

Sandeep informs me that Anil is living in rented accommodation in Malviya Nagar. 'You must go and see him and his family,' he says. 'Both of you were inseparable during our school days in Srinagar.'

'I have been looking for him all these years,' I say to Sandeep. In my heart, there is guilt and remorse, but my claim is not entirely true. Yes, I have missed Anil, but I have not looked for him the way I should have. The wise say that if you search with all your heart and soul, you will even find God.

I meet Anil one desolate evening in Delhi's Malviya Nagar. He shows me his stall by the roadside. The Delhi government has allowed many displaced Kashmiri Pandits to set up stalls by the roadside in the evening. Anil's stall belongs to his father. The stall contains several household and hosiery items for sale. Anil wants to gift me a t-shirt, a towel and a handkerchief. But I can't take them. We have juice at a roadside juice vendor.

Anil's father has taken up two rooms on rent. Anil's mother cries seeing me after years. 'You forgot about your brother and mother,' she says, hugging me and not letting me go. 'Ever since we got separated, your brother has not stopped talking about you. Every day, you figure in his conversations. He looked for you everywhere. I curse the militants for ruining our lives and forcing us to separate from one another . . .'

Anil's father wipes a tear from his eyes. 'You were his only friend,' he says. 'He hasn't made any friends here. Look at how we live now. Do you remember our house in Karan Nagar? You would stay with us for days together and refuse to leave . . .'

'How could I ever forget? Yours was a palatial house . . .'

Anil bares his heart out. He tells me how they were made to leave their home. 'Militants came and threatened us to leave or else . . .' he recalls.

This ghetto in Khirki Extension has become a refugee colony for hundreds of displaced Kashmiri Pandits. They make ends meet by running stalls and selling various things. Anil has also completed his studies. He had big dreams, but he must now support his father and mother to make a living by selling household things.

Pa has asked me to meet Dr H.K. Kaul, the secretary general of the Poetry Society, India. His office is in Malviya Nagar. Anil says he knows the place. Dr Kaul is also a Kashmiri Pandit. I want to show him some of my poems, but when we get there, the office is shut.

Anil and I promise to stay in touch. His mother gives me food to eat. She cries. 'If we were in our house in Srinagar, I would never have let you to leave like this. I would have made your favourite dishes and insisted that you stay for the night, but . . .'

Anil walks me to the bus stop. He can't stop talking about our school days and the time we spent in Kashmir. He goes on and on about the dreams we had as teenagers. 'Remember, we had promised to never part. We still have so many places to go and so many things to do. Will we ever go back and resume our lives . . . Will we ever get the lost time back? Will we ever do all the things we want to do? Will we ever visit all the places we want to? Will you take me back to my home in Kashmir some day?'

'You must come with me to Udhampur,' I say to him.

He is not the Anil I once knew. He's not that boy anymore, but the courage and wisdom I see in him are unmatched. It's something I have never known myself. Anil has sacrificed his future for his family's wellbeing. He has given up his dreams and aspirations so that his family can stay safe. He has become the householder now. He has taken charge of his family's affairs. He is bound by his duty to support his family so that he can someday rebuild everything that they lost.

There are many colonies in Delhi that have camps for displaced Kashmiri Pandits. Shadipur Depot, Amar Colony, Lajpat Nagar and Khirki Extension are the main camps. Many Kashmiri Pandits are working in private companies. Some are running eateries, while others have become stall owners. In Delhi, they are called Kashmiri Pandit migrants. Next to their ghettos, live the refugees from Afghanistan. They have been living here for years. Delhi is their home now. They are called Afghan refugees.

Some Days Later

Our landlords, the Bhatiyals, have a telephone now. I ring them up and ask for Pa to inquire about everything at home.

Pa says everything is fine and that I should not worry. I ask for Babi and Babuji. Babuji doesn't talk much over the phone, but Babi does. She ends up repeating herself. She asks if I am alright and if I'm taking care of myself by eating and sleeping on time.

I overhear Babuji talking about me and a mad dog.

'What's going on, Pa?'

'Nothing. It's just a dream he had.'

'And?'

'He thinks it's not a dream.'

'I am taking the first bus to Udhampur tomorrow.'

'Don't. It is not required.'

I know where this mad dog has come from. It is the same yellow dog that prowled the street next to our house in Srinagar. He chased me once and I ran and hid in Babuji's room. I shut the door behind me and didn't come out for hours. The dog is now mad. It is back and it wants revenge. I am his unfinished business.

That's why I must go to Udhampur tomorrow. I must not wait. I know what the mad dog is up to.

The Next Evening

I board a bus for Jammu at the interstate bus terminus in Delhi. I reach home the next morning.

Babuji is playing with a pack of playing cards. He's never been interested in card games, but now he is holding a pack of cards, uninterestedly and unwillingly, unsure of what to do with the cards. He can't tell the jack from the king. Pa is showing him how to arrange the cards in a sequence.

Pa explains, 'I know what I am doing. He's been a bit disoriented lately. The cards keep him busy and focused.'

'Look who's here. Who is this person who has come home?' Babi asks Babuji.

Babuji: 'He is Baijee (father).'

Babi: 'You think he's Baijee? Look again. Who is he? Talk to him at least. You were the one asking for him all the time. Now that he's here, talk to him.'

Babuji smiles an enigmatic smile. 'Which class are you in?' he asks.

Me: 'MA.'

Babi: 'Remember what he used to say when you would take him to school on your bicycle? "I won't go to school today. Not today, not tomorrow, not the day after tomorrow, but the day after the day after tomorrow." Remember how you carried him on your shoulders and he would refuse to get off?'

Babi looks at me. 'Remember those frequent trips to the forest behind Eid Gah? You would sit on his shoulders, refusing to come down and he would show you hoopoe nests and teach you how to mimic the sounds of the hoopoe. You must remind him of those days. He has forgotten everything, but not the time he spent with you. If you talk to him about those days, he will return to the present . . .'

Babuji smiles a strange smile. Then he turns to the pack of cards in his hands and looks at them blankly, unsure of what he must do with them.

Babi asks me to show him my leg. 'He thinks you were bitten by a mad dog outside our house in Srinagar.'

Me: 'I am perfectly fine. You shouldn't worry about me. How is your friend, Chajju Ram? Do you meet him often?'

But Babuji seems lost somewhere. I look at Pa.

In the evening, we sit on the terrace, talking about Babuji's dream. Some realities come back to haunt us in dreams.

The next day, Babuji asks me once again about the dog bite. 'Show me the bite mark,' he says.

* * *

January 1997
New Delhi

Pandit Arun Kaul sent for me today. Pa must have talked to him about me. He has asked me to see him in his studio in South Delhi.

When I enter the studio, I see people sitting and talking in a thick pall of cigarette smoke. Some youngsters are sitting in front of a bearded man who looks like a mystic. In front of the man is a large earthen pot brimming with cigarette ash. The man has two cigarettes between the fingers of his left hand. He is holding a pen in his right hand. There are papers on the wooden desk. He is sitting cross-legged on the floor. So are the others. He greets me with a smile and gives me a hug.

He is Pandit Arun Kaul, a screenwriter and filmmaker. He's the producer of *Kashmir File*, a popular television serial broadcast by Doordarshan India. Among the other critically acclaimed films he has directed, *Diksha* (The Initiation) stands out. It is based on a Kannada story by Dr U.R. Ananthamurthy.

Pandit Arun Kaul is Gasha's friend. He knows Pa and Babuji too.

'Go and take a look around the studio,' he says. He asks one of the boys to show me around. The boy introduces himself as Indraneel, his son.

'We make films. And we are in the process of making a documentary film about the exodus and exile of Kashmiri Pandits,' Indraneel says to me. He is sporting a ponytail. The two rooms are full of video tapes and film-making equipment. Indraneel points to an entire rack stacked with video tapes and books. 'All these tapes and books are about Kashmir. But we need to go to the camps in Jammu and capture everything on tape.'

'There is a camp in Udhampur too,' I say to him. 'The place where I live with my family . . .'

'Some day, I want to make a film on our exodus and exile. A film like *Schindler's List* or *Escape from Sobibor*,' says another boy.

A documentary film titled *Freedom from Fear* is in the making. So is *Echoes of an Ethos*. The film will narrate all the main events that happened from 1988 until 1997. There will be a chapter on our exodus and exile and the heritage and way of life that we have lost.

Pandit Arun Kaul has asked me to help his crew with research, writing and subtitling. He has also asked me to translate Dina Nath Nadim's Kashmiri poem 'Ba Gyev Na Az' into English.

The opening line is 'My song will remain unsung today'. This is how Pa has translated it.

A Few Weeks Later

I am handed a cheque for Rs 2000. 'This is for your work. Don't hesitate to accept it,' says Pandit Arun Kaul. 'A day will come when you will have to narrate the story of your exodus to the entire world. Jews are doing so even today. You must too . . .'

* * *

15 March 1997
JNU, New Delhi

My dear Papa,

I am anxious to see Babi. Now that you have had her cataract removed, I am sure she will be able to see things clearly and distinguish between ugliness and beauty. I share your happiness. Your patience, love and care are admirable. Didn't I tell you that pain, suffering and grief do not last forever? Nor do laughter and joy.

With love,
Siddhartha

* * *

A Day in August 1997
Sri Fort Auditorium, New Delhi

My classmate Hari's friend is a volunteer for the Society for the Promotion of Indian Classical Music and Culture Amongst Youth (SPIC MACAY). Recalling my earlier request to be part of SPIC MACAY's volunteer group and knowing my passion for classical music, she asks me if I would be willing to be part of her team in charge of a major concert of classical music to be held in New Delhi's Sri Fort auditorium. It's a special concert to commemorate the fiftieth anniversary of India's independence. Many *swarn jayanti samarohs* (golden jubilee ceremonies) are underway in Delhi and the rest of India. The mood among the people is one of jubilation and celebration. People are singing songs. But the most popular song today is:

> '*Sare jahan se achha, Hindustan hamara.*
> *Hum bulbulain hai iss ki, yeh gulsitan hamara . . .*'
> (Our Hindustan is better than the entire world. We are its
> nightingales and it is our garden.)

I am put in charge of Siri Fort auditorium's green room, where the great musician Pandit Ravi Shankar, his daughter Anoushka Shankar, tabla maestro Ustad Zakir Hussain, famous guitarist John McLaughlin and other musicians will spend some time before proceeding to the stage to perform. I am to wait on them. It's the happiest day of my life in years. I dream of performing at a concert like this someday.

The hall is brimming with people. Not a single seat is unoccupied. Even the stairs have been taken over. People are waiting in anticipation for the concert to begin. One by one, the musicians get out of their cars wearing colourful clothes. They are beaming. I welcome them and escort them to the green room. They briefly acknowledge my presence and allow me to serve them tea and snacks. I wait beside them in case they require anything. I am not supposed to move from my designated spot. I am to sit backstage, where they can spot me should they need anything.

The concert begins. Anoushka Sankar, the youngest performer, sits gracefully on the podium, strums at the strings of her sitar and plays the most melodious composition, sending the audience into a trance. The composition is a tribute to the nation and to the freedom fighters.

After the concert ends and the musicians are back in the green room, John McLaughlin starts talking to us volunteers. 'Where are you from?' is his question to us, seeing everyone in different ethnic attire.

The volunteers say: 'West Bengal . . . Manipur . . . Maharashtra . . . Kerala . . . Tamil Nadu . . .'

'And where are you from, young man?' he asks softly, looking at me. It is my turn to answer.

I pause briefly, not knowing what to say.

This question—where are you from?—has become the most difficult question of my life. I am sick of this question. But I know this is also the most important question. And it will be asked again and again. Perhaps this question will haunt me throughout my life in case I don't get to go back to Kashmir ever.

How should I answer? I am from Kashmir, but I don't live there anymore because . . . This is where I go blank.

How do I fill in the blanks?

'Kashmir,' I say to Mr McLaughlin, after a pause. 'I am from Kashmir.'

'Ah! Kashmir! Heaven on earth!' he says. 'You are lucky to live there . . .'

People wish one another a happy fiftieth Independence Day. The only thing I am thinking about is home. I want to go home. Not to Kashmir, but to Udhampur. I think about those people in the camp who must also be wishing one another a happy fiftieth Independence Day. They must have hoisted the national flag of India in the camp and sung the national anthem. Every year, on 15 August, they celebrate India's independence in the camp because they never got to celebrate the occasion in Kashmir. As far back as I can remember, many Muslims in Kashmir have been celebrating the Independence Day of Pakistan on 14 August.

But today, atop every tent in the camp in Udhampur will be India's national flag. On everyone's lips will be the song that we have recently discovered:

Vande Mātaram
(Mother, I bow to thee)

* * *

10 September 1997
Delhi

My dear Papa,

I'm sending you a few copies of my biodata and four passport-sized photographs for the state subject application form. You are right; the state subject certificate is an important document in these times—the most crucial one.[*]

Love,
Siddhartha

* * *

---

[*] An important legal document that acknowledges and certifies the special rights and privileges accorded to the domiciles of the Jammu and Kashmir state as enshrined in Article 35A (now revoked) of the Constitution of India.

27 November 1997
New Delhi

My dear Papa,

I was happy to learn about the exhibition that Henna organized at her school. Tell her that I will write to her soon.

How is Babuji? Keep me informed about his health. Hope he takes his medicines on time.

What about the plans to sell our house in Srinagar? Did you contact anyone? We must not wait any longer. It's already too late. We need the money. Do something about it. Well, there's so much to talk about. Take some days off and see me.

Love,
Yours ever,
Siddhartha

* * *

1 February 1998
Delhi

My dear Papa and Ma,

Living alone in rented accommodations is a wonderful experience. I sleep and dream at will. It's immensely exciting to taste freedom. I feel like reading Dostoevsky's novels once again just to know what it's like to live in a rented room. Dostoevsky's heroes live in rented rooms.

Mornings are usually quite rustic here. I can hear the sound of bells worn by cows and buffaloes in the neighbourhood. The smell of milk is always in the air here.

Nights are never quiet; they are always pregnant with the sound of trucks and airplanes. Living close to a national highway and the runway is quite an extraordinary experience. For me, it's reminiscent of old memories. Trucks come onto the highway from nowhere and disappear into a distant nowhere, leaving behind impressions of lost time and a half-lived past. All these things carry mysterious messages: messages of the never-at-rest world, of perennial migration, of change and of the futility of settled life.

The world seems very busy, but life in Rangpuri is very slow. I'm content with what I have now. Here, I live in blissful anonymity, dreaming of a pleasant hereafter.

I will try to visit Udhampur by the end of February. Until then, you must write to me at my office address:

231, HSIDC Industrial Complex

Udyog Vihar, Dundahera

Gurgaon, Haryana

It may not be a good idea to send letters to my room for fear of not receiving them at all or losing them since the room does not have a proper address. Houses don't have numbers here and streets are nameless in this part of town. The only thing I know is that I live in Rangpuri, which is close to Hotel Radisson. The village is on the Delhi–Gurgaon Road, about 1 km from Hotel Centaur and the airport.

I am sending a few visiting cards which mention my email address, fax and telephone numbers.

Yours ever,
Siddhartha

* * *

13 September 1998
Delhi

My dear Mummy,

You have not been writing to me at all. Are you that busy and overworked? Yesterday, Aishwarya invited me to her place for lunch. Her mother was eager to see me since Aishwarya talks about me at home. Her mother is extremely gentle, loving and affectionate. We talked at length about me. When you come to Delhi, we will visit Aishwarya at her place.

When do the Puja holidays begin for you? Inform me beforehand if you intend to come here. The weather is nice now. It's going to be winter soon. Is it possible for you to knit a full-sleeved sweater in a colour of your liking for me? Maroon would be perfect. Bring it along with you. Do bring my old sweater too. I need it for daily use at home.

I hope Babuji is keeping well. Do write to me regularly about his health. What about Henna? I wrote her a letter. She hasn't replied yet. Is she happy with college?

Ask Papa to write. Tell him that his poems are on an Internet website now. I will send him the printed copies soon. Why doesn't he come here for a few days?

Give me regards to Babuji and Babi.

Always yours,
Siddhartha

* * *

7 October 1998
New Delhi

My dear Papa,

I am sad that you kept me ignorant of the surgery you underwent. I do understand your love and care for me, but does that mean that I am not entitled to know whatever happens at home when I'm not there? The irony of it all is that I still don't know what exactly happened. Why don't you write? It is painful when I don't get to read your letters. I feel awfully wretched, estranged from home and lonely. And then you say everything is fine.

First, you must realize that Udhampur is no place to get treated. Please take your health seriously. I have nothing more to say. I hope you understand. Why don't you come here and stay with me for a few days?

I play the flute sometimes. I love to leaf through books as though they are old photo albums laden with dust and hazy memories.

I stare at the bare ceiling or gaze at the sky. Not that I like doing it, but it is the most convenient thing to do. Sometimes I think, sometimes I dream. I am most happy when I'm doing nothing.

Love,
Siddhartha

* * *

21 October 1998
Delhi

My dear Papa,

I received your short letter a few days ago. There was certainly more you could have written. You say that you are bored. Well, each one of us experiences boredom at some point. I believe it is somewhat ugly and brutal to not feel bored or to not relish and enjoy boredom whenever it comes. Isn't boredom man's secret companion? It is also the source of new ideas. What is boredom, after all? Is it man's ability to not be able to do anything? Is it that wisdom in us that tells us that whatever can be done is not worth doing? Is it man's expression of his profound contempt for this mad world? Or is it just an insane longing within ourselves to mould the stubborn world closer to our heart's desire? Boredom is a strange feeling. At times, it is borne out of excessive sadness or happiness. And many a time, it just springs from the very lack of these lonely treasures of life.

The only certainty about it is that it has no certainty. Isn't it wonderful that boredom keeps us occupied and busy even when we have absolutely nothing to do? And it remains man's true friend in loneliness and in pain.

If this is the case, then why must one try to get rid of it? What are our other comfortable and convenient alternatives, if not for boredom?

I'm happy that Ma, Henna and you have spoken to Aishwarya and her family more than a couple of times. I was too shy to tell you about her. Talking to fathers can be daunting sometimes, especially in such matters. Aishwarya's parents are eager to meet you. You must have figured that out by now. They (Mr and Mrs Pillai) keep asking me about you. I think you must tell Babuji and Babi about Aishwarya. We will see her when you come here. You can write to her at the same address as mine.

Take care of your health. Go for a complete medical check-up. Please give my regards to Babuji and Babi. Love to Ma and Henna.

I hope your writing keeps you busy. Remember your promise to complete the translation of Lad Ded? It's been quite a few winters now since you said you would.

Do keep me informed about everyone at home. And write to me positively.

With unbounded love,
Siddhartha

                    * * *

'A neurologist in Udhampur has diagnosed Babuji with Alzheimer's,' Pa tells me over the phone. 'Earlier, it was thought to be just age-related memory loss. The doctor says it is impossible to recover from this degenerative state. Nothing can be done.'

I go to a cybercafe in Munirka to search for information and read articles about Alzheimer's on the Internet. It is a dreadful disease. It leads to a no-memory, no-recognition state. It is an abyss that one keeps falling into until memory and recognition cease to exist. There is no coming back from it.

I return to Udhampur to see Babuji. He has been bedridden for almost a year now, unable to walk or even go to the bathroom. The trauma of the loss of his home, his laboratory and his Kashmir (which meant the world to him) has devastated him. It has rendered him hollow. The first shock he experienced was when he crossed the Jawahar tunnel in Banihal. When the truck exited the 3-km-long tunnel that day, the entire landscape had changed and so had something within him. And that tunnel became the tunnel of forgetfulness, not just for him but for countless other men and women who were forced to leave their homes in Kashmir for an unknown place, possibly for the first time in their lives.

For the first five years, he kept waiting for the situation in Kashmir to be normal so that he could return home and to his clinic, The Imperial Clinical Laboratory at Maharaj Gunj in Srinagar. If there is one word that he has not been able to come to terms with, it is 'migrant'.

He never gave up hope, but now he is beyond all hope.

Babuji mistakes Ma for Henna and Henna for his mother. He mistakes me for his father. He also mistakes Pa for his father.

Pa recounts horrific accounts about Babuji. 'Once he left the house and didn't return for hours. I brought him home after looking for him in all of Udhampur. It took me an entire day. He was sitting on a footpath by the roadside. But the worst day of our life was when he went to the toilet one afternoon and came out after an hour smeared with faeces. For him, the meaning of things has altered irrevocably. You can't imagine the sight! No one can. Ever since that day, I accompany him to the toilet every single time. One day, he went to the bathroom a hundred times. He just wouldn't stop. I was patient. I ensured that nothing went wrong and reassured him that I was around, though I was not sure if he recognized me any longer. I have never left him alone since that day. Not even for a fraction of a second. Some days ago, his earlobe fell off while I was giving him a bath. Look at him now. Look at what he has become. His body is full of sores. His skin is flaky and shrivelled. His fragile skin peels when I apply ointment to it. Babi is a strong woman. She's the strongest of us all. We should be grateful to her for who she is, for keeping us sane and for spreading cheer in her own way even in such desperate situations. She narrates parables to help me cope . . .'

Henna and I are mute spectators to this horror that has gripped us. We are falling apart as a family.

Exile has done terrible things to us, as it has to many others who are suffering in camps. Love deserts us every morning, only to return in snatches and disappear again. Yet, we wait for a better day and for that one moment of peace and calm. Waiting means never losing hope.

'Ronald Reagan also had Alzheimer's towards the end,' says Pa. 'It doesn't even spare presidents. But let us not lose hope. We will see better times. Waiting will keep us alive and sane . . . but we will and we must always remember this madness that brought us closer to one another and taught us how to love and serve.'

* * *

19 April 1999
New Delhi

My dear Papa,

Aishwarya likes your letters very much. She refers to you as her penfriend. You should see her smiling as she reads your letters. She says nobody else sends her such beautiful letters.

I'm looking forward to Henna's exams ending and then I will write to her. I dread recalling my examination days. I remember the day I took my philosophy test. I was the only one writing the test that day at the examination centre. The questions pertained to karma, existentialism and *maya*.

The temperature outside was about 45 degrees. It was the month of June. The worst summer ever. I finished the test and rushed to take a dip in the Devika.

When I reached home, you had lost your sense of reason. You sat with your head immersed in a bucket of cold water. Your expression was one of renunciation and resignation. Babuji was in a state of profound calm. He was half-naked, like a fakir. He was waiting for the end. Babi and Henna were hysterical. I don't remember anything else. What a day it was! That was a long time ago, but not very long.

You must not hide anything from me. You usually don't, I know. Write about everything. Write more often. Write about Babuji. You must be so dreadfully lonely there. I admire your will and determination. Sometimes I believe that your faith and devotion are stronger than steel. Nobody could ever do what you are doing or what you've done so far. Could anyone ever understand your sacrifices? I have much more to say, but I can't. You will have to read my silence. I hate to stop.

With unbounded love,
Siddhartha
P.S. I think of all of you when I am lonely.

* * *

8 July 1999
New Delhi

My dear Papa,

In our last phone conversation, you sounded very worried. I understand only too well what you must be going through these days. Our family is going through a crisis. All these years have been strangely sad and unhealthy for us. At times, it all seems like a nightmare to me. I'm frightened of certain things. I'm afraid of losing our laughter and happiness. Sometimes I have dreadful visions of death and desolation.

I can't accept, I can't resign and I can't reconcile. I'm helpless and lonely. But I rarely allow myself the opportunity to think about the whole thing. I do this deliberately because it helps keep doubt, depression and thoughts at bay. It is not that I have killed my consciousness, sensitivity and emotion, but that I have put them to sleep so I am not tormented by them. Who does not fear torrents? I am conscious of my own inferiority.

Wisdom lies in accepting old age, disease and death. It would be foolish to negate these ugly truths of life. Life is ultimately a burden. It deceives us. It knows no pity, no sympathy and no love. I don't know yet what supreme joy and profound satisfaction exist in knowledge. But ignorance and a simple attitude towards life seem desirable and tempting.

One must live and think like a woodcutter, a boatman or a farmer. To know is supreme, but to see, wonder and then smile is beautiful.

Well, these thoughts might seem foolish, but they are innocent. I'm too young and ignorant to know what lies beyond a carefree and foolish way of thinking. Doubt and a desire to know do lead to magnificent discoveries about man and life. But these paths can be dangerous. I live dangerously. Why think profound thoughts? Why fret? Why care about God and death? But then, I presume one must seek refuge in the shade of an old tree when one is old and lonely. The problem with the young is that they're young and have dreams. I shudder at the thought of a stage in life when one can't dream, hope or even wait. Where one is continuously dangling between hope and despair. That is suffering. What happens when dreams die and hope withers? What happens when you know that you are going away? We realize that our bodies are not ours. It's just a burden that we love to bear. We realize many things, but we realize them too late. We aren't prepared. We love to postpone things. Finally, nobody is granted a reprieve.

What is the solution? Is there a final solution? Could there be any answers? Should we be prepared? Should we begin to doubt our own existence? Should we start to negate and reject our own small hopes and dreams?

No, we mustn't do these things. We must neither rebel nor resign. We must neither tighten the string of life nor loosen it. We must tune it to the perfect rhythm, but that is difficult. After all, love and care are duties we must perform. Hope, happiness and struggle are glass beads in our pockets. They are fragile. They vanish.

Your incomplete, foolish son!

P.S. I wait for your letters. I hate to be away from home, from you, from Babuji . . . Let us pray for Babuji. My last goodbye to Babuji this time was tragic and sad. He didn't have any strength left in him to kiss me the way he always has. His eyes said it all. I still remember the afternoon he took me to Rainawari on his old bicycle. He was young. He was happy.

Yours always,
Siddhartha

* * *

October 1999
New Delhi

My dear Ma,

I got your letter a few days ago. I was happy to hear from you after a long time. Yesterday, I got Papa's letter. He says he has lost his sleep and that you are worried for him. Take care of him. He's written about Babuji. I hope he's stable. I think about Babuji and pray for his happiness and good health. Babi must be a sad woman. We must understand her and give her all the love and care that she deserves.

I'm sure Henna is enjoying her college life. She is a lonely girl. She has written me a letter containing thoughts that are philosophical in nature.

On Sundays, I go to Aishwarya's home. She sends you her namaste. She is here right now as I write this letter.

Your marriage anniversary falls towards the end of this month. My love and best wishes to Papa and you.

Please inform me beforehand about your visit to Delhi. But see to it that Babuji is not left entirely alone.

How is your schoolwork going? You work too hard in the kitchen. Rest is important.

I hope my sweater is ready. I'm looking forward to wearing it this winter.

I don't think I can come home now. If all goes well, I will be home for Shivratri* next year. Do keep me informed

---

* Shivratri is of great religious, social and cultural importance to Kashmiri Pandits. The festival is celebrated to mark the wedding of Lord Shiva with Goddess Parvati.

about home and yourself. Do write regularly or else I get worried.

Love,
Siddhartha

* * *

July 1999
Udhampur

Babuji's condition is deteriorating. Mentally, he's not with us any longer, but somewhere else—in a topsy-turvy world of dreams, memories and fantasies. He hops back and forth from one strange world to another. Some of those worlds are not even his. But they seem to be connected by a fine thread. A thread that is about to snap. And once it snaps, the world will come crumbling down.

Babuji mumbles, smiles and then talks to himself and to some people whom only he can see. He calls out the names of people who exist and those who don't and never will.

He's so frail and weak that we don't think he will survive one more day. He is unable to eat or drink. His body doesn't accept any food.

We rush him to a hospital in Jammu. He is kept in a ward. The doctors come one by one to examine him. Senior doctors bring junior doctors and even resident interns. They have an interesting case to study. A case so rare that the doctors refuse to leave his bedside. This is how they will learn to treat difficult and rare cases concerning people's mental states.

'Alzheimer's is not common in Jammu,' says someone. 'But lately, we are seeing more and more patients from the camps.'

At last, a senior doctor gives his verdict. 'Take him home. This place will do him no good. There is no merit in keeping him here and prolonging his agony.'

'Is there any hope?' asks Pa.

The doctor shakes his head.

We arrange for a van to travel back to Udhampur. Babuji mumbles throughout the journey. He calls out the names of people. He is delirious.

The journey from Jammu to Udhampur proves to be the most tumultuous of his life. His suffering peaks. It doesn't look good. Will he survive? A thought comes to my mind: he should not die in the van or on our way home. If something must happen, let it happen at home. This van is no place to die.

God listens to my prayers. We reach home. The last few days have been the worst of our lives and Babuji's life.

Once we are home, we place him on his bed and he goes off to sleep instantly. The stay at the general ward in the hospital has taken a toll and worsened his state. But now he's home and in bed, ready to depart for good. He has no strength left. Hope has abandoned him. We are next to him. He has the look of a tired man who wants to do nothing but sleep and dream. Babi holds his hand in an I-won't-let-you-go clasp!

Day after day, we watch him wither and wilt.

Days pass.

Our prayer for his deliverance remains unheard. It's better to go than to live like this in prolonged pain. He lies on his bed with a tube inserted into his nostrils. The other end of the tube is in Babuji's stomach. Babi makes soup every day and Pa uses a syringe to inject some of it into the tube. This is how Pa feeds him. This is what keeps him alive, apart from some mysterious force that none of us can understand. Taking the tube out of his nostrils to clean it and then re-inserting it is a nightmare. Only Pa knows how to do it properly.

Babuji has always been an independent person. He has always done his own chores. I have seen a time when he would do other people's chores too, such as cleaning the lane outside our house and polishing our shoes. His definition of cleanliness can never be understood by others, even the most trained sweepers. 'The drains have got to be sparkling clean,' he used to say.

But now he can't even lift himself up.

'He should go now,' Babi prays, unable to bear the sight of her husband's condition. Henna sobs. She has never known such desperation and helplessness.

To Babuji, none of us are who we used to be. We are different people now. He is another man. He looks at us strangely with his tired grey eyes. In a way, he's saying goodbye to us all the time. I don't want him to die a sad man. I want him to go at the exact moment when he is the happiest—smiling and dreaming.

31 July 1999

Pa is up for the whole night. He keeps checking Babuji's pulse every now and then. His heartbeat has been feeble for days now. But his heart is neither slowing down further nor stopping for good. It is just beating—one beat at a time, each beat separated by a long, long pause.

Sometime after midnight, Pa checks Babuji's pulse and then calls us quietly. 'He's gone,' says Pa, gently closing Babuji's eyes for the last time.

Babuji's face has an enigmatic smile, as though hinting at one last mischievous moment.

We wait for the sun to rise.

After the cremation, Pa and I stop at a shop. Pa breaks down. I comfort him. He comforts me. He reads my lips. I read his. 'Deliverance,' he says.

'What will I do now? What will I do from tomorrow onwards?'

'You know what to do?'

'We must learn to be happy now . . .'

For over three years, Pa did nothing except look after Babuji all the time. Not only as a son but also as a father and a mother. He was always there for Babuji, right next to him, every single moment. And during the last six months, he cared for him like a mother keeps an infant alive. But he suffered too. He endured not only Babuji's suffering but his own too. He took our share of suffering upon himself. He did it single-handedly and without any fuss. Such is his capacity for bearing suffering. I haven't heard him complain even once.

But Pa thinks otherwise. 'He not only took his pain when he left, but he also took away our pain. He delivered us of our agony too,' says Pa about Babuji. 'There's nothing for me to do now.'

'You must live your own life now,' I say to him. 'It is time . . .'

He asks me to return to Delhi and focus on my studies. 'Complete your MA and settle somewhere else. Build a life for yourself. Pursue the things you love—the things that mean the world to you. Don't give up on your dreams. Don't worry about us. We will be fine. Carve out your own destiny. Don't look back at us . . .'

Before leaving for Delhi, we donate Babuji's clothes to mendicants at the Devika Ghat. There is not much to give away: just four shirts, two sweaters, a jacket, a blanket, a quilt and a cap. I have all his letters.

Towards the end, Babuji lost all recollection of the things he loved the most and that meant the world to him.

* * *

8 December 1999
New Delhi

My dear Papa,

There has been a long silence between us. Long silences are strange. So much to say and yet one struggles for words. I don't remember the last word I wrote to you. We can now begin a new conversation. The last word may be lost, but it lives somewhere. We live and die in words. That's all.

The other day, Aishwarya and I were talking about words and the healing power they possess. During our talk, we spoke of 'greatness'. The basic question arose: what is greatness? Aishwarya made a very interesting remark. She said that great men are great because we are so ordinary. We finally settled on this thought.

I bought vegetables on my way home. We are happy in our small world. Simple things become very difficult sometimes. You can't grasp the essence. It's a good thing to not understand many things in life. It keeps pain at bay and keeps us happy in partial ignorance. We don't even know that we don't know. And we must know that we don't know.

How are you? I bet the winter is tempting you to remain as idle and sleepy as ever. There's been too much suffering and unhappiness in the past few years. 'I'm still, but I'm not still,' you once said to me. But this winter has got to be different. Why not make it a humorous winter? Why not make this winter smile like a madman? Why not proclaim, 'I am'. Why be happy? Why be sad? Why not just be?

Everybody is raving about the millennium. What does the millennium hold for the common people of the world? The people who are united in their lost hopes and dreams. The people who die daily. The people who should not have been born. Nothing. Isn't it just another day?

For us, it will be like any other day when you can get a haircut, watch a movie or simply do something meaningful and normal. I think the coming century is going to be peaceful because there won't be any time for war and evil. Well, who knows? Cruel moments have a habit of showing up unannounced. So do the happy moments.

Have you resumed work on the translation of Lal Ded's poetry?

I will end this letter now, leaving some small things unsaid. Until we meet again, goodbye and plenty of love.

Forever,
Siddhartha

10

Merge, Leave or Perish

Morning
July 1989
National High School, Karan Nagar, Srinagar

The assembly is going on. Students from all classes are standing at attention on the school grounds. Some are in the corridors outside the classrooms. Everyone is happy to see the school building renovated. At last, we have proper classrooms.

After reciting the prayer—*Lab Pe Aati Hai Dua*—we are all set to sing the national anthem. As soon as we begin, there is commotion next to the principal's office. Two bearded men barge into the school premises and start speaking to the principal in a threatening manner. All of us students are aghast. It's unsettling to even watch the two intruders speak rudely to the person who is feared by everyone because he stands for discipline and adherence to rules. Their body language itself is violent. Shortly after the two men leave, the principal hurriedly goes into his office and then leaves the school in a rush.

Some of my Muslim classmates speak in hushed tones as if they had prior knowledge that this would happen. They seem oddly happy. 'Serves him right,' is the look on their faces with regard to our principal. 'The Hizbul guys have done the job . . .' they say, elatedly. 'And they taught him a lesson for making us sing the national anthem of India. The only anthem we will ever sing here in Kashmir is the national anthem of Pakistan . . .' they go on and on. 'Pakistan is our beloved country, not India.'

All sorts of profanities are uttered against the principal and the Pandit staff. The Muslim students start singing the national anthem of Pakistan. The Pandit teachers stand terrified and mute. None of us Pandit students know how to react. We decide to pretend nothing bad or unexpected has happened.

Evening

On my way home from school, I stop by Basheer's hardware store, which is about twenty paces before Safa Kadal, the seventh and oldest bridge over the Jhelum. Basheer has supplied all the hardware for the renovation of our house. For years, my father has been collecting artwork to decorate the house. But a foreboding that the situation is going to take a terrible turn has been keeping us in a state of dilemma.

'What should we do . . . in case . . .?' we keep wondering.

'If you ever find yourself in trouble, just mention my name,' Basheer tells me. Besides being our hardware supplier, he is also Pa's student. He is grateful for the tutoring he received from Pa. However, education doesn't interest Basheer. 'Studies are useless,' he jokes. 'Real education lies in the political struggle for our people.'

Basheer is aware of the position, rank and authority he holds in the entire neighbourhood. He claims to have been appointed the area commander of the Jammu Kashmir

Liberation Front (JKLF). 'This part of Downtown Srinagar,' he says, 'is under my command.'

But Hizbul Mujahideen (HM) has lured the youth away from the JKLF—it has now risen to become the most feared of the insurgent outfits, given its links with the Jamaat-e-Islami, that advocates Kashmir's merger with Pakistan. HM is waging a war for Kashmir to become an Islamic State.

Basheer, however, dreams of azadi. 'My heart bleeds for Pakistan, but I shall live and die in azad Kashmir,' he says.

I confide in Basheer about a troublesome incident involving some miscreants near my school. The previous day, in school, I had blurted out that I was in possession of Salman Rushdie's *The Satanic Verses*. My uncle had brought the book for us from Melbourne. Little did I know that my foolhardy disclosure would put me in harm's way. Some classmates leaked the news to outsiders and I found myself surrounded by people who threatened to punish me for sacrilege.

'Do you want me to show it to you?' one man said to me, lifting the hem of his *pheran* (loose upper garment), revealing the nozzle of a gun. His partner, who people said was his younger brother and an HM boy, put his hand in the pocket of his pheran and fished out a pistol.

I mentioned Basheer's name and was let off with a warning. 'Don't ever spread such lies. And don't brag about the blasphemous book. You know the punishment for speaking against our Prophet?' they warned.

Basheer laughs and says, 'What a blunder! These Hizbul boys are dangerous. But they will not harm you as long as your big brother is around. It's a good thing that you told them about me.'

Luckily, no one believed my disclosure about having *The Satanic Verses*.

The Next Day

Basheer comes home to inspect the progress of the renovation of our house. The following afternoon, I stop by his shop again. He speaks of his ambition. 'I am going to be made the regional commander soon,' he says elatedly. 'And, Inshallah, if I meet the goals, I will be made the divisional commander of JKLF someday.' Heroism, idealism, utter contempt for school education, loyalty to his teacher and fondness for his teacher's son characterize Basheer.

'You will have to leave Kashmir soon,' he says, adding, 'but until the time comes, no harm will come to Professor Sahab and you.'

He lays out an ambitious vision for Kashmir. 'It is going to be a long struggle for azadi. It could take years, maybe decades.'

'What if it doesn't happen?' I ask, knowing fully well that most people have been made to believe that azadi is around the corner. Belief gives people hope.

The propagandist broadcasts from Pakistan have been encouraging. 'We will sip kahwa in Shalimar Garden in Azad Kashmir in March,' blare the voices on radio and TV.

Euphoria prevails in Muslim households. Pakistan TV and Radio Pakistan are the only sources of information. The only slogan that is heard: 'Kashmir will become Pakistan. Every child will scream: Islam, Islam, Pakistan, Pakistan . . .'

Inside Pandit households, men, women and children battle fear and trembling.

'Azadi is just a matter of days; you will see!' reveal the Muslim classmates at school.

But Basheer thinks otherwise. 'We Muslims are naive and impatient. Achieving azadi is not as easy as we think. It might take us years to see our cherished dream come true.'

'But what if it doesn't happen in your lifetime?'

'Our great leader, Amanullah Khan, has spelled it out in his vision,' says Basheer emphatically. 'The second wave will be more determined and primed for action than the present one because it will fight a battle on the soil smeared with the blood of their elders.'

* * *

The Summer of 2018
New Delhi
A letter to my daughter

My dear Amia,

Many years ago, on 14 September 1989, when I was going for my tuition class to Fateh Kadal in Downtown Srinagar, I heard about the assassination of Tika Lal Taploo, a prominent lawyer and chief of the Bharatiya Janata Party (BJP) in Jammu and Kashmir. He was shot dead outside his house in Habba Kadal, Srinagar. I was about your age at the time and studying in Class Nine.

Six weeks later, on 4 November, militants killed Justice Neel Kanth Ganjoo in Hari Singh High Street. His granddaughter was my friend and classmate. As the Sessions Judge, Justice Ganjoo had sentenced Maqbool Bhat, one of the founders of the Jammu Kashmir Liberation Front (JKLF),[6] to death for murdering a police inspector in Baramulla and also for murdering a bank officer. Thousands of people came out on the streets and celebrated the killing of Justice Ganjoo. 'Maqbool Bhat's death has been avenged,' our Muslim neighbours said. People in our neighbourhood chanted pro-Pakistan slogans, waved Pakistani flags and burned effigies of Indian leaders.

I never saw Justice Ganjoo's granddaughter after that. I didn't even have the courage to comfort her when her grandfather was killed. What face will I show her now? I hope she's happy wherever she is.

At the onset of the New Year in 1990, I witnessed a strange turn of events in Khankah-i-Sokhta, my neighbourhood. Known for the abiding friendships between Muslims and Pandits who lived there, the area resounded with the cries of Muslim men and women whose teenaged boys started disappearing from their homes to join militant outfits and wage war against the security forces deployed in Srinagar. Many of these boys never returned. A sense of fear grew among the Pandits as they saw Muslim youths glorify the armed struggle against India. When security forces killed militants, it was marked by grief as well as jubilation.

Anti-Pandit sentiment prevailed everywhere. It brought back the horrific memory of the riots in Kashmir's Anantnag district in February and March 1986, in which many Pandits were targeted and attacked and Hindu temples were desecrated and ransacked. While hundreds of Muslims came out on the streets in Downtown Srinagar, defying curfew and shoot-on-sight orders, to demand freedom from India, Pandits huddled indoors in fear and bewilderment.

In February 1990, militants killed Lassa Kaul, the director of Doordarshan Kendra, outside his house in Bemina. He was Dadu's (my father's) close friend. At his funeral, which was attended by hundreds of Pandits and the central minister of information and broadcasting who'd flown in from New Delhi, Muslim protesters chanted slogans against Jagmohan, the governor of the state, who had just assumed office. Pandits wept at Lassa Kaul's funeral, while

Muslims blamed Jagmohan for his death. They spread rumours that his killing was a conspiracy hatched by the Indian intelligence agencies to discredit the muhajideen and the Tehreek (the movement for the freedom of Kashmir). Before his death, Lassa Kaul had confided in Dadu about the threats he had received from militant groups. Some militants had visited him in his office and ordered him to stop broadcasting Indian TV programmes in Kashmir. Ignoring the demands and threats, he continued working, although many of his colleagues had advised him to leave Kashmir. He had been taking care of his ailing father.

The kidnapping of Soom Nath Saproo, our neighbour, terrified us. He worked in the Defence Estates Office of the Government of India and was posted at Shivpora. His daughter was my classmate and used to be tutored by Dadu at our place. Saproo had gone to buy milk when he was kidnapped. Dadu and I went to his house. Many Pandits and Muslims had gathered there. Our neighbour, Hafiz, told us that Saproo was on the hit list of a militant outfit because he worked for the central government. He had even warned Saproo about this. Saproo's family revealed that they had received death threats from a militant group. Two days later, at the behest of influential Muslims in the area, Saproo was released. He reached home with a gash on his head. He wouldn't talk. He fled to Jammu the next day. He died a few years ago. His last wish—to return home—remained unfulfilled.

September 1989

On my way home from school, I hear slogans blaring from a loudspeaker: 'Set the time in your watches to Pakistan Standard Time.' I look at my watch. The time is accurate.

It is set to IST, though. There is silence for a moment. A gunshot. Silence. A gunshot. More gunshots. A blast. There is pungent, gaseous smoke all around. A tear gas canister comes crashing next to me. A crossfire between militants and security forces erupts. A bystander next to me is hit. Some youths start hurling stones at policemen.

'Grab a stone and throw it at the police van. What are you waiting for?' someone screams. There are more gunshots and I run for cover towards a narrow lane.

'Shoot the boy in the red jacket!' someone screams. A policeman has his gun pointed at me. I take the red jacket off so that . . .

For a moment, I gasp for breath. I can almost feel the bullet of a .303 rifle inside me. It is about to explode. And I am about to die. I can't even scream, apologize or plead. I muster all my strength and lisp a prayer. 'God, please don't do this to me. Spare my life. I will do whatever you wish . . .'

I survive, but . . .

A Few Weeks Later

We wake up to the news of the death of a commander of the JKLF. He was idolized by Muslim youths, who called him a warrior, a rebel and a freedom fighter.

'Ashfaq has attained martyrdom; our hero has been martyred!' Muslim men and women scream in the streets and from the rooftops of their houses. The neighbourhood explodes with slogans; stories of Ashfaq's last encounter with the security forces are afloat. 'Death to the enemy!' women scream.

Ashfaq was twenty-three when the paramilitary forces killed him in Downtown Srinagar. Thousands of people attend his funeral procession and raise pro-freedom and pro-

Pakistan slogans. Babuji and I go to the rooftop of our house and watch the procession moving towards Eid Gah. Gunmen fire in the air as a mark of respect to their slain commander.

* * *

Autumn 1989–Spring 1990
Morning

A neighbour brings us a copy of *Al Safa*.* 'Read this,' says he, pointing to a press release.

> 'Pandits must leave Kashmir in thirty-six hours.'
> Issued by Hizb-ul-Mujahideen

Posters with the threat 'Leave Kashmir in thirty-six hours or else face the consequences' appear on the doors and walls of Pandit houses, shops and temples. Soon, they are pasted everywhere—on shop shutters and the walls of schools and colleges. Wherever we look, there are posters ordering us to leave or else face the wrath of Allah!

All this has happened overnight. The city was painted green while we were sleeping.

Our very own Srinagar just doesn't feel like it's ours anymore.

Night

'Green is the colour of Pakistan. Kashmir will become Pakistan; without Pandit men but with Pandit women.' We hear the slogans being shouted in the neighbourhood.

---

* An Urdu daily published in Kashmir in the 1990s.

Morning

The newspapers carry ominous columns referring to Pandits as untrustworthy and informants of the Indian intelligence agencies. More ultimatums and death threats to Pandits follow.

'Pandits are snakes. Whoever kills these snakes and brings us their heads will be rewarded.'
Allah Tigers

Aftab* brings out press release after press release issued by Harkat-ul-Ansar, Allah Tigers and Jamaat-e-Islami. The press releases carry warnings and death threats to informers, Indian agents, security forces and Pandits.

A poster pasted on an electric pole outside our house reads: 'Pandits in this lane must leave. This is the final ultimatum.'

'Who is this poster meant for?' asks Ma. 'Us? Because we are the only Pandits remaining in this lane . . .'

Suspicion, betrayal and mistrust divide the Muslims and the Pandits. Friends part from friends and neighbours from neighbours. Pandit families start to pack and leave. We spend nervy days inside our house with a foreboding that these are our last days.

Night

It is past midnight. We are in our room. Hushed voices lurk outside. There is a sound of digging. Pa and I peek from a chink in the window. Ismail and his two sons are in their

---

* An Urdu newspaper.

courtyard. Next to them are several tin trunks containing arms. The family members are wrapping guns, grenades and pistols in plastic sheets. Ismail's boys have dug two pits in the courtyard and are placing the arms in them. Before the sun comes out, all the arms are dumped in the pit. And the pit is covered with soil.

Morning

The Ismail family is planting saplings in their front yard. They wave to us as if nothing has happened.

Ismail is Babuji's friend. He rears pigeons for a living.

A neighbour brings horrible news. 'They shot him. They shot Nilla Kanth Raina . . .'

Our neighbour, Professor Nilla Kanth Raina, a retired professor of history, has been shot dead while loading luggage in a truck and preparing to leave for Jammu along with his wife. Ma is worried and doesn't allow Pa to go out now.

'They are killing professors and teachers now,' Ma says. She imagines the unimaginable.

People claim that Professor Raina was killed by his own students.

'His own students? My God! Who would have thought?'

'His killing is a clear signal for the rest of the Pandits to leave,' says a neighbour.

It is the beginning of the end.

Night

We hear whispers outside our house. Dadu, Dadi and I are in the living room on the first floor. Babuji and Babi are sleeping in their room. Pa peeps through a chink and sees two young men pacing the narrow lane. One of them is holding a pistol in his hand. The two are whispering into each other's ears. Dadi swallows her fright. One man lights a cigarette.

'What does he want?' Dadi asks.

'Nothing,' says Dadu. 'They must be mistaken. This is the wrong house. They must have come for those there . . .'

'But what have they done?'

'Nothing! But they are the ones to beee . . .'

'Shall we scream? Shaha! Shaha!'

'No, no. Be quiet! Not a word. They will leave soon.'

'What if they don't?'

Dadu has no answer.

We hear another knock! And then, a pause! Another one! A third one!

The other man whispers into the ear of the pistol-young-man.

The knocking persists.

Never has the knocking been more spiteful.

'What shall we do now?' Dadi asks.

'Nothing. Be still, quiet.'

Until 12.30 a.m., we sit still and whisper. Moonlight lights up the lane.

12.30 a.m. Our breaths are shallow.

Then we hear the whisper: Are you sure this is the house?

'Yes, this is the Professor's house,' says the other man.

Dadi wants to scream. But Dadu orders her not to utter a word.

Morning

Dadu meets our neighbours and informs them of everything that happened at night.

'Don't worry, Professor Sahib, they are outsiders,' say the neighbours. 'They mean no harm. Nothing will happen to you . . . We won't let anything bad happen to you. Look at the other Pandits living in the other lanes. Nothing bad has happened to them yet . . .'

'But . . .' says another neighbour.

'But what?'

'Whatever is said and done, you must realize that anything could happen from here on. Maybe we too will be targeted. Maybe even we will not be able to protect you. So it would be prudent for you to leave and go away from here,' he says.

Thereafter, every morning, we wake up to news of kidnappings, killings and unspeakable atrocities inflicted on Kashmiri Pandits.

A Raina, a Kaul, a Ganjoo, a Bhat.

What if they add a Gigoo to the list of those killed? Nobody will care.

'We will cut you to pieces if you . . .'

The neighbourhood is abuzz with news for us. All news is targeted towards us. 'So-and-so has been killed because he didn't follow the orders, because he worked for so-and-so or because he did such and such things.'

Professor Raina? Why him? He was a saint. Everyone in the neighbourhood respected him. He had taught thousands of students. He was leaving that morning. He was following orders. Then why him?

'Do you know why? To set an example. So that the rest of us will . . .'

'Don't say a word. We will leave tomorrow.'

'No, let us wait for some more time. Maybe this won't last. Maybe nothing will happen to us . . .'

'But then what if . . . what shall I do if something happens to you? . . . where will we go?' says Dadi.

Night

Kashmiri Muslims tune into PTV to listen to Benazir Bhutto's speech. Addressing the people of Pakistan and Kashmir, Bhutto says, 'the brave people of Kashmir do not fear death because they are Muslim. In their veins runs the blood of Muhajids and Ghazis. They are heirs of the Prophet Mohammad. They are heirs of Hazrat Ali and Hazrat Umar. The brave women of Kashmir are heiresses of Khadijah and Ayesha and Fatimah. They know how to fight and how to live. Kashmiris will win their freedom. From every village, mosque and school, only one slogan will emerge: Azadi.'

Songs and slogans rend the night sky.

'*Jaago, Jaago, Subah huyee,*
Roos ney baazi haari hai, Hind pey larza taari hai,
Ab Kashmir ki baari hai,
Jaago, Jaago, Subah huyee.'
(Awake O Muslims of Kashmir, for the promised dawn
is here,
Russia has been vanquished, India is under attack,
It is Kashmir's turn now,
Awake O Muslims of Kashmir, for the promised dawn
is here.)

'*Zalimo O, kafiro, Kashmir hamara chhod dou.*
Yahan kya chalega, Nizam-e-Mustafa.'
(O Monsters, O Infidels, Leave our Kashmir.
Kashmir will be under the rule of the Prophet
Muhammad.)

And then the call to arms, the ultimate war cry, the decree.

'Kashmiri Pandits,

Merge, leave or perish. Merge, leave or perish. Merge,
leave or perish.
Kashmir will become Pakistan.'

Morning

I am walking back home after buying groceries from the
Ali Mohammad and Sons shop. Two Muslim boys, who
are our neighbours, stop me. 'Panditji, what is the time on
your watch?' they ask me.

This is the first time they have chosen not to address
me by my name. I have become 'Panditji'.

I look at my watch and tell them the time. My watch
is now set to Pakistan Standard Time. We must follow
everything we are told to follow. After all, we are to remain
alive on their terms, not ours.

After satisfying their curiosity, the boys nod and let
me go.

* * *

15 April 1990

There is no end to the bad news. Sarla Bhat, a resident nurse
at the Sher-i-Kashmir Institute of Medical Sciences in Soura,
Srinagar, is abducted from her hostel. After four days, her
mutilated body is found in an area downtown. A handwritten
note is attached to it, describing her as a police informant.
Sarla Bhat was in her mid-twenties. After her body is handed
over to her father, Shambu Nath Bhat, in Anantnag, he is
not allowed to carry out the last rites during her cremation.
It is a rushed affair—the militants have ordered the people in
the neighbourhood to keep away from the family. Shambu

Nath Bhat takes his family to Jammu shortly thereafter. Indu Bushan Zutshi, the Bhat family's neighbour in Anantnag, recounts to me the horror faced by the family.

* * *

19 January 2016

(The twentieth anniversary of our exodus from Kashmir)
I receive an email from someone named Shilpa Raina. To my utter surprise, she reveals that she's Professor Nilla Kanth Raina's granddaughter.

'I saw you on TV,' she says. 'You talked about my grandfather. My mom told me about you and your father.'

We speak to each other over the phone. A conversation dotted with silences and sighs follows.

'Someday, I will write about everything,' Shilpa says.

* * *

19 January 2019

Shilpa's story is published in a journal. I know it is not fiction. The hero of the story is her grandpa, who was one of the most venerable professors in Kashmir.

I will pause now. But, Amia, there is more you must know. This isn't just my history. It is equally yours.

Yours always,
Poppy

* * *

May 2022
Home, New Delhi

I ring Ma up. Ma and Pa live in their own flat in Faridabad now.

> Me: 'Do you remember the moment Pa and you decided to leave home after you sent Henna and me away with Ratni Aunty and family in 1990?'
>
> Ma: 'How will I ever forget that day?
>
> Me: 'What happened that day?''
>
> Ma: 'The day Prithvi Nath Tiku, our neighbour, was killed by the militants right outside his home. It was a clear warning to us that we were next since we were the only Pandits left in the entire neighbourhood. Remember everything that happened during the previous days? The two boys who wanted to do the unthinkable. The day Tiku was killed, we locked the house and went to Indira Nagar. Saiba Dewani's house was vacant. They had left a few months ago. We moved in there, hoping that when the situation improved, we would be able to return to our home in Safa Kadal. But it was not meant to be. Who would have imagined that we would never get to go back. Had we known all this, we would not have left so many things behind in our house . . .'

* * *

It's been thirty-three years since Basheer's prediction came true. The second wave is here and it seems more menacing than the first. The first wave had battled an ill-equipped military force. But the second is up in arms against the best of the forces.

Kashmir is witnessing a 1990s redux, minus the azadi-seeking JKLF, which stands disbanded and defunct now.

The dreaded Jaish-e-Mohammed and Lashkar-e-Taiba, who have successfully altered the meaning of Islamic jihad, form the core of the second wave in Kashmir. Even if the second wave is contained or eliminated in the years to come, what assurance do we have that a third wave, which could inflict damage at a catastrophic level, will not rise? Indoctrinated by ISIS ideology, the present-day Jaish or Lashkar militant operating in Kashmir is willing to tackle the forces, spread havoc, put people's lives at grave risk, take a bullet and die for the sake of a lost cause—Pakistan, the Islamic State or jihad.

In recent times, Jaish and Lashkar militants have killed hundreds of security forces and civilians, including journalists, politicians and bureaucrats. Hundreds of commoners have committed suicide for unknown reasons. Several thousand people are suffering from mental disorders. People continue to get killed during encounters, combing operations and crackdowns. Children are the worst affected. People living in the border areas of Jammu fear for their lives on account of shelling by Pakistani forces. Infiltration remains unabated.

The Dogras of Jammu and the Muslims and Buddhists living in Ladakh are disenchanted; no one is concerned about them. The Gujjars and Bakarwals don't even care what the fuss is all about. They are better off migrating from one mountain range to another.

Kashmir, for the present-day militants, is an unfinished business worth fighting and dying for. For the security forces, Kashmir is just a posting to guard the 'crown'. For the ordinary folk who wake up in the morning and leave their homes to earn a living, not even caring whether it's safe to venture out or not, it is just another hopeless day. For those who're unable to make ends meet, Kashmir is an endless wait for a better tomorrow. For those who can't return to their long-lost homes even after a quarter of a century, Kashmir is a memory or a photograph. For the political parties, Kashmir is a scramble for power.

'Kashmir is a blank cheque in my pocket,' Muhammed Ali Jinnah, the founder of Pakistan, had once boasted. Clearly, the people living in Kashmir are a dispensable lot. But the exiled Hindus of Kashmir, the Dogras of Jammu and the Buddhists of Ladakh are the real trump cards in the hands of crafty politicians and arbiters.

The joker will be dealt, as they say in rummy, when it comes to any talks with those advocating separatism.

There are vested interests in India, Pakistan and elsewhere that don't want a solution because keeping the problem alive has, over the years, been incredibly profitable. A burning Kashmir generates a lot of funding in India and abroad. It keeps getting people elected to power. It keeps the security apparatus well-oiled. It keeps the coffers of zealots full.

What will the 'let-Kashmir-burn' people do when the fire is doused?

How will they derive sustenance?

The conflict has cost us Kashmiri Pandits our age-old way of life and rendered us bereft of hope. Over the years, more people have died in the streets, in hospitals and in camps than inside their homes. There is no information about many thousands. Society stands divided on religious, sectarian and political lines. Suspicion, mistrust and betrayals have created partitions within society and human relationships have lost their meaning. No one knows who's working for or against whom. No one knows what to believe and what not to believe. Daily life itself is paradoxical and full of absurdities and contradictions. To live there is to have your freedom snatched and remain trapped in an intricate web of insurgency, counter-insurgency, espionage and counter-espionage.

Is it possible for the people of Kashmir to ever come together and work towards reclaiming our lost way of life, notwithstanding our distinct identities, ideologies, perspectives, experiences, compulsions, aspirations, etc.? This, even at the risk of continued violence on the frontier and in the streets of Kashmir?

Countless people whose voices matter aren't even in the frame. Nobody knows of them and their dignified struggle for the basic, simple things of life. No one knows how they've lived, what they've gone through or what they've lost. The spotlight must be put on them. They are the ones who have experienced humanity in its purest form. Despite having lost a lot, they have quietly suffered and given others hope. The humanity of such people must be placed before the world so that future generations will know the cost these people paid to live simple lives. The humanity of these people should not be held hostage to the misadventures of those seeking to curb freedom and the right to live peacefully.

It is this humanity that could restore hope and happiness in the hearts of people and make Kashmir a peaceful place once again.

It should be salvaged before it is too late to even know that it ever existed.

* * *

January 2017
Srinagar

Swanky hardware stores dot the road leading to Safa Kadal. I can't locate Basheer's old hardware shop. I wonder what happened to it and to Basheer.

I am in front of our old house in Safa Kadal. It is undergoing renovation. Several other houses in Safa Kadal are being renovated.

'We Downtowners have been rebuilding our lives for years now,' says an elderly Muslim woman who instantly recognizes me. 'This is what we do. It is a perennial process here.' She points to our old house with tears in her eyes and says, 'That house is still yours and will always be. Don't you want to go inside? Shall I take you there? The owners are known to us.'

How do I tell her that I wish to live in the house once again? I wish for the old days to be given back to us.

Susheel, an old neighbour and friend, takes me to his home. His house is next to ours. Both houses share a common lane. His family is the lone Kashmiri Pandit family living there. His father, who's well known for having curated the only two one-day international cricket matches ever held in Kashmir in 1983 and 1986, has dementia. The October 1983 match between India and the West Indies is still remembered as the turning point in the history of Kashmir—the political leanings of the Muslims and their hatred for India came to the fore for the first time during that match. Every Muslim in Kashmir cheered for the West Indies and India's loss was celebrated for days.

Cricket continues to be Susheel's passion. He runs the Safa Kadal Cricket Club now.

His father's memory sparkles when he sees me after all these years. 'You must return home,' he says to me, looking intently into my eyes. History flashes in his grey, misty eyes.

It is that human history of being forced to live a life in isolation that I wish to examine.

Before bidding goodbye, I express the hope of seeing him again next year.

'I have something rare and precious to show you,' he whispers to me enticingly, with a glint in his eyes. 'You must return home in the spring when everything is bourgeoning.'

* * *

July 1989
Home, Srinagar

Fazi, our neighbour and Babi's friend, screams at the top of her voice, 'Uma Shori, don't drink water. It has been poisoned to kill us all.'

'A few more days and Kashmir will become Pakistan!' blurts another woman from the street.

* * *

A Cold, Wintry Day in December 1989
Srinagar, Kashmir

Babi takes me to the shrine of Reshi Pir (the great seventeenth-century saint) at Ali Kadal. Stray dogs are standing in front of the gate of the shrine. Like sentries, they seem to be keeping vigil, barking at every unfamiliar passer-by. The wind, which has been frighteningly menacing the whole day, is now mute and frozen like the leafless poplars dotting the avenue leading up to the shrine complex. Inside the shrine are two other women. One is sitting in devout contemplation in front of the idol of Reshi Pir. She is mumbling a prayer; her eyes are shut. The other woman—a newly-wed—is perambulating the idol with folded hands. She's going around the idol again and again without stopping, as if she were going away forever and never coming back. On her lips is a prayer, too.

Babi says her prayers and offers a *niyaz* (offering) while I sit in a corner looking at a pair of wooden clogs believed to have belonged to the Pir.

Reshi Pir's shrine has been Babi's go-to place in all circumstances. 'I am going to Reshi Pir's. Would you like to come along?' she asks me whenever she is about to go there. After all, I am her eldest grandchild—my sister is barely ten. Babuji isn't a templegoer. His laboratory—The Imperial Clinical Laboratory—is a ten-minute walk from the shrine in Maharaj Gunj, the trader area of Srinagar. He bicycles past the shrine twice a day but seldom stops to go inside. Not that he is an atheist, but that he is content with his own beliefs and doesn't believe in idol worship—he is a devout Arya Samaji like his father, who introduced the Arya Samaj to Kashmir.

Before leaving, the women exchange furtive glances. We are now headed home. But as we near our neighbourhood, Babi turns left into the Roopa Bhawani lane. At the end of the lane, by the bank of Jhelum, is a small temple. Next to the temple is a small house. It is the birthplace of Roopa Bhawani, the seventeenth-century saint–poetess of Kashmir.

We are the only two people inside the temple. A portrait of Roopa Bhawani (Alakheswari) is placed inside a glass enclosure by the window. Roopa Bhawani is sitting in deep contemplation at the feet of her father and spiritual guru, Pandit Madhav Joo Dhar. Babi sits in front of the portrait and prays. Once again, she prays for continuity and fortitude. 'May the darkness dispel. May we never get to leave our beautiful house and our beautiful land! May we live and die happily here. May my children and grandchildren flourish . . .'

She walks around Roopa Bhawani's portrait and the Shiv Linga next to it seven times while I sit by the window looking at the Jhelum. Nawa Kadal is to the left and Safa Kadal is to the right. The Jhelum flows quietly under the two bridges that are in sight. At a distance is Hari Parbat, the abode of Mother Goddess Sharika, who, as the belief goes, granted a boon to Madhav Joo Dhar that she would be reborn to him and his wife and known as Roopa Bhawani.

When we leave the temple premises, we see our cow and her calf waiting in the lane. Babi takes a piece of bread out of her bag and feeds them.

'Shall we stop by Ram Mandir?' Babi asks. 'We won't be long.'

We walk past our house towards Ram Mandir. In the summer, I used to play cricket in the courtyard of the temple complex. The courtyard is vacant today. The priest-caretaker's quarters are locked. There is talk in Pandit households that he was forced to flee after receiving a death threat from a militant outfit.

Babi goes inside the temple while I stand by the balustrade and look at the ghat below. The majestic Hari Parbat is still in sight. Whenever you look at it, you feel comforted. But everything is bleak today. It feels as though something terrible is about to happen.

Babi comes out of the temple. Sensing my childlike restlessness, she gives me a cheerful look. But I know what she is going to say next. We have one more temple to visit. Babi is good at coaxing people.

Janambhoomi is not a temple like other temples. A small wooden door opens to a large compound filled with nettles and shrubs. There is an old well at the far end of the compound. We walk down a flight of stairs made of tiles and reach a basin made of stone. In summer, it brims with water. And if you are lucky, you will see some goldfish. There is a Shiv Linga next to the stone idol of Lord Ram. An idol of Lord Krishna protected by small slabs of stone is a marvellous sight. Something about this place is ancient. The

stone structure resembles the stone structure of the Martand
Sun temple in Mattan, Anantnag.

Everything is floundering. The houses of Pandits flanking
the compound wear a sombre expression. The eagle nests atop
the leafless poplars are empty. Once again, I am overcome by
a strange foreboding that something bad is about to happen.

Babi lights a joss stick and places it in front of the idols.
A sweet fragrance fills the air. Babi mumbles the same prayer:
'May we always be happy in our homes! May our hearths be
warm and well lit! May our children prosper and flourish!
May Maej Kasheer (Mother Kashmir) always protect us!
May this Reshevaer (Valley of Saints) thrive!'

Babi: 'Do you think it will snow tonight?'

Me: 'Yes, I think it will.'

Babi: 'You're wrong. We are a few more days away from
the first snowfall of the season. You need to learn how to read
the wind.'

Me: 'When will you teach me?'

Babi: 'When you are ready to sit in front of me.'

Evening

Some of our belongings are lying next to tin trunks. Utensils,
bedding . . .

Babi is preparing for the inevitable. 'May we never be
deprived of our home,' she continues to mumble.

* * *

A Day in August 1996
Tourist Reception Centre, Srinagar

I reach Srinagar by road. I have grown a beard to pass myself
off as a Muslim. Nobody except my father and mother

knows that I am here. In my heart, there is a foreboding that something unpleasant is about to happen. Machine gun nozzles peek through tiny openings in camouflaged military bunkers. The road is dotted with bunkers, as if the city is at war. Soldiers in military fatigues are keeping vigil. They look like statues. The smiles on people's faces from the old days are gone. Now all you can see is a sense of doom.

At Lal Chowk, I conceal my identity when I ask an autorickshaw driver to take me to Safa Kadal. I start talking and behaving like a Muslim, but the act fools no one.

Autorickshaw driver: 'What are you doing here, Panditji?'
Me: 'I am here to see my house.'
He: 'You must go back right now or else . . .'
Me: 'Will you take me to Downtown?'
He: 'Where exactly in Downtown?'
Me: 'Ram Mandir Lane, Safa Kadal.'
He: 'I can't take you there. Go back to Jammu or Delhi or wherever you have come from. It is for your own good.'
Me: 'I am here only for a day. I will go back as soon as I see my house.'
He: 'But why did you come back here?'
Me: 'To see my house. That's all. No other purpose!'
He: 'I don't understand. You were not supposed to return. If anyone sees you in my autorickshaw, I will be in trouble. Leave now and do not come back. Don't take my refusal otherwise. I am saying this to you because I am your well-wisher.'

Lal Chowk resembles a war zone. There are military bunkers all around. It seems as if a battle is about to take place. A scene from the movie *Lion of the Desert*, which my father took me to watch at Regal Cinema when I was a kid, comes alive.

I have just one more hour and then at 6 p.m., the curfew will come into effect again until tomorrow. I assess the odds of walking all the way to my old house in Safa Kadal and then getting back before curfew. After assessing the risks, I give up.

The first announcement is made: 'People are directed to go back to their homes . . . Curfew is being imposed . . . All shopkeepers must shut their shops immediately . . . All vehicles are directed to stay away from the roads. Anyone found in violation of the curfew will be arrested . . .'

The announcement is then repeated over and over. People start dispersing and civilian vehicles disappear. The shutters of shops are brought down and armoured vehicles begin their patrolling.

A Muslim classmate from JNU meets me. We have made plans for me to spend the night at his place in Jawahar Nagar. His father has bought a Pandit house in the neighbourhood. We start walking. He says we should rush to his place.

A motorcycle stops next to me. The rider taps me on the shoulder. He takes the scarf off his face, revealing his identity. It is Susheel, our neighbour from Safa Kadal. 'Quick, hop on,' he says. In no time, he drives into a narrow lane and then stops at the gate of a house.

He throws the questions at me.

'What are you doing here? When did you come? Why didn't you tell me? Are you alone? What were you doing in the middle of the road while the curfew was about to be imposed?'

I explain everything to him. He takes us inside the house. 'This is where we moved some years ago. Safa Kadal is already like a liberated zone.* It is dangerous to live there. That is why

---

* Those days, some Muslims believed that some parts of the Kashmir Valley were already liberated because they were under the control of militants and no Hindus lived there anymore.

we are here. We didn't want to leave like you did. We never will, no matter what happens . . .'

His mother and sisters are sitting quietly in the room. They are shocked to see me. They start talking. The look of fright on their faces is worrisome.

More questions . . .

'How are your parents and grandparents? Where are they these days? I hope you have not brought them here with you. We heard you had to live in a camp. Is it true you are in a camp in Jammu?'

'I am in Delhi. Everyone else is in Udhampur.'

'Look what has become of this place and of us . . . Muslims have taken over everything . . . We are scared . . . You should not have come here . . . But now that you are here, you must stay with us for the night . . . Don't go out right now . . . It is too risky . . .'

Susheel contradicts them. 'Don't scare him. It's all right. I will be with him.'

'Don't listen to him. He's a daredevil. He goes to places where no Pandit should go . . .'

'Is your friend also from Jammu?'

'He is a Muslim and he lives here. We are classmates in the university.'

The look on their faces changes.

'Oh! Don't misunderstand us,' they say, changing the tone. 'We didn't mean all that we just said about Muslims. Muslims have been protecting us all these years. We have stayed safe so far because of Muslims. What will they do? They are helpless, too. They are caught between the mujahideen and army men. But they are brave. Our fate is now in their hands. They will decide the fate of Kashmir too.'

I should not have taken so much time to reveal my classmate's identity.

Babi's brother's family is also in Srinagar. They live in Shivpora, a relatively safer neighbourhood given that it is flanked by an army cantonment. But I don't go there. They will get worried if I drop in unannounced.

What if we too had stayed back and not left? I imagine the possibility. Pa tried but failed. He could never have succeeded. The unthinkable would have happened. What price are these handful of Pandits paying to stay back in Kashmir? We can never pay such a price. Their desperation is no less than ours. Militant organizations let them stay under certain conditions. They must pay money regularly and be willing to toe a certain line. They must follow orders. Their living there has come at a cost one can't even imagine.

I decide to take the bus back to Jammu tomorrow as soon as the curfew is lifted. There is no point in lingering here. I pray that I get to come back some other time to see our house and Ram Mandir.

* * *

A Day in the Spring of 1989
Home, Srinagar

It is Ram Navami. We are preparing to go to Ram Mandir. Henna and I are wearing new clothes. Everyone is dressed up for the occasion. As always, Pandit families from all over Kashmir will arrive here and the temple will be the centre of attraction.

Hundreds of thousands of Pandit families start arriving at Ram Mandir to take part in the festivities. By evening, they have said their prayers and partaken of the sacred *prasad*, or offering—kheer, halwa and puri—served in earthen pots. We call it *naveed*. Kids love it.

Muslims watch through the windows of their houses.

People part on a happy note. 'We will see you on Krishna Janamashtami now,' they say. Smiles reflect hope.

Janambhoomi resembles a fairground today.

Some Days Later

The priest's room is locked. He is nowhere. For decades, he has lived here within the temple premises. He has been the caretaker of the temple ever since I can remember. There are rumours in the lane. Some say that he was threatened by Muslims. Some say that he had a premonition of the dark times to come. Some say he went back to his village in Bihar or Uttar Pradesh.

* * *

A Day in January 2018
Srinagar

I am accompanying a documentary film crew to Srinagar. They are shooting a documentary film about the conflict in Kashmir. The film is titled *Kashmir: The Story*. After I tell them everything about the place, my growing up days and the conditions in which we were forced to flee, the crew decides to shoot in my old neighbourhood and inside the Ram Mandir complex. They want me to recount the memories of the old days once again. They want me to narrate everything.

I walk up and down the Ram Mandir lane several times before mustering up the courage to step inside. The broken gate—a familiar vestige from the past! From outside, I can tell what awaits me. Such is the condition of the temple.

I haven't forgotten anything. I never will.

I close my eyes—the temple is decorated. There are lights all around. Women are lighting diyas. Men are cleaning the compound. A boy and a girl are distributing prasad to the devotees. The idols of gods and goddesses are decorated. But the centre of attraction are the marble idols of Sita and Ram dressed like a bride and groom. The engravings on the walls and the murals are being cleaned and polished by the devotees.

I open my eyes and see the horror. The entire temple courtyard is now a garbage dump. Animal droppings are all over the place. The stench is unbearable.

What once was a hallowed place of worship—the sanctum sanctorum—where idols of our gods and goddesses were kept is now a damaged structure defaced with graffiti. Atrocious words are on the walls in English and Urdu—the telltale signs of hate and resentment towards the temple and temple-goers. Such words must not even be read or uttered. But such words, no matter how bad, must not be forgotten either, for such words changed the course of our lives.

The engravings, the ornate paintings, the venerable objects of worship and the symbols of our culture and heritage are gone as if they never existed! Such is the extent of the defilement. It's a devastating sight. The temple narrates the account of the desecration by those who deliberately wanted to erase history. It's not just an act of desecration of a temple and the temple complex. It's an act of willful obliteration of a centuries-old indigenous culture and way of life. Our way of life!

How do I keep my eyes open? But I can't shut them too, just to escape from this horrid reality, this ghastly truth. I must confront the truth.

Babi's prayer wraps me up yet again: 'May the darkness dispel . . . May we never get to leave our beautiful house, our beautiful land . . . May we live and die happily here . . .'

A boy is standing by the railing with his gaze fixed on Hari Parbat. Unlike me, he never left the place. He hid himself in the secret place near the ghat when the temple was pillaged repeatedly and when everything precious was stolen, damaged and destroyed.

As I leave the temple premises, an elderly man who has been keeping an eye on me all the while stops me and says, 'Do you think we Muslims did this? This is the army's handiwork. You must know . . .' He goes on and on about how the security forces were responsible for the devastation. How they occupied the temple in the 1990s and turned it into a bunker.

I have neither patience nor time for such distortions.

The film crew sets up the shot.

'The camera will start rolling when you come out of the lane, start walking on the bridge and stop to look at the temple,' says the director.

In front of me is Ram Mandir. It has turned golden in the light of dusk. Children are laughing and making mirth. Babi's prayer, which I have memorized, comes out and flies towards the temple.

'May you always protect us . . .'

Babi's dream is still alive.

* * *

4 a.m.
One Morning in March 1990
Home, Srinagar, Kashmir

The sun has yet to rise. Pa and Ma are getting Henna and me ready. A small bag is packed for us to take along. In it are a few clothes, some toiletries, a water bottle and a tiffin. Ma has rolled up some rotis in a towel. Babi and Babuji have not slept the whole night. Neither have Pa and Ma. I am keen to wear a necktie that Pa has bought for me. 'Not today,' says Pa. 'There will be another occasion for it.' An argument ensues between us. Henna is excitedly giggling, her favourite pastime. I am not convinced by Pa's arguments. What better day to wear a necktie than today? We are going on a trip. That too, just the two of us. 'Some other day, my son,' Pa says. 'One more word and the tie will be out of the window.'

Every winter, we would visit Delhi to spend a few days with my maternal grandparents.

Our neighbours, the Koul family, are getting ready too. The truck has arrived and is parked some fifty paces from our houses. The Kouls are making hurried trips from their house to the truck and back. They are taking their belongings out of their house and placing them in the truck. Ratni Aunty is sobbing but is afraid that the Muslim neighbours will hear. Her father-in-law, a retired police constable, is staring at his house as if it were his own child about to be snatched away.

Uncle and Aunty start speaking in hushed tones on the veranda of their house.

'Have you taken everything?'

'How many times will you make me repeat?'

'What about the mortar? Are we going to leave it behind? Did you check the attic? What if you have forgotten some things? Go inside and check one more time. What about the kitchen?'

'Why can't you keep your voice low? You will wake the neighbours and land us in trouble.'

'Check everything again.'

'There is no more room in the truck. What do you want me to do? Did you lock the rooms? Lock the gate now.'

The Sikh truck driver is constantly looking at his wristwatch. 'We must hurry,' he says, unhappy at the delay. 'We must leave before the light breaks or else . . . We have to cross the Jawahar tunnel before noon . . . If it snows, we will get stranded. If something unforeseen happens, we will have nowhere to go . . .'

'Do not leave your sister alone,' Ma says to me. 'Even for a moment. Do not let her out of your sight.'

We hop into the truck.

'Do we need to cover our faces now that we are leaving?' Ratni Aunty asks the truck driver.

Shaking his head, he says, 'Isn't it obvious?'

Aunty: 'Will you please drive through the lane next to Ram Mandir?'

Truck driver: 'It's too narrow there for the truck.'

Aunty: 'Then stop for a while when you are near the temple; I will get off and return in a jiffy.'

Aunty's daughter: 'Don't be mad.'

Aunty: 'I am not mad.'

There are no goodbyes. Everything is hush-hush and rushed.

'Wait, wait, wait for some more time. Let me go inside the house one last time . . .' says Aunty.

'Where are we going?' says Aunty's father-in-law. 'Where are you taking me?'

'Hurry now. We've got to be moving or else . . .' says the driver.

Tota, the cobbler's 'mad' daughter, isn't at her usual spot next to the gate of the Kaw house. It is too early and too cold for her parents to let her out of the house. Her mad laughter is nowhere.

Babi and Ma's eyes are fixed on us. On Babi's lips are a silent wish and a prayer. 'May Reshi Pir protect both of you! May Roopa Bhawani bless you and keep you safe.' They are holding tears in their eyes. When they go back inside, they won't be able to stop crying.

By the time I look back, the truck has already left our home far behind and the haze has swallowed everything. I want to get off the truck and run back home. Henna has fallen asleep on my lap.

* * *

July 1999
Udhampur

Babuji is dreaming a happy dream. His smile says it all. The sores on his body have turned ashen—a sign that the end is near.

Babi narrates a story about our days in Khrew, when we lived in Babuji's ancestral house located next to a hill atop which was the temple of Goddess Jwala (Zala).

'Do you remember teaching him how to make a slingshot?' she whispers into Babuji's ear. 'Standing beneath the vermilion-coloured rock, you taught him dangerous things like how to entice kites with the sacred offering—goat lungs. And then kites would swoop like arrows and snatch an offering from your hand.'

Babi is hopeful that her husband will die a happy death only when such stories are whispered to him. 'Someday, when we go back, we will start over . . .' she says.

* * *

24 June 2012
Jammu–Srinagar

Babi rings me up from Srinagar. She's on a short trip there. I coax her to go to all the places. 'Go to Reshi Pir's shrine,

Roopa Bhawani's shrine, Ram Mandir, Durga Naag, Kheer Bhawani, Zala Mata Mandir . . .' I say to her.

Babi: 'Will you come along too?'

Me: 'Go to Safa Kadal too.'

She: 'You mean to say home?'

* * *

Summer 2018
Home, New Delhi

Henna and her family are back from a trip to Srinagar. They go to Kashmir almost every year and spend some days in the ashram there. She sends me photos and videos of our old house and Ram Mandir. The graffiti, the wreckage and the desecrated walls of the sanctum—the saddest sight! The temple of my childhood, Babi's temple, is still in abject condition, in a state of neglect, evoking fear and anger, waiting desperately to be restored to its old glory.

'Did you see the photos and videos?' Henna asks.

'Yes, all of them.'

'You saw Babi and Babuji's room . . .'

I am sad and angry. But I must learn how to conceal my emotions and remain calm.

'Our memories . . . our childhood . . .' she says.

'Yes, but it is over now.'

'Don't say that. Nothing is over. We shall go back and rebuild everything that we lost and that once was ours.'

If you search for 'Ram Mandir, Safa Kadal, Srinagar' on Google, you will see some photos and videos of the temple as well as the condition it is in.

* * *

According to the survey conducted by the Kashmiri Pandit Sangarsh Samiti (KPSS), an association of Kashmiri Pandits, almost 550 temples have been desecrated, damaged and encroached upon in Kashmir between 1990 and 2020.[7]

According to the state government, of the 438 temples in Kashmir, 208 were damaged between 1990 and 2020.[8]

In 2019, the Government of India announced setting up of a committee to survey and reopen around 50,000 temples that were closed in Kashmir ever since the armed insurgency erupted in 1990.

Not a single temple has been restored to its old glory, though some temples are now being renovated by the authorities.

11

A Palace of Dreams

An Afternoon
Summer of 1994
The Camp
Udhampur

It is the onset of summer and there are flowers all around. I don't want to go back to our rented house. I am whiling away the time. There's nothing else to do and nowhere else to go. I am tired of making paper bags and selling them to shopkeepers. I am fed up with tutoring the wealthy landlord's son. I am not good at learning anything myself, let alone teaching others. Ma is happy that I get paid every month. A sum of Rs 300 every month is a good amount. I am sick of learning typing and shorthand, but I don't wish to be the cause of Ma's unhappiness. She is keen on me picking up such skills, as she believes they will sustain me in the long run. I keep dreaming, but I am tired of the same dream again and again. When I look back, a vast darkness stares at me mockingly. I wonder what the future holds for me.

I decide to wait for the sun to go down and then go to the tea shop by the highway. It's breezy there in the evenings. I have money for a cup of tea, an omelette and a cigarette. But I am a vegetarian and I have stopped smoking because I am learning how to play the flute.

A man is sitting on a mound of earth outside his tent, numbered 227. He lives alone. He doesn't talk about his family. No one knows where his family is. Initially, people indulged in banter. Some thought the man had lost his mental balance because he couldn't bear the trauma of being abandoned by his children. But now his neighbours and fellow camp-dwellers have their own worries. Perched atop an electric pole is a crow who has the man in his line of sight, as if he were waiting for him to pop off so that he can feast on his eyes. The 'I-know-what-is-going-to-happen-next' stare is frightening.

'Crows know about events before they occur,' the man says to me. 'They wait and wait patiently until everything is over and then they come down from their roosts to feast on the remains.'

The man is unruffled. He continues talking to the crow. The crow pretends to be interested in the man's monologue, as though to say, 'I am listening'.

'Listen, son, I have saved some money for my last rites and cremation. Don't tell anyone I gave you the money,' the man says, slipping his hand into the pocket of his trousers to take out the money. After counting the cash, he hands me a ten rupee note. 'Here, keep it safe.'

I accept the single note.

'Do whatever with it that day. Once, we were extravagant with such things in Kashmir. Sell my things if you run short of money. They are of no use to me now. But don't sell my house, my wristwatch and my transistor. You can keep them. And don't forget to buy some candy for yourself once everything is over . . .' he says, as if I am the only person in his life.

In front of him is Rani Dhar's tent. Rani is my classmate Kuldeep's grandmother. She lives with her son, daughter-in-law and two grandchildren—Kuldeep and a little girl whose name I don't know.

The man steals a furtive glance at Rani's tent. Then he begins again.

'Did you learn how to clean the toilet? Your mother must not get to see the filth. She deserves a clean toilet . . .'

His memory is sharp when it comes to some matters. He has been giving me some tips on how to be a dutiful son. He talks to me as though I were his son. I see no merit in correcting him. No good will come out of revealing the truth. If this is his truth, so be it.

'Yes, I did, but what if . . .?'

'No ifs and buts. You have no choice. Do it the way I do. Nobody does it better than I do. Nobody should do it better than you. It is an art and you must excel at it. Now go and get me a packet of Wills Gold Flake.'

I shake my head.

He surreptitiously places a cigarette between his lips as if he doesn't want anyone to see him with a cigarette in his mouth. His lips tremble, struggling to keep the cigarette steady.

'Aren't you going to light it?'

'I will, but what is the hurry? You know I don't smoke now. I was the greatest smoker in the whole of Kashmir. But I quit. Someday, when you grow up, you will also give up your most favourite thing for someone . . . even if your whole life depends on it.'

The crow begins to get impatient. Faced with the setting sun, he is now trying to estimate how much time is left before his wish is granted.

Looking at another mound of earth next to Rani's tent, the man murmurs to himself, 'You will know whom I am building this hill for. If only she touches me with her feet . . .'

Evening
Rani's Tent

As always, there is commotion in Rani's tent. Rani doesn't like anyone coming close to her. Not even her own daughter-in-law who feeds her after covering her face with a cloth. It's a trick that works some days. When it doesn't work, she turns the light off in the tent and forces morsels of rice into Rani's mouth. Sometimes she makes bird sounds. She becomes Rani's husband, father, mother. Rani then swallows the food.

Rani's son lifts her.

'Give me a bath,' he says to her while carrying her to the small basin in an adjacent tent that serves as a washing area for the camp-dwellers. After covering the entrance of the tent with a large sheet, he starts bathing her. Against her wishes, of course! The water in the drum is sparse, dirty and full of worms. Rani relents when her son reminds her of something. He must throw a tantrum for his mother to listen to him.

'Why are you doing this to me?' Rani cries.

'Have you forgotten? We're going home.'

'You're lying again, aren't you? I will die if you lie to me one more time.'

'I won't let you die. I will take you home.'

'When?'

'Tomorrow.'

She smiles and starts humming a song. 'What will happen to you after I go away? Is this where you say goodbye to me?'

'Look at your house—your room is still like a bride,' says the son, holding her hands, taking her from one room to another, showing her around, pointing to household things, marvelling at them as if they were precious stones. 'Look, nothing has happened to them. They are intact . . .' He opens the tap in the bathroom. Water gushes forth.

'I am not used to having everything,' she sighs.

Another Day

The son keeps a close tab on his mother's mental condition. He makes sure she doesn't miss a single dose of medicine. After dinner, he gives her a sedative so she remains calm at night. Then there is a memory booster prescribed by a homoeopathy doctor. Every now and then, he tests her memory by asking her questions and keeping her engrossed in conversations. This time, he is trying to figure out to what extent she's slipping further. Sometimes he runs out of patience and confronts her, suspecting that she does certain things deliberately to annoy him and his wife. He thinks all this might be an act, a charade and that, like a child, she derives pleasure in driving them insane and keeping them guessing. The adage—old age is a second childhood—is true for every old person, without exception.

'Who do you keep talking to?' he asks for the sixtieth time.

At last, she responds. 'You, who else?'

'I have seen you talk like a bird and imitate bird sounds.'

'My name is not Haer for nothing.'

'She does it intentionally,' the daughter-in-law mutters. 'She loves to do it. There is nothing wrong with her mind. She is misleading you on purpose. Look at how sharp she is . . . She remembers everything. Ask her who named her Haer . . .'

'Who gave you the maiden name?' she asks to test her memory and to check how she will respond.

This tit-for-tat between the mother-in-law and daughter-in-law has been going on for a long time. Kuldeep is fed up with it.

Her husband asks her to be discreet with a 'forget-it' expression on his face.

But she won't give up!

'Who are you expecting today, Rani? More guests, like every day? Answer me,' asks the daughter-in-law.

Rani's eyes light up. Her hair is auburn. Gold earrings dangle off her large earlobes. She's back in the palace of her dreams.

'What took you so long?' she asks when she sees me at the tent's entrance, mistaking me for someone else.

A crow flies from somewhere and settles next to her tent. When the crow caws, Rani starts complaining. She goes on and on, complaining to the crow about his delayed arrival yet again and about his bad habit of keeping her waiting.

'What took you so long? Do you have any idea what I go through when you don't turn up on time?'

She tells him things about others. It's mostly gossip that is not meant to be shared with anyone but a trusted confidante.

Then she comes out of her tent, holding a plate full of rice, vegetables and fried potatoes. She places the plate in front of the crow, who steps forward and eats his meal in peace while Rani talks to him about things as though he's a member of her family and not just a visitor.

Some Days Later

Rani is waiting outside her tent. Morning fades into night and night into the morning. But there is no sign of the visitor. Rani can't bear the torment any longer. She decides to go in search of him. But where will she go? She has never stepped out of the camp since she came here. She doesn't know what is outside the gates of the camp. Who will she turn to? She doesn't know what to do. She goes from one end of the camp to another. She keeps going. She calls out for him. Her voice is feeble. She can barely hear her own voice. She fixes her gaze on the sky.

Outside Rani's tent is the man who keeps smoking cigarette after cigarette, calling out my name again and again so that I don't go away.

Rani will always be in constant search. 'She will never forgive herself for leaving Sheermaal, the newborn calf, behind,' says someone.

Some days later, Rani goes missing from the camp. But thanks to other camp-dwellers who have seen her roaming aimlessly in the market, talking to herself, she is found and brought back.

Being the loneliest person ever was something that Rani learned to accept, but ever since that day, she could never bear someone else's loneliness . . .

* * *

A Day in the Spring of 1995

I am standing on a platform at the Jammu Railway Station, about to board a train to Delhi to join Jawaharlal Nehru University to pursue a Master's in English Literature. I am carrying a small bag containing some books and clothes. In my hand is my flute. In my heart, there is a void.

I am leaving behind a part of myself at home and at the camp. A part I will never be able to take with me wherever I go. No matter what I do, that part will not belong to me or anyone else. It will just remain buried in the soil or in the dust. I have a feeling that someday it will just vanish, leaving no trace of its existence.

* * *

Evening
August 1995

I am back in the camp in Udhampur, hoping to meet the man who called himself 'the greatest smoker in the whole of Kashmir'. The man who had mistaken me for his son.

But neither he nor Rani are in their tents. Both tents are now occupied by other families. I survey the camp, making inquiries.

'Vacant tents keep on getting re-allotted immediately to other families in case families relocate from here or, God forbid, something happens . . .' says a man. 'Who are you searching for? Do you have a name?'

I used to call him the Gold Flake Man.

'I am looking for the Dhar family,' I reply.

'There are many Dhars here in this camp,' the man says, sensing my desperation. 'One entire row of tents over there is the Dhar row. You should check with the camp commandant. He maintains a roster of all the families at the camp office. Perhaps the Dhars you are looking for have shifted from here and rented a place somewhere. People who have the means do move on to better places, you see . . .'

Men, women and children are going about their things. Not much has changed. Everything seems to be the same. Everything except the two tents, which, only a few months ago, were home to Rani and the Gold Flake Man.

Rani's palace of dreams is gone. But next to her tent is a small hill. On it are a few idols of gods and goddesses. Lord Krishna, Lord Shiva and Goddess Lakshmi.

It is evening. A swarm of locusts is approaching the camp. A crow is perched atop the same electric pole next to the tent where Rani once lived.

12

A Dream of Settlement

Autumn 1988
Ompora, Budgam, Kashmir

Pa and I are walking towards a residential colony, which he says is going to come up in 1990. He is taking me to see the plot of land he has bought—approximately three-fourths of a *kanal*.* Pa's lifetime savings have gone towards buying it. It's not just any other purchase! It is a dream.

'The plot is big enough for us to have a house with a garden and a backyard,' says Pa. 'You will have a room to yourself. All of us will have separate rooms. No more filthy drains. No more smelly lanes. This is going to be the poshest neighbourhood in all of Kashmir. But wait, you will be in for a surprise once we get there . . .'

It's a steep climb before we reach the plateau. We finally approach flat ground where plots have been marked. Some houses are already under construction, with the foundations being laid.

---

* A kanal is about 5500 sq. ft.

'We will begin construction in two years after we have saved enough money. To begin with, we need Rs 6 or 7 lakh. Just two more years. Come 1990 and we will start . . .'

We are now standing on our plot of land. It already feels like a dream.

This place is ours . . . This land is ours . . .

'Look at the sunset . . . this will be the view from the veranda,' says Pa, pointing his finger towards the setting sun. The sky starts turning vermilion.

'Can't we build the house this year itself or even next year?'

'Once you complete your matriculation, we can. The summer of 1990 will be the best time. We can move in before the winter sets in, provided we are able to complete at least one floor by autumn. It is possible. I will apply for a loan.'

I don't want to leave this place. I am already in our new house.

* * *

1992–93
Najafgarh–Bahadurgarh–Bhiwadi–Delhi–Gurgaon

Several Kashmiri Pandit families are looking for affordable plots of land in Najafgarh and Bahadurgarh. These are the only places on the outskirts of Delhi where land is relatively cheap because it is unauthorized.

We need at least Rs 10 lakh to buy a two-room house somewhere in the villages of Najafgarh or Bahadurgarh.

Every day, we go from one colony to another, from one neighbourhood to another. From Haryana, we go to Punjab and from Punjab, we go to Chamba in Himachal Pradesh in search of a house or a plot of land we can afford. If only . . .

Pa takes me to meet Arjan Dev Majboor in Palam colony. He is a poet. He lives in Udhampur, not very far from where we are, but his son is living in rented accommodation in Palam village. He works for a firm in Delhi. Pa is translating some of Majboor Uncle's exile poems into English. We meet Majboor Uncle's son.

There is no other discussion apart from the daily troubles that we face: house hunting, settlement, the situation in Kashmir, destiny, children, jobs, security and the future.

'Go to New Palam Vihar,' advises Majboor Uncle's son. 'You can buy a small plot for Rs 50,000 or Rs 60,000. At least, you will secure your children's future. The colonies will be authorized soon; don't worry.'

We take a bus to New Palam Vihar and meet the property dealers there. The place is full of people involved in the selling of land and houses. Wherever you look, you see vacant plots and an abundance of houses under construction. There are hoardings all over the roads soliciting people to invest.

'Book your dream home today. Pay 10 per cent now and the rest on possession.'
'Ready-to-move-in houses available.'

Day after day, we find ourselves here, looking at the plots for sale, desperately trying to find an affordable one.

Some days later, Pa signs the papers after paying Rs 55,000. He is now the owner of a small plot of land in New Palam Vihar.

As we leave, the sun begins to set behind the railway track at a distance. An old song is playing on the radio at a dhaba. It is *'Jeena Yahan Marna Yahan, Iske Siva Jana Kahan'** from Raj Kapoor's 1970 film *Mera Naam Joker*.

---

* You live here, you die here/Where else can one go but here?

Pa is happy. So am I. There is silence between us.

In a few years, we will build a small house here. The dream I've been dreaming will come true. But I've been having nightmares too. The nightmares are about us owning a house here, but it is about to cave in because the foundation is not strong enough.

I don't want to have that dream again. I just want the nightmares to end, but they're not stopping.

* * *

Autumn of 2003
Udhampur

'We will have to sell our plot of land in Ompora if we are to buy a house in Jammu,' reveals Papa. 'How long will we live houseless and homeless? Someone has offered us Rs 3.5 lakh for the plot. I know it is nothing, but we must take whatever is offered at this stage. We need the money for Henna's wedding.'

A Few Days Later

Pa sells the plot of land at Ompora for Rs 3.5 lakh. All our efforts to demand the market price for the plot go in vain. The going rate in the area for a similar-sized plot of land is Rs 40 lakh, but none of the Kashmiri Muslim buyers are willing to pay us the right price for our land.

We have no option but to accept whatever money is being offered.

'We will add some more savings to these Rs 3.5 lakh and buy a small house in Jammu. It is time to kiss goodbye to Kashmir,' says Pa.

One more dream comes to an end.

13

At Least We Are Alive and Together

A Day in the Summer of 1991
The Camp
Udhampur

Pa and I are at the entrance of the camp. A swarm of locusts has descended on this arid piece of land upon which stand about 1200 canvas tents. Here in this camp, over 1200 Pandit families are battling for survival. Everywhere there is desolation. Pa and I try to make sense of the human condition.

'What's going to happen to us?'

'At least we're alive and together . . . Think of those who aren't . . . At least we're still . . .' says Pa.

Carrying the burden of the community's history marred by six enforced exoduses—the first having taken place in the fourteenth century under Shah Mir (an invader and the founder of Muslim rule in Kashmir), we nurture the hope that our predicament will end soon and that we will witness happy times once again.

* * *

240

Three decades later, Pa and I remember our days in the camp when we thought that the end was near. 'I wish I had a camera in those days,' laments Pa. 'That horror should have been captured for posterity.'

Very few photographs of our camp life exist today. The few possessions that people had were destroyed. In camps, there was no room for people, let alone for things essential for human survival.

When people are uprooted from their homes, they not only lose their identity and a sense of belonging, but they also lose language. A new vocabulary characterized by dispossession has now taken birth. 'In the camps, we learned new words and their meanings,' says Pa. 'Ration card, migrant, tent, relief, dementia, delirium, diabetes, arthritis, tumour, sunstroke, snakebite, malignancy, heatstroke, hypertension, amnesia, myopia, thyroid, senility, cardiac arrest, depression, cholesterol, cataract, echo, viral, conjunctivitis . . .'

Time, space, memory, home and relationships have assumed different meanings altogether.

The years since 1990 have been the darkest period in the history of our community. Some are still languishing in the darkness because they remain in camps, waiting to return to Kashmir. But most are resigned to their fate. The hope they kept alive in their hearts for over a quarter of a century is diminishing. They are not even sure what they will be going back to, even if they do get the opportunity to return. Nothing remains of the homes in which they once flourished and nurtured dreams of living and eventually dying. Not even ruins.

* * *

31 December 2018

It is New Year's Eve.

Pa sends me a letter with a photograph that I've never seen before.

'Look at what Nancy has given us,' writes Pa. 'You remember Nancy Bhat of Ladhoo, don't you? She's my grandmother's sister's daughter-in-law. She visits us sometimes and ends up remembering her days in Ladhoo. The lavish wedding ceremonies, us visiting them in spring and celebrating Navreh (New Year) in the temple of Goddess Zala at Khrew. The woman on the left in the photograph is my grandmother's mother.'

My great-great-grandmother looks at me with wonder in her eyes, as though she is about to reveal the deepest secret of her life. I can't take my eyes off her. Diamond-shaped gold ornaments are dangling off her large earlobes. She's wearing a piece of headgear and smiling an enigmatic smile. Next to her is another woman—a sibling or a close relative. A child, aged three or four, with a glint in his eyes, is throwing me an inscrutable smile. There are more people around the two women and the child, but they are outside the frame. What could have happened on that day and later in the life of my great-great-grandmother? What is she hiding in her heart?

Thus, begins the quest to decipher the woman I have never seen in my life. I want to know everything about her. Who she was, what she did, how she lived, how she died . . . I want to know about her children. grandchildren, sons-in-law and daughters-in-law. The mysterious look in her eyes betrays her awareness of me.

The people in the photograph come alive. She's at a wedding that took place a hundred years ago. Women are singing a wedding song. They whirl around the bride and take turns to be at her place—the coveted place in the centre of a colourful sawdust circle made by the bride's uncle. They kiss foreheads. A man throws a handful of marigold petals up in the air. He blows a conch to announce the bridegroom's arrival. Under a yellow umbrella, ushered by seven aunts and six uncles (one died while crossing a river), the bridegroom steps into the courtyard. He is wearing embroidered headgear and a garland of green cardamom pods. The eldest uncle blows the conch seven-and-a-half times. The groom lifts the veil of marigolds and reveals his youthful smile. He is wearing a coat—the same tweed coat that his father wore on an excursion to Verinag, the holy spring from where the Vitasta flounces. The chorus goes on and on. In the courtyard, honeybees flutter over hyacinths floating in a pond. A matriarch steps forward, kisses the groom's forehead and applies a vermilion tilak to it. A girl comes out of hiding to dance. This isn't the first time I have seen the little girl. Next to her is a young man with a mole on his chin and a beautiful woman with a scar on the bridge of her nose. Their belongings are packed—a bundle of clothes and kitchenware.

My present-day reality intrudes into the pleasant picture. Suddenly, I see the petrified shadows of people behind them. They are leaving for good. Where are they going?

The air is heavy with camphor fumes. Camphor fumes remind me of death. The persecutors throw these people into the river with heavy objects tied to their ankles. The sacred threads are removed from their bodies, fed to flames and the ashes are buried deep into the ground in order to erase the traces. The pockets of these hapless people are emptied. Some of these people plunge into the Vitasta to evade death. The only two people who survive are a woman and her infant son. Carrying her son in her arms, the woman scrounges for refuge in a distant land. When she falls asleep, she dreams of a spring amid a cluster of huts and windmills. Fountains of water gush forth from the spring. She rushes towards the spring to quench her thirst.

She addresses her son: 'After I die, you will find a stone in my pocket. I have carried it all my life, hoping that someday you will chance upon it and take it back to the place where it belongs—a ruin atop the sacred hill. The stone is the last vestige of our age-old existence. The endless summer has turned it black. Worship it, for this is the stone from the very hill against which the heads of your ancestors were smashed. The land that once belonged to me is not mine anymore. It is claimed by wandering nomads, by the animals that graze there, by the dead whose remnants are in its soil, by foreigners who have never set foot on it, by conquerors who are not able to conquer it and by the stars whose light falls on it. This land belongs to our shadows now and to the shadows of people who sacrificed their lives to nurture it. They left no progeny. The land is their progeny. Someday you must go in search of the land under which I have buried a gold earring. Go in the spring when the ice is melting. Go with a seed and sow it there. On the day of your return, smear yourself with the ashes of your ancestors and drink the nectar of the holy spring. On that very day, you will know who you really are and where you have come from.'

On the first day of the New Year, when the light of dawn lights up the photograph in front of me, I read Pa's letter.

My dear Siddhartha,

For twenty-five years, you kept asking me a question. I brushed it aside and told you anecdotes that no one else knew. Now, here's the truth—plain and simple, like spring water. I can't hold it in any longer.

Balak Ram Gigoo, my great-great-grandfather, owned a provisions shop in Srinagar, Kashmir. His son was Gulab Ram Gigoo. Balak Ram's sister, Sangri Devi, was the wife of Sudarshan Mian, who lived at Rainawari in Srinagar. Gulab Ram Gigoo managed the estate of Ved Lal Dhar who owned lands and orchards. His monthly salary was Rs 90. Ved Lal Dhar would give him seventy mounds of rice and fruits a year. Gulab Ram spent most of his life as the manager of Ved Lal Dhar's estate. He would visit Maharaja Pratap Singh, who respected him. Once, a person named Dr Bal Krishen took him to Allahabad to meet Moti Lal Nehru. The two of them stayed in Anand Bhawan for five days. It was actually Ved Lal Dhar who had requested Dr Bal Krishen to do so. Gulab Ram knew Arabic, Persian and Urdu. He had studied the Quran and Persian and Urdu poets. The family had a domestic helper named Krishen Das who had served the family for thirty years. He looked after the two cows, made butter and ghee, and occasionally distributed these among the neighbours. Adjacent to the house was a big piece of land on which Krishen Das grew vegetables and fruits. Each time Gulab Ram went to the orchards, he got fruits in abundance for the family, relatives and neighbours. One day, at the age of sixty-nine, Gulab Ram suddenly died while smoking his hookah in an orchard. He had two sons, Madhu Ram Gigoo and Nand Lal Gigoo.

Madhu Ram Gigoo was born in Srinagar in 1893. He studied up to matriculation at Tyndale Biscoe School. He was a skilled swimmer who had twice crossed the Wular Lake and received recognition from Tyndale Biscoe. After passing matriculation, Madhu Ram Gigoo learned laboratory work from Dr Doon who had come to Srinagar from London. Tyndale Biscoe had asked Dr Doon to take on Madhu Ram as an apprentice. The boulevard had been constructed. Dr Doon constructed a house at the foot of Shankaracharya Hill. He opened a clinical laboratory in a room in the house. Madhu Ram would go there every day. He was fluent in English. Two brothers, Dr Nev and Dr Alter, came from London. Dr Nev became very popular in Srinagar. He was very kind to all and treated his patients with love, understanding and compassion. All the Englishmen were Christian missionaries whose objective was to convert people to Christianity. Dr Alter made Madhu Ram Gigoo read the Bible and learn psalms and took him to church on Sundays. Then, one day, Dr Alter asked Madhu Ram Gigoo to embrace Christianity. He told him that he would be able to visit all the places in the world. Madhu Ram Gigoo was baptized as a Christian at the Roman Catholic Church in Srinagar and given the new name Michael Bhan. That day, there were festivities in the courtyard of the church. Christians were happy and celebrated the event. Four English ladies and a Muslim from Bihar came to Madhu Ram's house at Khankah-i-Sokhta in Srinagar. Madhu Ram's wife, Dhanawati, and mother were there.

Photos were taken and a relative of the family spread a rumour that Madhu Ram Gigoo had married an English Christian girl. However, Madhu Ram was already married to Haer from Khrew, a village in Kashmir. Haer was an ace horseback rider. The new name given to Haer in her husband's house was Dhanawati. (Her mother is the woman on the left in the photograph.)

One day, Madhu Ram Gigoo told the members of his family that he would go to the house of his mother's parents in Rainawari and stay there for four days. But he told his grandmother that he was going to Punjab in connection with his job. He went to Kabul, Sialkot, Peshawar and some other places by bus. In Afghanistan, he went to a tribal area, where he met the head of the tribe. From there, he went to Rome and met the Pope. He studied Christian literature there and also learned Greek and Latin. He went to Denmark, Switzerland, Turkey and other countries. In Turkey, he met Mustafa Kemal Pasha Ataturk and those who were leading Turkey towards modernity. He wrote a book, *The Snake in Kashmir,* which was published in Rome. On the orders of the Maharaja of Jammu and Kashmir, the book was banned in Kashmir and its copies were burned on the road.

Madhu Ram Gigoo came back to India and stayed in Mumbai, where he met Dr Annie Besant, who asked him why he had converted to Christianity when Hinduism was so vast. She asked him to learn Sanskrit, read the Hindu scriptures and then re-enter the Hindu fold. There, Madhu Ram Gigoo met K.M. Munshi, Leelawati Munshi, Rahul Sankrityayan and many other Sanskrit scholars. He spent some months in the company of such people. Then he returned home. Three years had passed by then. The news spread in the city. One day, Pandits assembled at Raghunath Mandir, called Madhu Ram Gigoo and asked him to explain why he had converted to Christianity. He replied, 'I did what I wanted to do.' He did not listen to Dr Bal Krishen, Ved Lal Dhar, Hargopal Kaul and all others, including the secretary of Maharaja Pratap Singh. Such was his stubbornness and arrogance.

A few days later, he was asked to present himself before Maharaja Pratap Singh in his court. The Maharaja, on the advice of some influential Pandits, asked him for a written apology. Madhu Ram Gigoo held the pen in his toes, signed the document, left the court and went home. After some time, Diwan Munshi Dass got him appointed food inspector and he was posted to the government hospital.

After some months, Madhu Ram Gigoo met a Pandit Sanskrit scholar at Ganpatyaar and requested that he teach him Sanskrit grammar and the Hindu scriptures. He studied the elementary Sanskrit learning books by Damodar Satwalekar and Panini. Then he devoted time to the study of the Vedas, the Gita, the Upanishads, other scriptures and the commentaries on them. He memorized the Rig Veda, which took him four years. He studied Persian and read books written by Urdu and Hindi writers. He studied the Quran under Maulvi Abdullah, who lived at Nawab Bazar in Srinagar.

Madhu Ram Gigoo became an ardent Arya Samaji and introduced Vedic philosophy to the family priest Lassa Bhayu. He directed Lassa Bhayu to go to Ladakh and convert the people of that place to the Arya Samaj philosophy. Two people laid the foundation of the Arya Samaj in Kashmir: Janki Nath Vidyarthi of Habba Kadal and Madhu Ram Gigoo. They would go to the Mughal Gardens on Sundays, deliver lectures and propagate Vedic thought. They were against idol worship and abstained from eating meat. On some days, Madhu Ram Gigoo went to Kheer Bhawani (Tulamula), made speeches and was beaten for propagating a thought that did not believe in idol worship.

A person named Gowri Shanker offered Madhu Ram Gigoo and Janki Nath Vidyarthi a place to carry on the activities of the Arya Samaj and hold meetings with those inclined towards religion. Discussions were held there about Vedic dharma and social reform. The aim was to free the minds of the Pandits from outdated customs and rituals. A person named Maulvi Ahmad Shah was taught Sanskrit and Hindi. He studied the Hindu scriptures, too.

In 1934, Rabindranath Tagore visited Kashmir and
read out poems from his book *Gitanjali* in the auditorium
of S.P. College. He danced on the dais as well. Later, he met
the poets, writers and intellectuals of Kashmir in the house
of P.N. Kaul Bamzai. Mahjoor, Master Zinda Kaul, Gwash
Lal Kaul and all the luminaries of Kashmir were present,
too. Madhu Ram Gigoo introduced himself to Tagore as
an Arya Samaj member.

Madhu Ram and Janki Nath Vidyarthi would walk
through the streets and along the roads of Srinagar with
torches in their hands at night and shout at the top of
their voices, 'Back to the Vedas. Vedic dharma is the best.'
They would also deliver lectures at various places, reading
out passages from Swami Dayanand Saraswati's *Satyarth
Prakash*. This continued for several years. They read books
written by the great Arya Samaj members of Punjab and
Gujarat. Madhu Ram Gigoo and Kashyap Bandhu tirelessly
worked towards social reform. They saw to it that the
Pandit women gave up wearing the complicated pheran and
switched to saris. The people did not take it lightly and, in
fact, reacted vehemently. Madhu Ram got in touch with the
Arya Samaj members in Punjab and Gujarat who came to
Srinagar and held talks with him on religion, Indian culture
and social reform. Anand Swami (Khushal Chand, editor
of *Milap*), along with other Arya Samaj members, would
visit our place at Khankah-i-Sokhta, Nawa Kadal, Srinagar,
every summer. K.M. Munshi and Leelawati Munshi
came to our home when the former was the governor of
Maharashtra. He used his influence in Punjab and saw to
it that Dayanand Anglo Vedic College was established in
Srinagar in 1944. Dr Sri Ram Sharma was appointed the
principal of the college. Every Sunday, he went to the Arya
Samaj centre at Hazuri Bagh and conducted the hawan. He

was made the president of Arya Samaj, Maharaj Gunj. He even got a few Pandit widows remarried.

Madhu Ram Gigoo retired from service in 1950. He started the first pathological laboratory in the state of Jammu and Kashmir at Maharaj Gunj in Srinagar and named it The Imperial Clinical Laboratory. He passed away at the National Hospital in Srinagar in 1968 after a brief illness. Netra Pal and other Arya Samaj members performed a hawan. Throughout his life, Madhu Ram Gigoo had utter contempt for the complicated rituals performed after the death of a person.

I found Rs 14 in the pocket of his shirt when he died.

With unbounded love,
Papa

* * *

In the pale winter morning in Delhi, a bright star appears in the sunless sky and it is my turn to understand who I am and where I have come from. A descendant of the child in the photograph my father sent me is still languishing somewhere in exile. Years from now, people will look at the photograph and know that we existed and were a happy lot before being blotted out. It will serve as proof of our existence when everyone else tells us we never existed.

The photograph conceals another startling truth. A century ago, a woman gave up her dreams, aspirations and happiness for her great-great-grandchild's survival and happiness. The great-great-grandchild, until now, had forgotten his origins and did not realize that his happiness had come at a cost.

How am I to reconcile the torment my elders faced in camps where they perished without remembering their agony and without realizing the enormous loss they had been made to suffer? How am I to save myself from obscurity? How am I to go on without history?

Pa still remembers the day he saw his great-grandmother happy. 'It was a beautiful day in the summer of 1964. She had come to attend my Yagnopavit.* She sat in a corner and sang happy songs the entire day. That was the last time I saw her.'

About the winter of 1990, when we were made to leave our homes in Kashmir, Pa says, 'When the climate did not change after twenty days, the twenty days shrank into twenty years, then a hundred years and then hundreds and hundreds of years.'

Years from now, photographs such as the one Nancy Bhat and her family have preserved for over 100 years will hold the only clue to the genealogy and history of Kashmiri Pandits.

---

* Yagnopavit refers to the thread ceremony which symbolizes a Hindu man's initiation into performing his threefold duties to the household, his devas and his ancestors.

14

Don't Leave Me Here. Take Me with You!

A Day in the Summer of 1991
The Camp
Udhampur

I am at the camp school. But there are no classes. Someone in the camp has died today as well and people are preparing for the cremation. Deaths are a daily affair here. So are school closures.

'You can leave today,' the headmaster informs the students. 'We will resume tomorrow.'

Where do I go? I come here to the camp thinking I won't have to go elsewhere. What do I do with the day? What am I to do with myself?

The hourglass is empty. It is useless. I have no use for it anymore.

At a distance, there are two tents. Outside them are a man and a woman. The bald and reedy man is sitting opposite the woman with elephant legs. Their gazes are fixed elsewhere. They seem unruffled by the death that has taken place in a nearby tent.

They are always outside their tents. They seldom talk to each other. I have always thought of them as a widower and a widow. Their tents are empty. An empty tent is a rare sight. Maybe their families are dead. Maybe they are gone. Maybe they have deserted them like some children desert their parents once they are all grown up.

'Don't go over there,' Pamposh gestures to me with a look. Pamposh is my classmate. His family is from a remote village in Kashmir. He lives in the camp.

'Why?'

'Haven't you figured it out by now?'

It seems he's once again alerting me to my situation, which is very different from his, though I may think otherwise. 'Don't you dare . . . You are grossly mistaken. Do you think you belong here? Do you think you are one of us? You have no idea what goes on here during the day and at night. You can never imagine. Nor will anyone else. You will never survive here for more than a day. Go now. Leave. Come back tomorrow for the class.'

'But the widow and widower over there . . .'

'They are husband and wife, not widow and widower. But they have forgotten that they have been married for forty years. Now tell me, don't you think they are pining for each other despite being married for forty years?' he remarks.

* * *

Today, sixteen people . . . one after another, in a span of a few hours . . . just like that . . . before the sun has even risen . . . sixteen men and women are gone. Mostly men. As if they never existed.

A fatal day follows a fatal night.

'He is just sleeping,' says a woman about her dead husband.

A man from the adjacent tent shakes his head while examining the dead man's pulse, hoping against hope to find a trace of life. Just one sign, even if it is the last one. The dead man's wife is adamant. 'Give him some time. He is always up to such antics! It is deliberate.'

'There's been a mistake,' another woman says about her man, who is lying lifeless on the floor. People have gathered around him to give him the final bath, but his wife is adamant and stops them.

'Look, the food is almost ready,' she says. 'He won't eat without me . . . I have prepared his favourite dish . . . He can't do a thing without me, let alone close his eyes . . . He quit smoking for me . . . Are you listening? I know you are . . . You have things to do today, don't you? You will blame me if I don't remind you . . . Don't blame me then . . . You know how he is . . . He's a child . . . Always up to pranks! He will never grow up . . .'

I look into the man's eyes. The woman is right. The man is almost alive. Maybe he's pretending to be dead just for his wife's attention. Just to check whether or not she loves him.

'I wish they were saying all these things about me . . .' the man's sobbing mother says. 'I wish I were the one to be taken by Lord Yama . . .'

The man was the strongest man in the camp. He had renounced almost everything except his sense of duty towards others. He cared little about himself. People had always wished him a long life. But now others see no hope because they're shocked to see someone as strong and blessed as him die.

'Go, call the miracle man,' someone says.

Pa's friend, the miracle man, is the noblest person in all of Udhampur. He must have helped with at least 1000 cremation rituals. Every day, he shows up at places where deaths have occurred. He single-handedly arranges everything and helps the families with the last rites. Very few camp-dwellers can afford the last rites of the dead.

The worst part of dying in a tent in the camp is preparing the body for cremation. There is no room to even give the man his last bath. The dead need room; the living can adjust. The dead demand dignity; the living can eat shame.

'God, put him out of his misery, please,' is the prayer on everyone's lips.

'We don't even have ice to keep the dead bodies from decaying in the heat. Death comes easily here. Death is all around here. I could be next. Nothing terrifies us now. There is nothing left to grieve over. There are no tears . . .'

Sixteen families switch the lights off in their tents in the evening. They might never see the light again.

Husbands don't touch their wives; wives cannot touch their husbands. Love seems to have deserted the camp. It will never set foot here. Humanity cries inside this wretched den of human suffering.

The miracle man has given up everything to serve others. Cremating the dead with dignity and in accordance with Hindu customs is his only purpose in life now. It offers him solace. He performs the last rites of the dead as if they were his own flesh and blood. He doesn't cry. He speaks of immortality and the transmigration of the soul. He speaks of redemption. He comforts those who are left behind with nothing to live for. He is going through a crisis, but his crisis has metamorphosed into hope. And he passes on hope to those who have nothing. His own suffering has vanished because his life isn't his any longer—it belongs to others who have no life of their own.

He sits with the grieving families in the evenings and speaks to them about the importance of moving on with their lives and duties. He speaks of human virtues. He speaks of freedom. Of deliverance. Some believe him, while others know he's just trying to distract them.

A woman sobs. She seems to have lost her reason. 'You think this is a dream,' she says to the miracle man, mistaking him for her husband. She partly realizes he's not her husband, but she goes on addressing him as if he were her husband, blaming him for her plight. 'I am not in your dream . . . This isn't a dream . . . You don't allow me to go out . . . You forbid me from doing things . . . You are trying to cage me . . . I don't like this . . .'

He listens in silence. There is deep compassion in his moist eyes. These are tears of love. I hope you never understand the unsaid, for the unsaid will torment you even more.

* * *

An old man who resembles Babuji is dying. His wife is made to sit next to him for the last time. She whispers something into his ears and the old man smiles an enigmatic smile as if he hears the confession for the first time in his life.

'Don't leave me here . . . Take me with you . . . Take me with you . . .'

And then he closes his eyes.

Their son and daughter-in-law have left them alone. They haven't slept for the entire night because they know their father and mother won't have another opportunity to be together. They spend the night on a mound outside their tent.

The next morning, when they open the flap of the tent, they see the woman's head on the old man's chest. A happy smile has come to settle on their faces. Is it the first day of their love in exile? Or the last day?

The son cremates his father the next day. In the evening, he sits on a mound. He is free now. Free from burden, from responsibility, from guilt, from everything that had kept him occupied and given meaning to his existence until now. He cries and then stops, realizing that he has cried enough.

Here, in the camp, one death equals ten deaths. The one who dies takes with him ten more people.

* * *

June 1999
Udhampur

Death keeps evading Babuji. It betrays him and keeps him waiting, much like life has done so far. We don't know what to do. The rash on his hip is getting worse. Babuji asks me to sing a song and cook him his favourite meal—rice and fish. Then he looks into my eyes. A strange look conceals a question I know I will never be able to answer. He grabs hold of my hand and places it on the rash, begging me to rid him of it. He has no other wishes. The regret of not being able to fulfil his last wish will torment me for the rest of my life.

Ten Years Later

Babuji appears in my dream. He is happy; he has no desires now. He is filled with only goodness and happiness. I seek his forgiveness. I tell him what I couldn't tell him when he was alive.

I kneel in front of him and kiss the rash on his leg. He would do the same if I were the one with the rash.

I whisper into his ear to tell him quietly that this rash is nothing but the sting of a flower that blooms once every 100 years, its scent having entered his bones through the pores in his body, leaving him with this yellow rash, causing no pain.

I tell him he can still dance his youthful dance. That he can do everything that he wishes.

My dear Babuji,

You can do anything you like.

Nothing can prevent you from watering the evergreens in the courtyard of your house.

Nothing can keep you from doing your favourite things: polishing our shoes and arranging them aesthetically on the shoe rack as though they were books.

You can eat your favourite meal—rice and fish—with your hand, even if, sometimes, your hand reaches for your right ear instead of your mouth.

It's all right. I do it all the time these days. Our weary hands often betray us.

You can use the old centrifuge to separate the good cells from the bad and to determine the true cause of any affliction.

This rash will go away. It's not harmful; it won't do a thing to you. You now know how to live with it. I may inherit it, too. Then, the two of us will do the things we always wanted to do: dig the earth in the garden; run away to the woods to listen to the songs of the hoopoe and play poker even if the cards deceive us.

You now know that the fragrance of this strange flower has entered your body and killed the very cells that cause fear. You now know that the name you no longer remember is not worth remembering. The memory of me, too, will fade away. You may forget your way back home if you ever go to the market. But now you know that all roads lead to your old house. You will never lose your way in the world. You may forget everything you ever possessed, even the symbol tattooed on your arm. But one day, you will become a flower and, as the days progress, it will rid you of your rash.

Forever yours,
Siddhartha

* * *

Udhampur–New Delhi

We learn that the government has taken over the plot of land we purchased in New Palam Vihar as the entire colony is not authorized and regularized.

Pa and I rush to New Palam Vihar to meet the people there. The property dealer shakes his head, saying, 'Nothing can be done now; we are helpless. It is God's will.'

'But we wanted to build a house here . . .'

Our plot of land is bang in the middle of a soon-to-be-constructed expressway, which is part of the government's master plan to connect Dwarka to Gurugram.

We meet Babi's relative there. They had built a house here a few years ago and love it more than anything else in the world.

'Everything will be razed to the ground,' they say. 'All the houses and buildings that are right in the middle of this proposed highway . . .'

Even imagining the fate of house and the family is no less than a punishment. A death sentence would be better.

'Is there any hope for a solution?'

'This is our fate. We won't get our money back. The court case will drag on for years. Compensation will take decades, too. In this country, justice can take up to several lifetimes . . .'

'What do we do now? Where do we go?'

'What can we do? We are back to square one.'

Yet again, the dream of a home comes crumbling down. The land documents no longer mean anything. The savings of a lifetime . . . gone once again.

* * *

Kashmiri Pandits, whose land has been taken over by the government to build the expressway, form an association and hire a lawyer to take the matter to court. Their only demand is fair compensation—land for land, home for home.* They plead before the authorities: 'Give us land somewhere nearby so that we can build our houses there. Don't just look at us as people who bought land to build houses. We have been thrown out of our homeland. We are refugees in our own country. Our dream is to create a Kashmiri Pandit colony in New Palam Vihar or somewhere else and settle there. Don't crush our dreams.'

Year after year, the government doesn't even bat an eyelid. No compensation. No justice. No home! It's just an endless wait for us.

We are still awaiting compensation for the losses we have incurred.

---

* My family is among the affected parties. We have formed an association and hired a lawyer to represent us in the case.

15

Home Tourists

Autumn of 2004
Udhampur

My dear Siddhartha,

I retired from college today. It was my last day there. I don't need to go to college from tomorrow onwards. I am happy. I will draw a decent pension every month. You needn't worry.

We are finally kissing goodbye to Udhampur. We are buying a house in Jammu. The Bhatiyals are sad to see us leave their house in Udhampur for good. We will keep visiting them from time to time. You should too. They have been good to us. They love us.

We will always miss Udhampur for a variety of reasons. We've seen the best and worst of times there. We've learned so much about life—almost everything there is to learn. We've learned what struggle is and how to live with it. We've experienced goodness, horror, beauty and compassion. We've understood the true meaning of humanism. We will never forget our time in Udhampur.

The house we are buying in Jammu is in Lower Roop Nagar, which is a good and upcoming neighbourhood. It is a nice, spacious house with two bedrooms and a large drawing room with dining space. There is also parking space for a car. Babi will have a room to herself. We can add an additional floor to the house in the future.

Babi is very happy now, as the new house will be her own home. She is excited at the prospect of moving to Jammu so she can be near her relatives and visit them almost every week. She has always wanted us to move to Jammu.

Next year, I will buy a car and hire a driver. So we can travel comfortably from one place to another and avoid buses and autorickshaws. I will also apply for a telephone once we move into our new house. We can start afresh now.

Yours,
Papa

* * *

6 October 2004
New Delhi

Amia is born to Aishwarya and me. It is the happiest day of our lives.

* * *

24 June 2007
Srinagar

Aishwarya, Amia and I are in Jammu. Amia is three years old. We are here to spend a few days with Pa, Ma and Babi.

On impulse, Pa suggests making a trip to Srinagar. He rents a taxi and takes us to Srinagar. We visit Gulmarg and spend a day there. We become 'home tourists' for a day. We take Aishwarya and Amia to Tulmul and offer prayers at the Mata Kheer Bhawani temple there. On the third day, we ask the taxi driver to take us to Safa Kadal. We stop in the lane leading to our house.

Aishwarya sees the abandoned houses of Kashmiri Pandits who were once our neighbours. We walk past a row of houses—desolate, forlorn and derelict. One such house is ours. The windows of some houses are open. The latticework has come apart. Years of neglect have taken a toll. The taxi driver is quiet. He senses our anguish.

We click pictures. From a distance, we can see our house. It is the tallest house in the neighbourhood. You can spot it even from as far away as Eid Gah, which is a fifteen-minute walk. The tin roof of our house is all rusty now. Once, it shimmered in the afternoon sun.

Babi is overcome by a strong urge to get out of the taxi and run towards her house. She is gutsy and brave. But this time, she's cautious. She knows we are strangers in our own land. She points to our house and begins to tell Aishwarya everything about it—anecdotes and stories that I don't even remember!

'This is where we . . .' begins Babi, unable to contain her excitement. Once again, she's the little girl in our household. Her stories go on for days, even after we are back in Jammu. 'When we were there, we used to . . .' she goes on.

Will the weeping houses of Safa Kadal ever get their happiness back?

* * *

Time: Unknown
Year: Unknown
Place: Home

I am home. Babi and Babuji are in their room. Babi laughs her
hearty laugh, watching me tiptoe into her room. Babuji smiles
his old smile. It is the smile of a child who is about to crack
the secret behind a magic trick. He is making the bed—one of
the very few things he loves doing.

'Remember this quilt?' Babi says, taking a quilt out of
Babuji's wooden box. 'It is 100 years old today. Come and
smell it. Do you know why it still smells the same? It's because
of this box; it preserves everything. Your Babuji got it made
some days before our wedding . . .' she goes on, marvelling at
her belongings.

'Sleep early tonight; you have to be ready very early
tomorrow,' says Babuji, giving me a hug and a kiss. The
hug and kiss of a man who is reuniting with a grandchild
separated two lifetimes ago.

'Don't worry! I will wake you up early tomorrow,' says
Babi. Her old habit of interjecting her husband.

'Salama is going to be here with his tonga at dawn,' says
Babuji.

'And then it will take us until lunchtime to reach Ladhoo,'
says Babi, cutting him off yet again. She does it for me, not to
irritate him. Babuji is never annoyed. He doesn't mind such
things.

'Triloki Nath's children are going to be there,' she says,
sensing my reluctance to go anywhere. Half of her world is
outside, in the countryside and in other people's homes. 'They
will take you to the orchard. Don't be a pest and steal plums
the way you ransacked their orchard last time.'

'This isn't the season of plums,' says Babuji. 'Winter isn't
over yet.'

'Don't teach me about seasons,' says Babi. 'I have seen summer in winter and winter in summer, haven't I?'

'There she goes again—the greatest raconteur ever,' Babuji whispers to me.

No one narrates anecdotes and stories the way Babi does. She will make you believe the unbelievable. For instance, she will tell you about the day a crow whispered into her ear and spilled the beans about her husband. Something nobody knew. Not even the husband. And then her tryst with an elephant when she carried her calf across a river.

'Take this along,' says Babuji, handing me his transistor. 'It should work after we get the batteries replaced.'

I turn the transistor on. A song plays. And then the unthinkable happens.

'Babi, Babuji, where are you?'

Babi and Babuji are sitting next to each other in their room with smiles beaming on their faces. On the wall are two paintings—The School of Athens by Raphael and Krishna taming the five horses of Arjuna's chariot. The window frames a willow tree.

* * *

Babuji is working in his laboratory, examining samples of blood. I am waiting for him to break for lunch. That is when he will teach me how to identify cells using his microscope.

'Look how beautiful these cells are,' he says, pointing to their dance-like movements. 'You should learn how to cure the sick ones.'

Babuji has never been sad in his life. He has always known boundless happiness because he finds joy in the happiness of others. He sees beauty and goodness in every human because the very cells that give them life are made of nothing but beauty and goodness. He has deep love for even those who have never loved and for those who don't know what love is. He is the messiah of humanism in the entire neighbourhood.

'What will you do with my memory after I am gone?' he says, as we begin cycling back home.

Babi is in the courtyard, making apple jam. The first person to taste it will not be her husband but her grandchild.

I am sitting on the branch of a plum tree, listening to a song playing on Babuji's transistor. Plums hang low on the branches, tempting me to pluck them. But I promised Babuji and Babi that I wouldn't even touch them. Triloki Nath's family is preparing for the wedding feast. In the courtyard of the house, a boy is chasing crows away. 'Crows are harbingers of bad news,' his mother says. 'Don't let them near us.'

Triloki Nath comes out of the house with saplings in his hand. 'Come with me, all of you,' he says to the kids. 'I am going to teach you how to plant a sapling. Years from now, these trees will be yours.'

From inside the house comes laughter. Everyone is laughing at Babi's jokes. Babuji is sitting in a corner, lost in his own solitary world, content with being a sunrise-to-sunset man.

I close my eyes, thinking that this day will last forever.

* * *

When the history of the happiest people who ever lived is written, Babi and Babuji, to whom home meant everything, will prominently feature in it. The eternal smile on Babuji's face proved that he left this world satisfied after tasting the sweetest nectar of life. Babi breathed her last in a hospital in Srinagar, just one day before having her final wish fulfilled— to be home one last time.

16

Once We Had Everything and Then . . .

Morning, 8 September 2016
New Delhi

Ma and Pa have come from Jammu for the festival of Vinayak Chorum. We call it *Pann* (thread). The day is associated with the spinning of cotton. On this auspicious day, roth (sweet bread) is prepared and an age-old story is narrated. The day marks the end of deprivation and the beginning of prosperity. Ma cleans the kitchen, washes the utensils, kneads the dough and makes roth. Then, in accordance with the ritual, she does what all Pandit women do. She assembles us—Pa, Aishwarya, Amia and me—in front of a vessel containing the roth and recounts a story that has been narrated for generations:

'Once upon a time, in a village in Kashmir, lived a woman, her husband and their daughter. They made a living working in the households of the rich. One day, while working in a house, the girl saw the women making roth. She had never seen such a beautiful sight. When she returned home, she narrated the incident to her parents. Her mother told her about their past. "When we had everything," said her mother, "we celebrated Pann, too. Then, our fortunes changed and we were left with nothing." Sensing her daughter's despair, the mother went in search of some wheat and condiments. All she was able to collect were five grains of wheat. She washed them, ground them and made roth. She placed the five pieces of roth in a basket and covered them. Then she offered a prayer for the good times to return. When she lifted the cover off the basket, the five pieces of roth had turned into five gold coins. "You've returned to us whatever we had lost," she said to God. "From now on, we shall always celebrate Pann on this day."'

Ma pauses. 'What happens next?' I ask her.

'If Babi were alive, she would have told us what happens next,' Ma says. 'May we always be happy and flourish. May we always be together!'

* * *

A Day in September 1989
Home, Srinagar, Kashmir
Morning

Babi is cleaning the house and preparing for Pann. The thread she has spun from cotton wool is dangling off her right earlobe and holding the gold *dejhor* (earring). I am eager to eat the roth and other sweets and listen to Babi's story. She asks me to sit beside her. She begins:

'Once upon a time, in a village not far from here, lived an adventurous little girl with her mother and father. Once, when she was collecting walnuts in a forest, a lion descended from a mountain and blocked her way. The girl wasn't scared. Just as the lion was about to pounce on her, she raised her hand and gave him a smack. Stunned at the girl's valour, the lion ran for his life. The girl returned home and narrated her encounter with the lion to her parents . . .'

Daytime

Babuji, Pa, Ma, Henna and I gather in the kitchen for the prayer. After the prayer, Babi resumes narrating the story of the family who lost everything due to difficult circumstances. As always, she doesn't finish the story. She ends by offering another prayer. 'May the darkness dispel. May we never get to leave our beautiful house, our beautiful land. May we live and die happily here. May our children flourish.'

Elsewhere in the Valley, women across 50,000 Pandit households narrate the same story and offer the same prayer.

Evening

We sit next to empty tin trunks. We stare at our household possessions: utensils, bedding, clothes, rugs, jewellery, documents, certificates, bicycle, photographs, books, paintings, boxes, mirror, etc. Babi is chanting a prayer.

Shamboo Nath, our neighbour, has sent his granddaughters to Jammu.

'We shouldn't leave yet,' a Pandit says.

'We will be killed if we stay,' says another. 'Don't you know what militants did to Niranjan's son? They won't spare us if we don't give in to their demands. Ismail and his two sons have arms in their house now. What do you think they intend doing? This is a signal for us to leave . . .'

'What if, God forbid, something was to happen to . . .' whispers Ma. 'I know what you are thinking. You don't want to . . . even though many others are already preparing to leave . . . but you very well know what is going on outside . . .'

'The very thought of leaving is unsettling. Where will we go? We will wait it out . . .'

'May we never be thrown out of our home,' Babi prays. She tells the story of the brave little girl once again. I know who the little girl in the story is. Fear has forced its way into our house.

Outside, a frightful night reigns.

'In the spring, Kashmir will become part of Pakistan,' a Muslim neighbour has said to us. 'What will you do that day, Panditji?'

* * *

A Day in September 1996
Udhampur, Jammu Province
Morning

I have come to Udhampur to spend some days at home. Home is where everyone is. It is my semester break. Babuji is sitting in a corner like a child. Pa has given him children's games to keep him engrossed. At times, Babuji expresses himself in baby talk. Babi is the only one who understands his desires and tantrums. Home is where Babuji wants to go. Babi gives him the good news once again. 'Stop worrying; we're going home one of these days. We will celebrate Pann at our house. You will have things to do. You must start preparing. Do you remember everything or not? Don't tell me you don't . . .'

A smile appears on Babuji's face. His eyes light up like a child's. He wants to stand up, rush to the closet, get dressed and be ready for the departure. 'Not yet,' says Babi. 'Tomorrow!'

Out of desperation and helplessness, I look for ways to see improvement in Babuji's condition. He has developed an uncanny ability to be in different places and different eras at the same time. A time traveller performs similar feats! Whatever I do, I will never be able to see or know those places or join him on his travels. Such is the nature of Babuji's affliction. It's left him with an estrangement, which has led to a terrifying state.

Daytime

Babi gathers us in the kitchen. After performing the ritual, she recounts a story different from all the stories she has narrated on previous occasions.

'We are in Tulmul,' she begins. 'It is springtime and everything is bourgeoning. Temple bells are pealing. Children are swimming in the *naag* (pond). Jigri comes running. Devi has given birth. What shall we name the newborn? Evening falls. Jigri is still undecided. 97,777 names aren't good enough for Devi's newborn calf . . .'

After finishing the story, Babi offers a wish. 'May the darkness dispel! May we never get to leave our beautiful house, our beautiful land!'

Babi pauses. We sit still. She begins again: 'May we return home soon. May we live and die there. May our descendants live happily and never be forced to leave again. Till then, may we remain together!'

Evening

I visit the camp, as I often do whenever I'm in Udhampur. There are 1200 families huddled inside the tents. The women have finished telling the story to their families. Had it not been for the story, they would have perished out of despair. The story has kept them going through the dark times. It has kept hope alive.

Dawn

Babuji doesn't wake up on time for the first time in his life. He has been an early riser ever since his childhood and ever since we can remember. A mysterious smile is dancing on his lips.

'This has never happened before. Is he okay? Shall we wake him up?'

'Let him dream. The happy dream mustn't end,' says Pa.

* * *

September 2016
Jammu

Raging mobs of Muslim youth pelt stones at transit camps set up in Kashmir for displaced Pandits employed under the prime minister's special employment package. About 4000 Pandit youth, whose parents are in camps in Jammu, live in these transit camps. A friend, Sushant Dhar, working in a government department in Srinagar, informs me of his decision to leave Kashmir.

'For good?' I ask him.

'My worst fears have come true,' he says. 'Our camp was attacked by stone-pelters.'

'What next?'

'I will return home to Jammu.'

Sushant's parents live in Jammu in the Buta Nagar Camp for displaced Pandits. For a decade, they lived in a one-room tenement in Muthi.

What kind of homecoming has the government thrust on us? Once again, we're being forced to leave our homeland. We are the twice-displaced people. Many youngsters who spent their early years in squalid camps in Jammu were later given jobs in Kashmir and then, because of persecution, forced to leave Kashmir once again and return to the camps.

Sushant, too, dangles between two 'homes'—a long-lost home in Seer, Kashmir and the one in Jammu, where, after the exodus in 1990, he spent his exiled childhood. He has had a life of strange departures and arrivals. In his camp, lived a Pandit woman whose relatives were massacred by militants in Wandhama in 1998. She, too, died last year. She had been suffering alone, carrying the burden of the martyrdom of her relatives. It is this burden of history that all Kashmiri Pandits will have to live with for the rest of their lives.

* * *

A Day in October 2016

Ma informs me of the fate of her cousin. With nowhere else to go, he and his paralysed wife have sought refuge at an old-age home run by a charitable hospital in Jammu. Their children reside elsewhere.

The question of what will happen to thousands of displaced Pandits who have been languishing in camps and old-age homes for a quarter of a century should haunt the nation.

For over twenty-five years, we've celebrated memory and kept hope alive in our hearts. But are we to accept rootlessness as our natural condition forever?

The mendacious designs of the secessionists in Kashmir include obstructing our efforts to return. Successive state and central governments have failed and betrayed us. Indian human rights activists have ignored us. But we won't let Kashmir slip out of our existence and memory. We will rise and rebel against those who are hell-bent on preventing our homecoming. But our rebellion will be through our writings and activism, not violence and propaganda.

Bhatta Mazar (the graveyard of the Pandits) in Rainawari, Srinagar, still bears testimony to the brutal repression of Pandits by Muslim dynasties that ruled Kashmir in the fourteenth and fifteenth centuries. A generation of Muslims who have no clue about the Pandits now reside in Ratnipora, a village near Pulwama, where twenty Pandit families lived until 1990. Laar, a beautiful stream, flows quietly through Ratnipora. The remnants of an ancient temple stand tall among thirty new mosques that have come up over the last twenty-five years. They bear witness to a history that has been erased by the locals.

The Kashmiri word pann means thread. The thread holding the story of our ancestry, our history and our future has started to wear off. Yet, our part in the story is not over. For centuries, in our ancestral homes in Kashmir and for the last two-and-a-half decades in migrant camps and rented tenements in Jammu, our grandmothers and mothers have recited the story to us. It is time the world heard our story.

Babi's story will remain unfinished so long as it's narrated outside of Kashmir. Will I be able to keep the story alive with the same hope, the same conviction and the same compassion? Ma thinks I will.

17

My Life Has Become Long. I Want to Go Now

July 1994
The Camp
Udhampur

I am back in the camp. I keep returning for reasons I don't quite understand yet. I come here almost every day, although I am done with the school here. I ran away from other places to be here. This is where I must be. I wish there were other places to go, but there is something about this camp that pulls me towards it. It has been ever since I first came here in 1990 and saw these tents, these people and how they live and go about their lives.

There is an inexplicable force at play. I dislike coming here some days, but there are days when I find myself trapped in the most surreal and bizarre situations. Life is not normal here; it is something else. Things happen here the way they are not supposed to. Take, for instance, the way water is supplied in tankers, distributed, collected and consumed. The way men and women wash clothes or utensils, use the toilet and bathe. And the way they cook and sit down to eat. The way the students attend classes and study in their tents in their attempt to clear their exams. The way the teachers teach. The way the women stay awake and cry at night while the men are asleep. The way they lick the tears off their cheeks. The way they fall silent. The way they breathe and get ready for the day. The way they wait for a moment's rest. The way that moment never comes.

You can witness everything that happens here with your own eyes, but you still won't understand it. Not unless you live here. And not just for one day or two days or a week or two weeks or a month or two months, but for an entire year, perhaps two years. These people have been living here for four years. Four years in tents with less than four buckets of water per tent per day on some days. You must live here to understand how these people stay alive.

I could not attend regular college because displaced students were admitted only to the camp college, where they were taught by displaced college lecturers. Unlike the camp school, which is about a dozen shabby canvas tents erected in the camp, the camp college is atop a hill overlooking the town. The students attend classes in the afternoon when the regular college closes. The students at the camp college benefit from the college library, the playground, the canteen and most importantly, proper classrooms. Classes in the camp school are still held in tents. There are no benches, but the authorities have provided blackboards. Students sit on tarpaulin sheets while the teachers don't have proper chairs to sit in. There is very little furniture. During rainy days, most students do not come to school. At lunch break, the students go back to their tents to eat with their families.

The days are mundane. When deaths occur in the camp, people assemble for funerals and offer words of comfort to one another. The sight of funeral processions is unsettling. A grim silence descends on the families living here. The young and the middle-aged live in constant fear of losing their elders.

Four years have passed since our ouster from Kashmir. We wait and wait for a better, hopeful and happy tomorrow. We haven't seen our homes in four years now.

The school headmaster's office is in a tent with a few plastic chairs, a plastic table and a ramshackle cabinet to store things. The headmaster is from Anantnag, Kashmir. He speaks fondly of his house, which he was compelled to desert barely a year after he renovated it. It's the same story as ours and everyone else's. He has stopped boasting of the intricate and artistic woodwork of the ceilings. But his eyes still shine when he talks about the cherry and walnut trees in his old garden. He misses those trees and their shade because in the camp there are no trees. There is not even a sapling in the camp. Not a single flowerpot. Nothing will ever grow here, for the land is barren. The soil is home to rodents, worms, scorpions and all sorts of creatures we've never seen in our lives. Some of them crawl out of the holes and crevices and get into the tents at night. And you can hear the screams of women and children. The men are too tired to even throw them out or do anything about them. The women curse their luck. They go to any lengths to protect their children from these dreadful creatures.

There have been days, full of exhaustion, when I have fallen asleep next to these scorpion and snake hills. Not just out of exhaustion and a sense of submission, but out of a strange sense of bravado, just to see what will happen. Will I get bitten, too? Or will I be spared? What happens when a scorpion bites you? How much pain does it cause? Is it greater than the pain we live with every day? I've known people who have been bitten by snakes and stung by scorpions and somehow survived. And I've known those who died painful deaths. When they were about to be cremated, they seemed to scream, 'Don't burn me yet . . . I don't want to go . . .' Their children covered their bodies with wood and, just before the pyres were lit, they peeped one last time. On their faces was a glimmer of hope to stay alive for one more day, even if it meant spending it in the most wretched circumstances. I want to be able to hold their hands and embrace them, praying for a miracle. I have desperately wished to lay next to them on the funeral pyres. I've longed to invoke the god of death, Yama and plead to him to take me instead and let them live longer so that smiles will return to the faces of their children and their ageing parents, who curse their luck for outliving their children.

A mother whispers to her son, 'Will you be near me when I start burning and when I become ash?'

The school headmaster's family is a large joint family. Some members of his family are renting a two-room set nearby. They have a cooler there. Some families in the camp, too, have coolers in their tents. Others must make do with table fans. These gadgets work only on days and nights when there are no power cuts. But where is the power in summer? No one knows. Some camp-dwellers pooled in money to buy a used diesel-powered generator set. But you need a constant supply of diesel to keep it running.

The problem with table fans is that you can't have them on while gas or kerosene stoves are on. You can either cook or have the fan running. You can't do both at the same time. People use hand fans as the temperature can go up to 45°C. Blisters appear on the arms and necks of children and elders. On such days, women curse their fate and pray for the strength to carry out their chores. They do everything from cooking and cleaning to washing, with no time for rest. The queue for kerosene and ration gets longer and longer. Men wait for their turn with empty sacks and containers. If you don't get kerosene today, there won't be any dinner tonight.

The headmaster carries himself with decorum and poise. He takes classes religiously, despite the increasing administrative workload. He is completely possessed by his subject—mathematics. The blackboard in his class is the most wondrous sight with mathematical problems and solutions, geometrical drawings and equations scribbled all over it. He solves the problems without referring to any of the textbooks. The look on his face, after solving a problem, is that of a saint's. Nothing gives him more pleasure and satisfaction than teaching and seeing his students solve complex problems. Yet, there are a few students who don't understand anything. He smiles forgivingly and says, 'Mathematics is not everything. There are other subjects too.' He also tutors students in the mornings and evenings. Many students have benefited from the tuition, including me.

The camp school is a fifteen-minute walk from our rented two-room house in Barrian. A portion of the ground is also used as a garbage dump. The fence is in shambles. The Jammu–Srinagar National Highway runs nearby. Many shops dot the highway on both sides—car, truck, bus and bike repair shops, petrol and diesel stations, tea shops, fruit sellers and roadside eateries. In the rainy season, the camp is covered in thistles. It is the only thing that grows there. It is an ordeal trying to do anything without getting yourself stung. Anthills erupt by the dozens and buffaloes and cows stray onto the ground to feed on leftovers. And then there are the snakes—cobras and vipers all over the place.

Staying inside tents means being exposed to the risk of snakebites, suffocation and depression. Stepping out of the tents and spending time outside could give you heatstrokes and sunstrokes. A wretched barrenness prevails. At night, an eerie silence blankets the camp, only to be broken by the baleful howling of dogs.

Now that I am back here, I find myself overcome with a sense of futility. It has been a few days since I last visited, even though I walk past this place every day on my way back home after tutoring a shopkeeper's son. The shopkeeper owns two electronic appliance stores in the market. We bought a television set from his shop. I've stayed away from the camp because of the heat. The summer heat has been atrocious this year; it is unbearable. So I spend more time tutoring the boy because the room where I teach him is air-conditioned. He is preparing for the Class Ten board examination that is going to be held in a few months. He asks difficult questions. But I don't get the impression that he will clear his exams. He seems lost in his own world. Some neighbours say that he doesn't need to clear his exams and that even if he fails, it won't be such a bad thing. He has his father's shops and business to look after. His future is secure. The boy wants to know more about me. He's interested in how I cleared my board examination. I don't tell him anything, even though he keeps insisting. So finally, just to motivate him, I tell him it wasn't easy. I say that studying hard is crucial and that one must pay attention. I lie to him. I would never do what I tell him to do, but then his father is paying me Rs 500 per month, which is a big amount.

The canvas of the tents is fluttering vehemently in the wind. A dust storm hits the camp, throwing pieces of paper and cloth, leaves, plastic bags and garbage in different directions. Camp-dwellers rush into their tents and fasten the flaps with ropes. Some of the torn tents have plastic sheets sown onto them.

The tents of the camp school are empty. At night, some people from large joint families use these 'school tents' to sleep in or to discuss the affairs of the camp. Their own tents are too cramped. Sometimes, they buy a bottle of whisky, disposable tumblers and tandoori chicken and spend a few hours inside the tents. And then they talk. It's the same old talk about their glorious yesteryears and their homes and hearths. They talk about the fields, the brooks, the rivulets and the springs running by their houses in Kashmir. They talk about the cold water in the well at the temple in Mattan. They talk about the smell of pinecones and the fragrance of myrrh. They long for just one tiny whiff of the fragrance again. They talk about making apricot jam in the summer and exporting produce. They talk about the days when their barns were full. They talk about the time when their cows and oxen were happy, too. They go on and on. They don't stop. Not even when screams come out of the tents nearby.

They are but a moment away from ecstasy.

One of them mentions Abdul Ahad, a Muslim neighbour whom he trusted and who in turn betrayed him, his family and all other Pandits in the village in 1990.

'The apples and pears that arrive here are from our orchards,' he says. 'We can't even afford our own apples and pears . . .'

They paint these pictures to comfort one another and keep hope aflame in their hearts. They cry. They make promises. They make vows.

'Mata Sharika, take me home and I will renounce everything and build a temple for you in our village,' they pray.

'Lord Krishna, take us back and we will never ever leave . . .'

'Lord Shiva, help us get back to our homes and I will spend the rest of my life in your service . . .'

They sing hymns. They chant. They sing praises about their villages.

'When Lord Ganesha takes me home, the first thing I will do is kiss the soil in my courtyard. I will smear myself with it.'

'Look, I am home . . . Over there is our house and our temple and our brook . . . Come and look . . . We are back home . . . The bad times have ended . . . Lord Shiva has answered our prayers . . .'

They go on and on while a dust storm rages outside their tent.

* * *

Why are we drawn towards the sufferings of others? Why do we gaze at those trying to stay alive while fighting adversity on a daily basis? Why do we derive pleasure in witnessing the battle between life and death? Especially when the battle is not ours.

A giant cloud of dust hovers and momentarily eclipses the sun, providing respite from the blinding light and scorching heat. Specks of dirt stick to my face. The dust storm abates after a while. Evening falls and the sky turns scarlet. Some migrant men and women come out of their tents to inspect the condition of their tents and attend to them. Fortunately, on this occasion, none of the tents have fallen apart, though some of the bamboo poles holding the fabric have dislodged.

I have seen worse storms and worse days. This is nothing. I have seen tents come apart in the heavy rain with families still inside them. I have seen tents get blown away in the heavy wind. I have seen household things fly about and some of them become reduced to nothing. But today, we are lucky. Everything seems intact, by the grace of God. It could have been worse. People thank God.

The runway of the Udhampur Air Force base is close by. Flying sorties and drills take place at night and during the day as well. The MIGs land and take off one after another. The deafening sounds drown out all the other sounds.

An old classmate comes out of a tent, looking dishevelled. We're meeting after a long time, but he greets me with an unusual expression. His eyes meet mine. He lives with his family in a tent. I inquire about the welfare of his family. He looks around desultorily. It is a congested cluster of shanty tents. They look the same. Each tent has a number. It is difficult for an outsider like me to tell one tent from the other. For him and others who live here, I am an outsider.

Every morning, he walks down to a spring at the bottom of a hill to bathe. On his way back to his tent, he carries along a bucketful of spring water for drinking. Pa, Ma and I went through the same routine after we moved from Chabutra to the house in Barrian, where the landlord derived a sadistic pleasure in denying us water by closing the valve of the pipe that supplied water to our bathroom and kitchen.

I will never forget the sight of Babi collecting and storing water even in the smallest of utensils, such as bowls and tumblers, so that we wouldn't need to make frequent trips up and down the hill to ferry water from the spring. But the six of us would not have had adequate water for drinking, cooking, washing and bathing if we didn't carry at least ten buckets of water from the spring every morning. There were days when we would use up the ten buckets of water before noon and then have to make more trips up and down the hill to fetch more water.

Water is the most precious commodity; you can't afford to waste a single drop when it's not easily available to you. You think ten times before using even a little bit. This means you drink less, you don't bathe at home and you go to the spring instead; you really do save every drop. And in the rainy season, going up and down the hill is a perilous activity. Not only is the path to the spring slippery, but it is also full of snake hills. You've got to be lucky to stay alive without being bitten or breaking a bone.

For my classmate, it is a torment to watch his mother and sister struggle for space and privacy in the cramped tent. Almost every man and woman living here is battling spondylitis, dermatitis, gastroenteritis and hypertension. Some elderly people have developed dementia, but their families don't even know what it is. Memory loss and dementia are inconceivable. Why would anyone not remember anything? Such things were unheard of in Kashmir.

Then there are ailments that no doctor in Udhampur can either understand, diagnose or treat.

'We have never seen such outbreaks here,' the doctors say.

They ask the family members of these patients with strange conditions to take them to Delhi or Chandigarh for treatment. But how will they go anywhere?

These diseases are now called 'camp diseases'.

The camp does strange things to people—to their minds and souls. Camp life renders them bereft of many things.

I go near a tent. The two canvas flaps are placed on either side of the tent for light and fresh air to enter. An old man is lying on a bed. He is in his shirt and pajamas. An old woman, his wife, is fanning him with a hand fan. I go closer. The man is delirious. The expression on his face is one of acute sorrow. He seems caught in a reverie. He mumbles some words, the meaning of which I'm unable to decipher. Except for the old couple, there is no one else in the tent. The old woman mutely fans her husband and wipes the drool off his mouth with a towel. Nothing distracts her, not even the presence of a stranger standing at the entrance. She caresses her husband. He smiles and lets out a cry. A touch is all he needs.

I look at the couple one last time and then leave them alone. I will never come back here.

* * *

I will eat only once a day from now on. I will skip the second meal. I have committed the worst sins. I will starve. I won't eat and drink after 3 p.m.

'Why are you doing this to yourself?' asks Babi. She is the only one whom I can confess to and the only one who listens without passing a judgement.

'The only person I can tell everything to is you. But this . . . this I can tell no one. Not even you! I must undertake penance. I don't deserve to live . . .'

'If you go on like this, I will starve too . . .' says Babi.

Six Months Later

I continue to face my own trial. I go on inventing excuses to exonerate myself. There is no justification. There is no exit. I seek solace in the thought that someday my grief and guilt will fade away and that the days of repentance will be over too. But then, yet again, comes the dark night when I am face-to-face with myself. And I hear the same dreadful yet familiar voice. The voice I don't wish to hear ever again for the rest of my life.

> He: 'No matter what you do, you must never tell anyone about this. Not even God. No one will believe you. No one will believe you are capable of such an act. I don't believe you either. Did you really do this or are you lying to me for some reason? Or maybe it was a dream and you've mistaken it to have actually taken place.'
> Me: 'I wish you were right.'

He: 'But then why did you break your own vow?'

Me: 'I am fickle. I give up too soon. I am not meant for such vows . . .'

He: 'Forget that this ever happened. Forgive yourself.'

Me: 'Will you forgive me?'

He: 'Yes!'

Me: 'Would you say the same thing to anyone else who commits such an act?'

* * *

A wintry chill has descended over the camp. It feels as if it is going to snow. Yet again, the season is deceitful! A clan is kept waiting. A family has cooked fish. It is Gada Bhatta, the day when rice and fish are offered to the *ghar devta*—the presiding deity of the house and of the land that has belonged to the people who now live far away from home with nothing.

Some children have painted a portrait of the deity. They claim to have seen him. He is wearing a *pheran** and has a beard. His mane is long and brown in colour. They say he looks like their father when they lived in Kashmir. He diligently partakes of the offering of rice and fish and leaves some behind on the plate for the family members to finish. By doing so, the family will be bestowed with happiness, longevity and prosperity. The house will always be protected. No harm will come to the people who live in the house. But that was in Kashmir and it was how Gada Bhatta was celebrated there.

In the camp, a woman places a bowl full of rice and fish outside her tent–house. The next morning, she finds the bowl empty. The rice and fish have been eaten. She believes that the Lord visited them in the form of a cat. But the woman is wrong.

---

* Pheran is the traditional outfit for both males and females in Kashmir. People wear it in winters.

It is not a cat that came out of nowhere to eat the rice and fish kept outside the tent. It is the Lord of the house, who travelled a long distance from the mountains of Kashmir to the camp in the plains to partake of the promised feast on this special night.

This isn't a fairy tale. This is the story of hope and of the truth we live by. It keeps us alive.

The previous night, the women of the camp narrated tales about the ghar devta answering their prayers. They continue: 'This is our kitchen. This is our living room. This is the barn. This is another barn. This room is for our grandsons when they grow up and get married. This is our bedroom. This is the cow shed. This is Gowri's room. This room is for the guests. This is for the wayfarers. This room is for the ghar devta when he visits us . . .'

The realization that their families are now permanently scattered fills their hearts with longing and sorrow. The distance between them is growing wider and wider even in these tiny tents with not enough space. Sons have deserted their fathers and brothers have parted ways. But there is something that keeps them together. They recount Lord Shiva's boon to the ghar devta. 'Wherever these people live, no matter how big or small their houses may be, you will protect them and they will always worship you. And they will cook fish and rice for you when you visit them once a year . . .'

However, not every family is able to celebrate Gada Bhatta. 'Don't cook meat or fish in this house,' many Dogra landlords have said. This has been their condition for renting the rooms to Kashmiri Pandits.

Some months later, on the eve of Khechi Mavas,* the head of a family narrates the tale of the *yaksh*,† who will knock at

---

* Khechi Mavas, also known as Yaksh Amavasya, is a Kashmiri Pandit festival which is held to satisfy the demands of the ancestors and aborigines.
† The aborigines who lived in the forests during the ancient times.

the door of their house in Kashmir and call the man's name two-and-a-half times. Whoever opens the door while the yaksh is calling the name will be thrown into a sack by the yaksh and taken to a cave in the mountain.

'We will make a snowman in the courtyard,' says the man. But there is no snow in the camp. It will never snow in Udhampur. He starts teaching his grandchildren how to make a snowman.

'Here, take this story,' he says to them. It is from his chest of memories. He hands over the chest to his grandson, asking him to preserve it and keep it for posterity. For his children, grandchildren and great-grandchildren. 'They must know how, on a day like this in Kashmir in the winter, we made snowmen and cooked khichdi and placed it in the courtyard of our house for the yaksh to feast on.'

On these two nights, when the moon is just a black dot in the sky, people almost forget they are in the camp. They believe they are back home. The camp compound becomes the courtyard of their ancestral house. The tent becomes their home in Kashmir. They pray to the ghar devta, imploring him to protect their house from all invasions, intrusions, destruction and calamities. They implore him to partake of the feast—a humble offering of rice and fish! In the morning, they wake up and see foot impressions.

* * *

2010
New Delhi

Rahul Bhat calls me from Bombay. He's now an actor in the film industry. 'Did you know that our friend Anil died?' he says.

After a long pause, I ask, 'How? What happened?'

'A terrible disease. He couldn't be saved.'

'And all this time, we didn't know. We were not with him . . .'

It wasn't a disease that killed Anil. It was the separation from Kashmir that was responsible for his death. His life was destroyed the day he and his family were forced to leave their home. They had nowhere to go. His father lost his business. He lost everything. Everything he had built over the years. All gone! And now he has lost his only hope. His son who had promised to rebuild everything. The entire family has nothing to live for anymore. But I know they will gather pieces of their lives and live. They have no other choice.

I imagine his last moments. He may have wanted to see me. He may have wished for me to meet him one last time—to hold my hand and ask me to hold his. I imagine his last words. 'I don't want to die . . .'

I wasn't by Anil's side during his loneliest moments . . . I wasn't holding his hand at the time . . .

* * *

18–19 April 2011
Winter Hall
Sher-i-Kashmir International Convention Centre (SKICC),
Srinagar, Kashmir

I am in Srinagar at the invitation of the Government of India's appointed group of interlocutors to Jammu and Kashmir. It is a round-table conference with the intelligentsia.

Formerly Hotel Centaur, now a convention centre, SKICC, is situated by the Dal Lake, opposite the Mughal

Gardens and provides an ideal setting for such a conference. It is a beautiful spring day.

I am the only displaced Kashmiri Pandit in the palatial Winter Hall of the convention centre. The rest are prominent Kashmiri Muslims. There are at least twenty people from the rest of India and they are from the fields of law, politics, academia, journalism, art and culture, and the security forces.

At the outset, the interlocutors remind everyone about the expected outcome—that the round-table conference and these dialogues are meant to pave the way for reconciliation and peace processes, and eventually help arrive at a solution to this seemingly unresolvable Kashmir problem. Even if the solution may not be a lasting one.

'How do we build a consensus?' ask the interlocutors. 'How do we understand one another's issues? How do we propose possibilities and solutions? How do we shun narrow perspectives and think of common Kashmiris and humanity? How do we stop the bloodshed? How do we save Kashmir from further deterioration?'

Everyone speaks in turns. Kashmiri Muslims go on and on about Jammu and Kashmir's special status. But soon, the divergences and paradoxes become evident.

Everyone is in conflict with each other.

Where must I begin? How must I begin?

How do you build a consensus and talk about peace and solutions if you haven't even seen how Kashmir's special people—its indigenous minorities—have been living for the last twenty-one years? None of these people have even seen the camps we have been living in for the past twenty-one years. They haven't the faintest idea of what we've been going through and what our issues have been. They don't even know the simplest of our issues.

In such a scenario, how will they understand the real issues facing Kashmiri Pandits and how will they propose ideas and offer solutions to address the problem?

Earlier, the prime minister's Working Group on confidence-building measures had recommended making the return of Kashmiri Pandits a part of State policy.[9] But the State did nothing.

* * *

May 2012

The final 176-page report titled 'A New Compact with the People of Jammu and Kashmir', is submitted by the group of interlocutors to the Government of India. Kashmiri Pandits are mentioned only a few times in the report and only once in the ten-page executive summary. The report contains passing references to two demands—namely, monthly relief money to be raised and reservations for jobs. And that the jobs are to be made available in Jammu. It suggests having the problems of Pandit women addressed through an NGO.

Kashmiri Pandits are referred to as 'migrants', suggesting that we migrated out of Kashmir on our own accord.

Yet again, we stand marginalized, ignored and insulted.

* * *

April 2013
Jammu

I am in Jammu to meet Ma and Pa who live here. Vinod Veerakumar has also come along with me. He is a cinematographer from Mumbai. We are here to make a short film.

We go to the Muthi camp nearby. It is an apartment complex consisting of two-room flats. Almost everyone living here has lived in tents for ten to twelve years (from 1990 to 2002) and then in ORTs for eight to ten years (from 2002 to 2010). That is, half a life, in camps. The children you see here were born in these camps. They call these camps their home. But when they grow up, they will understand what they've been through.

We are greeted by some old men lazily sitting on the porches. Some camp-dwellers are sitting idle and some are playing cards and chatting. Some are ambling aimlessly.

The president of the camp takes us to a flat to meet an old couple. Their children live elsewhere. The old man is smoking a cigarette. Wrinkles criss-cross his sunken cheeks. He smiles a mysterious smile and doesn't speak a word.

My aim is to get him to talk about his house in Kashmir, his childhood and youth, the circumstances leading to his exodus, his early days in the camp and, most importantly, how he feels about the present and future.

'What is in store for us now?' I ask him. He barely speaks a word. Then, after finishing his cigarette, he lisps two sentences. 'What else can happen to us? We're ruined, but we must go on for the sake of our children.' He turns his gaze elsewhere.

We meet another old couple. They offer us tea. The old man adjusts his cap and spectacles as soon as he sees my camera. 'Newspaper wallahs and television wallahs would come in the initial days, take pictures of us, ask us questions and then leave. But there was no mention of us either in the newspapers or the news on the radio. No one comes here any longer. What can I do for you?' he says.

The old man reminds me of Babuji. His karakul cap[*] is exactly like the one Babuji wore. He sits exactly the way

---

[*] A cap made from the fur of the Karakul breed of sheep found in the upper reaches of Kashmir.

Babuji used to sit by the window, holding his cherished transistor in his hand and waiting for a cup of tea. An uncanny resemblance! The cheekbones, the nose and the forehead!

This hopeless wait for the glorious past festers within the hearts of these people. The present is oppressive.

P.N. Kabu, who is in his eighties, is worried that when the time comes for him to depart this world, he shouldn't become the cause of other people's discomfort. Like many others, he, too, lives alone in the camp. His only son, who taught in a school in Gool, was killed by militants in 1997. Kabu epitomizes resilience. In his heart, there is nothing but compassion and forgiveness, even for those who killed his son. Like everyone else, he speaks fondly of his home in Kashmir. His eyes sparkle when he talks about his youth in his village.

We look at photos of a village in Kashmir. Wandhama is a beautiful village situated in the lap of nature. The picturesque views of nature all around make one believe in fairy tales. It's a small hamlet where people live peacefully and quietly. On their faces is innocence. Even death doesn't step foot in this hamlet, let alone talk of people massacring each other. Such is the power of make-believe. You don't feel like taking your eyes off the photo. It casts a spell and you are transfixed. You see stillness. Time was supposed to have protected us, but even time was helpless before the mercenaries, who came masquerading as security forces, butchered innocent people, including children. The worst of massacres! 'A curse,' say people. But this is hatred. This is the result of people's hatred towards us hapless Kashmiri Pandits.

Look at the trees around the abandoned houses. They haven't withered or fallen off. They have grown twice as big. They are still in bloom. They remember everything, don't they? They look old but happy. They, too, are waiting for those who once sat in their shade.

Once again, I go back in time. I remember the day an elderly woman sat crying next to a pile of rubble that had been her dwelling for a decade. I wonder where she is now. She must be here. I pray she is still here. I pray she is happier than she was that day when she sat crying next to the demolished one-room tenement where she lived.

* * *

July 2010
Campsite with ORTs at Muthi, Jammu

Hundreds of ORTs at the camp in Muthi are being demolished. It is the saddest sight, but the outcome will be happy and reassuring for those who have lived here for many years. Sad, because some people are crying—this too is uprootedness. Happy, because people are going to live in a complex now—another camp, but instead of ORTs, they will have two-room flats. Each family has been allotted a flat in the new camp complex in the same neighbourhood.

'Prime minister Manmohan Singh visited us some time ago and cried,' say people. 'Only one refugee can ever know the pain of another . . .' they say. 'He promised to have a better complex constructed for us after seeing us live in such a miserable condition for years. No human should live in such a place. This place is not fit even for animals. We are grateful to him for life for honouring his word to us . . .'

The demolition is going on. People are looking at the structures turn to dust. What do we call these structures?

An elderly woman is sitting on a mound next to a heap of rubble, which a few moments ago were four walls and a roof—a place that the old woman was never able to call home. It was just a temporary dwelling where she lived with her husband for almost a decade. In the woman's lap, is a piece of brick. She holds it close to her chest and refuses to discard it, as if it were her own child. The brick is from the wreckage of her demolished shed. The entire camp is nothing but a huge pile of debris now. Smashed bricks and tiles, blocks of concrete, iron sheets, rusted iron rods, broken frames of doors and windows, decaying wooden pillars, plastic and potsherds cover the plot of land. The woman sits there with the brick in her lap. She can't seem to leave. Her son is busy gathering and moving things, loading the luggage into a vehicle. The brick in the woman's lap is the last remnant of the shelter where she spent one-fourth of her life with her husband. In this place, they grew old, nurturing hopes of a better tomorrow. And now, when it is time to move to a new place that promises better amenities, she can't just leave and forget the old 'miserable' one. The wretchedness and misery have come to grow on her.

* * *

After spending a few days with Pa and Ma in Jammu, Vinod and I travel to Srinagar by road. We stop at the dhabas on the Jammu–Srinagar National Highway. I recount some old stories so that Vinod can frame an image in his mind and even understand the true story behind the film we are about to shoot.

We shoot at Ram Mandir in my old neighbourhood, Safa Kadal in Srinagar. The temple is now in a dilapidated condition. I walk through a lane so narrow that even the rays of the sun don't enter it—a lane sandwiched between clusters of old houses.

Observing me taking photographs and looking around the neighbourhood, a Muslim woman comes out of a house.

She comes in front of me and asks me to recognize her. When I can't place her, she slaps me gently out of affection and bursts into tears.

'I used to carry you in my arms when you were a small boy. You were like my son. You still are. Your grandmother, Babi, was like my mother,' she says.

This is happening for the second time. What are the odds of such a thing happening for the second time? The first time it happened was when I was here some years ago. I can never forget that day and what happened here at this very place.

The woman wipes away her tears. 'Don't stop me today,' she says. 'I have not cried in years. These eyes have had no tears in them ever since Tota died . . .'

She is not the same woman I met the last time, but she looks like her. Such things don't happen in real life. Vinod is stunned. He can't believe what he just saw. He goes on taking photographs.

'You are not going anywhere,' the woman says to us.

A young man with a horse comes out of a house.

'You remember Salama, Doctor Sahab's friend? This is his son . . .'

'Is Doctor Sahab still . . .'

* * *

Salama—the only person whose name was on Babuji's lips when he lay dying and when all other names were forgotten. On his deathbed, Babuji remembered the name.

* * *

During her last years, Babi would often say to us, '*Wumber ha gayam zaeth.*' (My life has become long. I want to go now.)

She rediscovered her love for her husband, my grandfather, when he was fading away.

In her heart, Babi didn't want to die. She wanted to live. She was a lover of life. The greatest lover I have ever known. All she wanted was her Kashmir. The Kashmir which, for her, stood for eternal seasons, for love, for mirth, for life, for happiness, for togetherness, for warmth, for laughter, for sunshine, and for all things that are beautiful and desirable.

18

Babi Is Home Once Again

24 June 2012
Jammu

Pa, Ma and Babi are on a trip to Srinagar. Babi has been to Kashmir four times in the last twenty-two years, each trip lasting five or six days. Twice, she stayed at her brother's place near the army cantonment. On one occasion, she stayed at a hotel in Srinagar and the fourth time, she accompanied some of her relatives on a pilgrimage when they visited temples and a Sufi shrine on the outskirts of Srinagar. During that trip, they spent some days in quietude, found in abundance in temple complexes. Everyone returned with small presents—packets of assorted dry fruits, condiments like saffron and spices and walnut wood and papier-mâché decorations. Upon their return, they fondly spoke of their stay in the familiar locales of the land of their birth—their homeland—where they once lived, where their ancestors were cremated, where they dreamt of nurturing their children and grandchildren and where they wished to die in peace. They recounted the days spent there, gossiped about people and then, with a certain degree of certitude, thought of the trip as the last one in their lifetime. Even with the passage of time—in weeks and months—these trips were not forgotten. The memory of these visits became a source of regular conversations during family get-togethers. Nothing about these journeys faded.

Babi's eyes sparkle when we ask her about her life and her parents. She comes from a vast joint family and still remembers everything about her brothers, sisters, uncles, aunts and cousins. She traces the entire genealogy of her family—the names of relatives, their ages, hobbies, tastes, likes and dislikes, the yarns they spun and the riddles they made up. Every person has more than one name. She even knows intricate details about the relatives of her relatives, including the distant ones! Her memory is a cage from which nothing escapes. We are baffled by the infallibility of it all. She loves to talk about her mother-in-law. We call her *Dyed*—a common term of endearment for a grandmother. She teaches Aishwarya and Amia the Kashmiri language and the two of them converse with her in her beloved mother tongue.

Earlier, Babi would visit us in Delhi twice or thrice a year. As the years go by, it becomes challenging for her to travel. Travelling by train, especially, is out of the question now, given her advancing age and health conditions. She walks with great difficulty and requires support to climb stairs. She has turned frail.

The last time she stays with us is a few weeks before the onset of summer in 2012. She takes a plane from Jammu to Delhi. I bring her home from the airport. She spends most of the days in bed, reciting hymns that I neither understand nor pay attention to. Upon my insistence, she spends an hour or so in the drawing room every evening, particularly after dinner and looks at the television screen with utter disinterest. We sit together and watch various shows on television. She sits silently and waits for the opportunity to start a conversation about something that took place years ago.

She enjoys sharing anecdotes from her youth. When the conversations end and we get busy with household chores, she lingers, pretending not to feel bored.

She complains of indigestion and nausea and heavily self-medicates. She makes frequent phone calls to her nephew, Dr Kamlesh Dewani, asking him to suggest some tablets or syrup. Every night, she gets out of bed an hour before dawn, quietly tiptoes into the kitchen, switches on the light, surveys the cabinets, takes a saucepan from the drawer, turns on the gas stove and makes sheer chai for herself. The rest of us are fast asleep. Then she washes the utensils and sips the tea in the dead of the night, sitting all by herself in desolate silence and stillness and then goes back to bed, content and at peace. She bathes at dawn and in the mornings, she says, 'I made some tea in the night and the ache in my tummy disappeared.'

She doesn't do anything significant during the day. Small things keep her busy—fixing buttons on a shirt or darning a torn sari. There was a time when she performed extraordinary feats, such as walking miles to meet her relatives or travelling to places all by herself. She never complains of boredom. She just waits for the moments to pass. All she owns are a few saris, a towel, a purse, some spools of white thread, a box of needles, a prayer book, a comb, a bottle of hair oil, a toothbrush and a medicine kit. She also has some money—relief money that is deposited in her bank account by the government every month. It's her money, but she gives half of it to Henna, Aishwarya and me. She uses the rest to buy us presents. She rarely buys anything for herself.

Other household items that we typically treasure do not entice her. Nothing appeals to her except our company. She has never exhibited signs of attachment to any of her belongings. Having conversations with people, indulging in gossip, attending weddings and participating in family functions interest her more than anything else. Even though she narrates the same anecdotes repeatedly, the renditions are different every time. Each narration is a consummate tapestry of enchanting tales about people and strange happenings during her youth.

I am often amazed at the way she conjures up tales of adventure, deftly weaving them partly from strands of memory and partly from her rich imagination. One wonders if any of those events have ever taken place. Such events mostly occur in dreams. In one such story, a lion makes a grand appearance. In another, a viper keeps coming home every now and then to sip milk from a bowl in the kitchen.

One night, she has a panic attack. She starts trembling; her hands and forehead are cold; her breathing is laboured and her voice is feeble. Despite the terrifying sight, we manage to remain calm and call Dr Dewani. He arrives immediately, examines her, talks to her, cracks a few jokes while we watch nervously and finally reassures her that we are around and won't let anything happen to her. She chuckles and then flashes a tremulous smile, partly out of fear and partly because she is relieved to see all of us around her.

I feel a shiver while clinging to her trembling arm. Anything can happen now or in the days to come. This isn't the first time she has suffered an attack at our place.

She calls me to the room and hands me a woollen shawl.

'Get this dry-cleaned,' she says to me. I notice that the shawl doesn't need any dry cleaning. It is clean and in immaculate condition—almost as good as new. It smells fresh as well. She still insists that I get it dry-cleaned. The next morning, I take the shawl to the dry cleaner. After a couple of days, I return the dry-cleaned shawl to her. She places it back in her bag.

'Aren't you going to wear it?' I ask. She smiles at my question. 'The shawl is for you to place on me when I am gone,' she says casually. A strange smile plays on her lips. 'Who knows, you might need the shawl tomorrow itself!' she adds.

'Don't say that. Never say such things . . .'

'After I go, I will still see you in my dreams,' she says. 'And I will be in your dreams . . .'

'May we always be in each other's dreams . . .'

She is not prone to anxiety and is energetic and zestful when it comes to visiting her relatives or hosting guests at her house in Jammu. The house that Pa bought for her. She is happy now because of the house. She still misses her old house in Safa Kadal, Srinagar. Her conversations are laced with wit and humour. Her laugh is hearty.

She's the same Babi she was a few years ago. But she is not able to do certain things.

* * *

In 2009, when I went to Kashmir, I didn't tell her about the trip, thinking she might get worried. But when Pa informed her that I was in Kashmir, she insisted on speaking to me on the phone. She called me and said, 'You didn't tell me that you were going home.'

Even after twenty years of being in exile, *home* was still Kashmir.

As she grew older, her memory became stronger and her renditions more intense. Pa would call her Zeenat Aman. One day, at the wedding of a relative, she dressed up in a new blue sari and resembled a bride.

* * *

I am delighted at the prospect of her spending some more time in Srinagar again. Henna and her family are there too. They are on a pilgrimage to the Holy Cave of Amaranth. I make a few calls to them while they are on their way to Srinagar. They talk excitedly about how fragrant the air is there.

They have arranged for a couple of rooms in a developing residential neighbourhood in Srinagar. A visit to our old ancestral house is on the itinerary. It's been twenty-two years. Ever since the exodus in 1990, Babi has not visited her old house. Despite having visited Srinagar four times previously, she has not been able to go to the house. The place is still a hub of militancy, so it isn't safe for Pandits to go there. I've always prayed for such a visit to happen. I have dreamt of this day—when she sees her old house after all these years. This time, I'm hopeful of the dream turning into reality. I am more excited than she is and I want to be with her right now. I want to watch her look at her house. I want to see how she will react and what she will do. I am not sure if she will be able to go inside the house. But perhaps she will figure out a way to do it. The new owners may let her inside the way they allowed me some years ago.

Anything is possible when Babi is around.

They reach Srinagar in the evening. I call Pa to inquire about Babi's health. 'She was fine throughout the journey. She braved the ordeal. She's okay and resting now. But she wants to be up and about,' he tells me.

A grand plan awaits them the next day—a drive through the city, a visit to the old neighbourhood and then her 'home'. A visit to other places too.

But the news from Srinagar is disturbing. A 200-year-old Sufi shrine of Sheikh Syed Abdul Qadir Jeelani—locally called Dastgeer Sahib—is set ablaze in Downtown Srinagar. Violent clashes between the people and the police forces are ongoing. Some parts of the city are under curfew. Thousands of policemen are patrolling the streets. The residents are indoors as unrest grips the city. The situation is bad, but it's no surprise—days of peace are rare in Srinagar.

I keep calling Pa every hour to find out how Babi is doing. At night, Pa calls me and reveals, 'She vomited and had stomach cramps. We took her to a private hospital nearby. The doctor examined her, administered dextrose intravenously and said there was nothing to worry about.'

I speak to Ma, who is worried because Babi has fallen ill there and they had to take her to a hospital where they didn't know anyone. But Ma is relieved when Pa's Muslim friends come to check on them. She says, 'Two Muslim nurses attended to Babi. One of them was kind and compassionate. When her shift ended, the other one took over. For some reason, this nurse first hesitated to stay close to Babi. She feigned ignorance when it came to changing the drip. But later, she changed her attitude and attended to her with utmost care.'

Pa rings me up again to say, 'We've taken her to SHMS Hospital now. There were a few complications. Don't worry. I will keep you posted.'

It is past midnight. I pass the phone to Aishwarya and she talks to Pa. I can no longer sleep.

An hour later, the phone rings again. It's Pa.

'The doctors did a scan. They now say she needs surgery immediately. But the chances of survival are slim. Her intestines are a mess. If she survives the surgery, she won't live for more than a few days. We've got to decide quickly.'

'What do we do?' I ask.

'What do you suggest?'

I am clueless and don't know what to say.

'What should we do?'

'We should opt for surgery. It is the best thing to do. We should take a chance. Miracles happen.'

Within a few minutes, the phone rings again.

Pa now says that Babi is not doing well. 'She has gone into a semi-conscious state. Let's not go in for surgery,' he says.

A nursing orderly in the ward walks up to him and says, 'Why take on the risk of surgery when her chances of survival are slim? Keep your mother with you. Serve her well during this difficult time. Let her live a few more days. Let her be with you.'

'Let us bring her home tomorrow. To Jammu,' I say. 'But in case she is in no condition to travel, either by air or road, then we stay at the hospital there. For as many days as it takes.'

At 2.30 a.m., I book a flight to Srinagar for the next morning.

My flight lands in Srinagar at 1.30 p.m. I don't know what awaits me. At the airport taxi counter in Srinagar, I ask for a taxi to the hospital. The taxi drivers and the taxi booth operator inform me that no one will go to the hospital because the area is under curfew due to ongoing violence. The taxi drivers refuse to take the risk of ferrying passengers to the city. I make frantic inquiries and plead with the taxi drivers, some of whom are taking tourists to other places in the Kashmir Valley. There are taxis going to Gulmarg and Pahalgam, but none to SMHS Hospital in Karan Nagar. After moments of desperation, a kind-hearted taxi driver finally relents. 'I'll take you to the hospital. Hop in.'

He is a godsend.

The road leading to the city is deserted. The shops are closed and not a single pedestrian is walking on the road. Fortunately, the policemen keeping vigil in the armoured vehicles parked on the roads don't stop us. The taxi driver talks to me and, sensing my anguish, tries to comfort me.

'God will be kind,' he says. 'Humans are powerless, but we must be fearless in times like these.'

When we reach Lal Chowk, I call Babi's brother, Mohanji. He asks me to rush to the hospital immediately. 'I am waiting for you at the gate,' he says.

I tell him I am on my way. I reach the hospital in forty minutes. I rush to the ward. Grand-uncle is waiting at the gate. His nose is bleeding.

'What happened?' I ask.

'Don't pay attention to my nose,' he says. 'Rush upstairs. She's waiting for you.'

It takes me five more minutes to reach the general ward on the second floor. I enter the ward, which is a vast hall with beds on both sides. Some injured people with bandages and casts on their bodies are being wheeled into it. I walk thirty steps and reach the end of the ward. A matron comes out of an adjacent hall on the left. Pa's uncle points towards me. 'This is her grandson,' he says.

The matron looks at me with compassion and says, 'She passed away a few moments ago.'

I enter the hall and go to Babi's bed. My mother is sitting next to her. She lifts the white cloth from Babi's face and asks me to pour a spoonful of water into her mouth. I struggle to keep my hand steady while pouring water into Babi's mouth. Her lips are grey and her tongue is curled.

I inform Aishwarya. She books a flight to Jammu.

I go to look for my father downstairs. He is standing outside the hospital gate, talking to some people and making arrangements for our travel back to Jammu.

He breaks down when he sees me. The matron and her staff wrap Babi in white cloth and hand her over to us.

A thought crosses our minds—that of cremating her in Srinagar, the place of her birth, her homeland, where she was born, got married, gave birth to her only child (my father), reared her grandchildren and lived for years. The crematorium is not far from the hospital. But the area is under curfew. 'Jammu is our home now,' says Pa. 'Let us take her home.'

The ward staff see us off at the hospital gate. They are crying. 'She died in her home,' a Muslim woman says.

There are no ambulances available to Jammu and the local ambulances cannot leave the Kashmir province. A private Chevrolet SUV is available for hire. We lay Babi down in the middle seat. Around 4.30 p.m., we set off for Jammu. On the way, we make a brief stop at the house my parents and sister's family had rented. We collect Babi's belongings—a bag and a pair of sandals.

We make calls to friends, neighbours and relatives in Jammu. Some of them begin preparing for our arrival. Another strange journey! Bringing Babi home! From one home to another.

A day earlier, she had plans to visit her home in Safa Kadal. But it was not destined to be so.

She had survived three previous attacks. Why couldn't she survive this one? Or live just one more day to be able to see her old house one last time and spend some time talking to her neighbours, some of whom would certainly have recognized her. But then she survived the three previous attacks, only to see this day.

She died in the land of her birth, her homeland. My only regret is that I couldn't make it on time to see her, talk to her during her final moments and kiss her one last time. A kiss in return for the thousands of kisses she'd given me. A familiar smell wafts in the air. It's the scent of her hands.

'Muslims are responsible for our plight,' she said to people there in the hospital. Pa says everyone laughed because they understood the emotion in her caustic expression. They called her 'Mother'.

We drive past Pampore, famous for its saffron. Babi's town. Every town is her town.

Pa falls asleep soon after we have tea at a highway tea shop. He hasn't slept for sixty-three hours. Ma is tired too. She refuses to eat or drink water. She can't sleep. I clasp my palm around Babi's feet, which are tied together firmly with a string.

We reach Jammu at 1.30 a.m. At last, we are home.

Family and friends are waiting. I spend the night next to Babi in her room. Tired and drowsy, I eventually fall asleep.

The Next Morning

Aishwarya and Amia reach Jammu.

We wrap Babi up in a shawl. The same shawl that she had asked me to get dry-cleaned a couple of months ago. We take her away for cremation amidst the chanting of Vedic hymns and prayers. Her final wish has been fulfilled. During the last few months, she would always say, 'Why am I not dying? I have lived enough. This life is long.' She must have told Pa hundreds of times, 'I have only two wishes. I shouldn't be ill for a long time. You should be by my side at the time of my death. I want you to carry me to the crematorium and light the pyre.' Pa would respond in his own characteristic manner, 'I will burn you with my own hands.' She'd laugh and bless him.

The funeral pyres at crematoriums have always fascinated me. The smell of burning flesh and bones, the cinders and the ashes that remain in the end! The deep loneliness of the pyres after the mourners leave. The flames consume the bodies and, at night, the embers, last traces and remnants—pieces of bones—remain intact. These remnants crave a human touch. The bones crumble in our hands when we pick them up and put them into earthen pots. The warm ash settles down in a small heap, losing its warmth as the night progresses. Nothing else exists. Yet a strange scent wafts through the air. A scent that is quite distinguishable from any other that one has known. It is neither the scent of life nor death, neither being nor non-being. At the crematorium, people become spiritual and philosophical. It is as though wisdom and enlightenment dawn upon them, not by chance or accident but by means of some divine intervention. This feeling is transitory and vanishes the moment people step out of the crematorium. For a moment, I find myself caught in this magical spell of transient wisdom and knowledge. The unsettling realization that everything perishes in the end and that life is not to be spent worrying. If only we could visit the crematorium for a short while every day, many of life's beautiful secrets would be revealed to us. Revelations that could lead us to a more fulfilling and purposeful existence! One could become detached and, therefore, experience joy and bliss. Perhaps the constant thought of death turns us into beautiful beings.

Two days later, just after dawn, we go to the crematorium to collect Babi's ashes. A familiar scent of new life is hidden in these warm ashes. Pa's friend, who is an Arya Samaj scholar and teacher, performs a Vedic ritual. The ashes are still warm. We pour water on the ashes. Another family is performing a ritual, too. A young woman is crying inconsolably. She is referring to the mound of ash as her loved one.

We collect Babi's ashes in two earthen pots, decorate them with marigolds and set off for Akhnoor, a village not very far from our house in Jammu. The Chenab River runs through this village. We cross a steel bridge and reach the ghat of the Chenab. During the monsoons, the transporters who work for timber merchants throw hundreds of logs of timber into the river and the waters ferry these logs from one place to another. Some youngsters dive into the river, even when it is in fury, to gather driftwood.

I hold a fistful of ash in my hands one last time before placing it back in the pot. Offering a prayer, we immerse the ashes in the water and watch them float instantly. The water changes colour for a moment. The flowers float in a zigzag movement and slowly move away from the riverbank. I watch the flowers until they are no longer visible.

'One day you will hold my ashes in your hands,' Babi had said. 'I will be happy that day.'

The river flows into Pakistan. For those of us who witnessed our elders pine endlessly for one last homecoming, it was Pakistan we always cursed for creating a mess in Kashmir—our homeland—and for making us leave and spend the rest of our lives in waiting and in exile. For many of us, it would take years or even decades to fathom the impact of the loss of a generation that traced its ancestry to a unique people who originated from the land of *rishis* (sages) over 5000 years ago. Now, the descendants of these people struggle to keep the consciousness of this fabulous ancestry alive.

The people of Babi's generation are fast fading into oblivion and nothingness.

Babi's death has made me realize how little I know of her life, which spanned over eight decades. Whatever is left must be preserved with the utmost care.

The elderly nurse a yearning to return to their homeland; the middle-aged and the young oscillate between a strange past (which was once beautiful but then changed for the worse) and an uncertain present; the children born in exile are grappling to assimilate into the new and carve a new identity. They are growing up with a fragmented memory, which is the only thing their parents and grandparents have.

In a cameo titled 'Thirty-Six Hours', Pa sums up the story of Kashmiri Pandits in two sentences: 'He gave me freedom for thirty-six hours; I gave him freedom forever.' (Referring to the 1990 ultimatum to Kashmiri Pandits to leave Kashmir in thirty-six hours.)

The river takes Babi far away, beyond the imagined borders of hope, despair, pain and longing. Yet, there are a few more places where she would have desired to go. For her, there was always one more place to set foot on and explore, even when, for many of us, there was nowhere else to go.

The next day, Pa writes an obituary for Babi. It reads:

'Uma Shori Gigoo passed away in Srinagar, Kashmir. She was cremated in Jammu and the ashes were immersed in the Chenab at Akhnoor. The next day, a *hawan* (fire ritual) was performed at home. That was the last day of mourning. Rice and water are not offered to the deceased. Neither is a lamp lit in the evenings. Other rituals will not be held at all. The dead don't eat anything; they don't drink water and they don't need a lamp when the evening sets in. They don't hear the melodramatic, horrible, fearful and weird wail. This family tradition should and will continue.'

* * *

Pa informs the relief commissioner's office of Babi's passing. The money deposited in Babi's bank account every month is no longer needed.

19

We Will Go Back, Even if It
Takes Us Several Lifetimes

An Evening in the Summer of 1991
Udhampur, Jammu Province

I am sitting on the steps of a ghat by the river. In front of me flows the Devika, the River Ganga's younger sister. The light is fading. A body has been burning on a pyre for a long time now. There are no people. Smoke from the burning pyre is rising to the sky. The smell of burning flesh and the crackle of burning bones are the only signs of life and time.

The sun has set. The moon is out.

Notes from a flute waft in from somewhere. My gaze doesn't leave the burning pyre. The flames are dying at last. Only a heap of ash is left, with a crown of embers adorning the pyre. He who may have lived for almost a hundred years is gone and will never come again to the ghat, as he may have been doing every morning and evening to offer prayers and to take a dip in the holy waters of the Devika—his only saviour and the saviour of all those who live and die here. 'All those who come to her and bathe in her waters are redeemed.' So goes the belief!

The sound of the flute gets closer. A flute seller stands in front of me, playing a flute. His gaze is fixed on me as his fingers rhythmically tap on his flute. The melody is beguiling. Looking into my eyes, he stops playing and hands me his flute without saying a word. His expression conveys everything.

'I have no money,' I say to him.

'Don't worry about the money,' he says. 'Keep the flute and pay me some other day when you have anything that you wish to give me.'

By the time I place my fingers on the six holes of the flute, he is gone. The song comes to an end, but the melody is still playing in my ears.

Some Days Later

Sitting in a corner, I try to play the flute. A jarring sound is all that I hear. I try again and again. Still the same jarring sound . . .

Some Days Later

Pa takes me to meet 'Masterji', his friend and colleague, who teaches music at his college. His name is Bushan Lal Kaul. He's tuning his sitar when we enter his quarters. 'My son wants to learn the flute,' Pa says.

'Are you ready?' Masterji asks. 'It will take years.' I nod. 'Come tomorrow for your first lesson,' he says.

The next day, he teaches me how to hold the flute and produce sound. 'We will get you a new flute sometime. This one is out of tune and not meant for serious learning,' he says, referring to the flute seller's flute.

One Year Later
The Terrace of Our Rented House

I practise the notes Masterji teaches me every day. That's all I do. Sit on the terrace and play the flute. Nothing else. There is an expression of worry on Ma's face.

* * *

A Day in the Summer of 1992
Delhi

Despite being blind (having lost his sight to small pox in his childhood), Masterji leads the way in the dark and dingy lanes of Delhi's Chawri Bazaar. We are on a trip to the capital to get his sitar repaired at a music instrument shop. Buying a new flute is also on the cards.

Having nowhere else to stay, we spend the night at a makeshift camp for migrants in Delhi. The next day, we take the train back to Jammu. I am the proud owner of a new flute.

* * *

A Day in the Spring of 1993
Masterji's Quarters

Masterji says, 'I will speak to Omkar Nath Raina's son. You go to him to learn the nuances of the flute.'

* * *

A Day in the Summer of 1994
A Village on the Outskirts of District Udhampur, Jammu

I'm waiting for my guru, Anil Raina, son of the illustrious sitar maestro and music composer of Kashmir, Pandit Omkar Nath Raina, to return from his school, where he teaches music. I am thinking about what he will teach me today. I am hoping he introduces me to a new raag. But deep in my heart, I know he will stick to the usual notes. 'One mustn't be impatient,' he has been saying to me ever since he agreed to take me under his tutelage. I am bound by the *guru–shishya parampara* (teacher–student tradition) to not do anything on my own.

Shortly before sundown, he returns home. 'I am going to take a nap, but you start practicing,' he instructs. I lift my flute and begin:

> *Sa, Re, Ga, Ma, Pa, Dha, Ni, Sa*
> *Sa, Ni, Dha, Pa, Ma, Ga, Re, Sa.*

I practise for two hours, hoping to be taught something new. Even in his sleep, my guru nods every now and then and winces at every false note. When he wakes up, he doesn't waste even a moment to begin his practice.

Birds start chirping outside—a sign they are back in their nests after flying all day long. I sit at my guru's feet with my eyes closed. Afar, in a shanty along a mountain slope, a Gujjar woman is lighting a lamp. This happens every time my guru plays Raag Yaman.

The next day, I am to go down a hill to the spring and ferry water. Mother's spondylitis has been aggravated. She wears a belt; there's no other way out. Babi lines up the utensils. When we return from the spring with two buckets full of water, she starts pouring the water into empty vessels—first into the big ones, then into small containers. Then, to Pa's surprise, into small saucepans and spoons. 'I am not mad,' she says. 'Every drop must be stored or else . . .'

Babi is the most sensible and practical of us all. 'Stop intervening in the kitchen affairs,' she says. 'You must focus on yourselves. Learn to live and be happy. We still have one another and we still have the means to live. Think of those who don't have what we have. Learn to stave off bad thoughts. Can't you even do this much? If you do this much, we will be a better lot.'

Thanks to Babi's relentless efforts, Pa doesn't cry anymore. Babi has achieved what no doctor could have.

The summer is turning out to be horrid, with no proper water supply in our rented accommodation. Our days are spent getting water from outside. Water tankers, public taps on roadsides, other people's houses, a spring at the foothills. But we are not alone. Around twenty displaced Kashmiri Pandit families in the neighbourhood are facing a similar ordeal.

'We should look for a better place,' says Ma. 'A place where we don't have to carry out this uphill task every day.'

I find it difficult to stay home. My music lessons take place on alternate days. I want to be at my guru's place all the time so that I don't miss out on lessons. On weekends, my guru goes to Jammu to spend time with his family living there. I'm happiest on Tuesdays, when I can be back at his place for lessons. Still no luck with being taught a new raag!

At last, after several months of teaching me Raag Yaman, he takes a compassionate stance. 'We will start Bhairav today,' he says. Little does he know that I have already copied it from him and have been secretly practising it at home. Yet, my fingers tremble at the very thought of getting the *komal rishab** right in front of him.

Adjacent to our two-room set is a one-room tenement with another Pandit family of six members—grandfather, grandmother, father, mother, son and daughter. The ten-year-old son comes to meet me on the terrace, bringing his flute and pestering me to teach him. My excuses—I am still learning and I am not good enough to teach anyone, not yet at least—fall flat.

The boy is adamant. His eyes conceal a fiery look, as though he's burning inside. He wins me over by playing an intricate piece that I've been struggling with. I wonder how he has managed to do it. He blurts out the truth. 'I listen to you whenever you play the flute,' he says. 'I don't know what else to do but copy you.'

His mother complains to Ma, 'My son is going astray. All he wants to do is play the flute. He keeps bunking school. I am worried. What will he do in life? My daughter, too, supports him. She says we must let him do what he wants. Will you ask your son to drive some sense into him? What will this flute playing fetch him? Doesn't he realize what we are going through? His father remembers everything about his childhood but can't recall his last meal . . .'

Ma comforts her, saying, 'Don't worry. He will realize soon . . .'

The family is from Bandipora, Kashmir. Just another displaced Kashmiri Pandit family living in Udhampur.

A Day

I am sitting by the roadside, waiting for my guru to return from his school. Two small girls are bathing a calf in a pond.

---

* Komal Rishab is a note in the Hindustani classical music scale.

The sound of splashing water and the laughter of the girls have me in a trance.

'Why are you sitting idle and wasting time?' my guru chides, breaking my reverie. 'You should be practising all the time . . .'

A Day

I am sitting in a corner at the terrace of our house. At the far end is a newly married woman combing her hair. She's from Jaipur. Her husband is a fighter pilot and posted at the Udhampur Air Force Station. They are new arrivals in Udhampur and have recently moved into the house.

> She: 'Where have you been the last few days?'
> Me: 'I have been around. Where else will I go?'
> She: 'Then why haven't you been playing your flute?'
> Me: 'I was unwell.'
> She: 'Can you play today if you're feeling better?'
> Me: 'How about tomorrow? I still have a cold and cough.'
> She: 'I haven't been able to comb my hair properly ever since you stopped playing.'

* * *

One Day in the Summer of 1994
Pandit Bholanath Prasanna's House, Allahabad

I play a composition in Raag Multani. Panditji listens quietly. 'You play for the radio?' he asks.

'No, guruji, I am learning . . .'

'Who is your guru?'

I tell him everything.

I touch his feet and seek his blessings. I muster courage and tell him the purpose of my visit. 'Guruji, I have come to you to buy some flutes for my guru and myself. There is no music shop in Udhampur that sells good-quality flutes.'

He points to a pile of flutes in his room and asks me to choose any flute. I pick up four flutes of four different sizes and scales. Two for myself and two for my guru.

'Take these two, but leave the other two which are my personal flutes. These two are from 1968.'

I throw a tantrum like a mad person. 'Guruji, I want these two . . .'

After a lot of negotiation and yeses and maybes and nos, he relents. 'You are obstinate, but I like your tenacity and choice,' he says. 'I would have chosen these very flutes if I were you.'

I play the flutes to check if they are well tuned. I inspect the holes, their size, position, alignment and distance from one another, just as my guru has taught me. 'The seven holes should be in a straight line,' my guru had said.

Panditji observes me keenly as though he's testing me. After some time, he stops me. 'The only instrument you will ever need to tune is yourself, my son. Tune yourself well and you will even play the most defective of flutes. Take these flutes and surrender to them, and they will always remind you of me and my younger self when I was your age, learning music from my father and learning how to make flutes and tune them. This is what my father taught me: one must learn how to tune oneself first and the instrument will take care of itself. I am passing on the secret to you.'

Two of the flutes bear his finger impressions. 'Always sit at your guru's feet,' he says before letting me go. 'Someday, music will save you.'

While roaming the streets of Allahabad, I hear music coming from a decrepit house. I am unable to keep myself from barging in. In a large hall, several children of varying ages are sitting on the floor and facing a young man playing the flute. Some of the children fidget with small flutes in their hands, while others play. After a while, the man stops playing and walks up to me to find out the reason for my intrusion. I explain how his mesmerizing recital led me into the house and tell him how lucky I think his students are to have him as their guru. 'You're wrong,' he says with an inscrutable expression on his face. 'You don't seem to have noticed these children carefully. They are homeless children suffering from cerebral palsy. First, you must learn to pay attention; only then will you be able to hear the music.'

The man permits me to spend the rest of the night in the house. At midnight, I play my flute hoping to attract the attention of some children.

However, not a single child looks at me. My presence is immaterial, as is the presence of any other person. Music is their only companion.

'I don't know who God is or where he resides, but I know for sure that if you wish to be heard by him, music is the only way,' says the young teacher when I am about to leave in the morning. He gives me the impression that he doesn't want me to leave yet. 'Stay for some more time,' his eyes seem to say.

'These children are my teachers,' he whispers.

* * *

Banaras–Sarnath

I have a room in a *dharamshala* (shelter for travellers) at Godowlia in Banaras. The *maharaj* (caretaker) says I might have to share it with other guests if they run out of rooms. The dharamshala overlooks a ghat. The window frames the Ganga.

I am dejected and heartbroken after facing rejection at the Services Selection Board, Allahabad. Not being selected has jolted me. Therefore, I have come to Banaras. I don't want to go back to Udhampur. I don't wish to go anywhere else now. Banaras is the only place for me now.

All I do the whole day is roam around the city. In the morning and evening, I sit all by myself on the steps of the ghat next to the dharamshala. I look at people—pilgrims, mendicants and swamis, who come to the ghat and go about their chores. People perform puja, rituals and last rites. They take a dip in Ganga, meditate, hum hymns and take boat rides.

Along the ghat are several other dharamshalas. Some for tourists, some for the homeless and the elderly, and some for those who are waiting for their last breaths. They have no other purpose or dream left to be fulfilled. They are just waiting to die. Given a choice, they would prefer to die at this very moment.

Many elderly women with shaved heads sit by the windows, looking at the Ganga the way I do. They are widows. They have nowhere else to go.

The ghats are dotted with both burning and burnt pyres. These widows are waiting for their final call before they find a resting place on one such pyre. Their children have already made arrangements for their cremation and some basic rituals once they are gone. Their families may not even attend their last rites or the post-cremation rituals now that the money for the same has been paid to the caretakers of the dharamshalas. These widows have a lot to give to the world. Their eyes are full of love. But the world has nothing left for them.

The maharaj of the dharamshala is a wise man. He is unmarried and doesn't like to talk about himself. He says his happiness is in serving others, especially the guests at the dharamshala. The owner of the dharamshala lives in another place.

I wish to let go of my worries and forget the rejection and sadness. I wish to let go of my burdens. Perhaps I am not meant for the army. Perhaps I am meant for a variety of things. I go to the ghat and play my flute. Some people sit next to me for a while and listen quietly. There are some who notice the flaws in my flute playing.

'Do you know, young man, our Banaras is the land of music and devotion?' says a bystander to me. 'You must find a good guru in life.'

I ask the maharaj the way to Ustad Bismillah Khan Sahib's house. He laughs and says, 'Just hop on a rickshaw outside and ask to be taken to Khan Sahib's house.'

I do as I am told. The rickshaw wallah takes me through the lanes and bylanes of Banaras. People chew paan and spit everywhere and the paan-stained streets lead to Khan Sahib's residence. We enter a narrow lane. A sign board reads: Padma Vibushan Ustad Bismillah Khan Sahib Lane.

The narrow lane is dotted with butchers and meat shops. The smell of meat is all around. The drains are red with the blood of slaughtered sheep, goats and chicken. Goat heads stare at me with bloodshot eyes as I try to look away to avoid the gory sight. Chickens' throats are slit and they are left to bleed and die in plastic drums. They are then chopped into pieces, packed in black plastic bags and handed over to customers.

We arrive at a wooden gate leading to a house. 'This is the house,' says the rickshaw wallah. 'That will be Rs 5.'

The door is half open. As soon as I enter, a cacophony breaks out among some boys and men. '*Bane Miya bhaag gaya, Bane Miya bhaag gaya.*' (Bane Miya has run away.) I'm afraid that a child might have run out of the house and gotten lost in the lanes. As I lean against one of the pillars in the veranda, a boy comes running and screaming into the house, 'Bane Miya mil gaya, Bane Miya mil gaya.' (Bane Miya has been found.) What a relief!

The next thing I see is a middle-aged man entering the house with a white goat in his arms. He is stroking the goat's mane and saying, 'Shaitan hai Bane Miya, bhaagte rehte hain.' (Bane Miya is naughty like the devil; he keeps running away.)

'Who are you?' the man asks.

'I am here to meet Ustad Bismillah Khan.'

'Khan Sahab does not meet journalists during Muharram. Come back after Muharram.'

I explain that I am not a journalist and that I've come all the way from Udhampur to see Khan Sahab.

'Udhampur?'

'It is near Kashmir.'

'Kashmir? You have come all the way from Kashmir to meet him?'

'Yes, I am a big fan of his music. I'm also learning the flute.'

'Sorry, but these days Khan Sahab spends most of the time all by himself, praying and fasting. He is in no mood to see anyone. Come back after a few days.'

Bane Miya starts grazing in the courtyard. He is tied to a pole with a rope.

I don't want to leave, so I keep returning to Khan Sahab's house day after day. Days go by without any luck. Then one day, when I'm back in the house, someone yells from the staircase.

'Kaun hai bhai?' (Who is it?)

And then comes the moment I've been waiting for. Ustad Bismillah Khan Sahab is in front of me. He is dressed in black. A black lungi and a black half-sleeved shirt. He has a sombre look on his face—a mourner's face!

'You've come from Kashmir?' he asks, patting my shoulder. 'Kashmir . . . I remember it vividly. So many fond memories, concerts at the foothills of the Zabarwan mountains, the serene Dal Lake and the autumn leaves all turning the good earth auburn . . .'

A smile appears on his face. 'I should not be smiling these days, young man . . . but tell me more about why you are here . . . that too all the way from Kashmir . . .'

I clarify: 'Actually . . . I don't live in Kashmir anymore. I live with my parents and grandparents in Udhampur. We had to leave Kashmir in 1990. It's been my dream to see you in person . . .'

'I am just an ordinary man.'

He tells me all about how he was hosted several times by eminent politicians in Kashmir and how he enjoyed performing at concerts there years ago. The male members of the family gather around us and listen to him as he recounts his memories of Kashmir and other places.

On the walls of the room, there are photos and the framed Padma Vibushan award certificate.

What follows is a conversation about life, music, places, Banaras and Kashmir. Time stands still.

'You're the first person to come to meet me from Kashmir. Here, take my card.'

'I want to hear your music. Perhaps I could learn something from you.'

'I don't play at home during Muharram, but I play in the evening after returning from the Muharram procession . . .'

I tell him about my meeting with Pandit Bholanath.

Time stops again as Khan Sahab launches into telling me about his experiences on tours to various places across the world and recounting his own boyhood days.

I touch his feet to seek his blessings. He places his hand on my head.

'I will see you again.'

'Where will you go now?'

'Godowlia.'

'You are staying in Godowlia?'

'Then wait.'

He gestures to someone. The man rushes out of the house. He returns in a couple of minutes with a rickshaw.

Khan Sahab asks me to hop on first and then joins me.

The rickshaw wallah starts peddling. I am numb. I am in a rickshaw and sitting next to me is a god of music.

* * *

Sarnath

A boy introduces himself to me, insisting I hire him as a guide for the day in exchange for some money and lunch at a dhaba. He turns out to be a history buff. He gives me a ten-minute overview of the last 400 years of the history of India. Then he talks about Gautama Buddha!

'Since you are named after him, are you also going to follow in his footsteps?' he playfully asks. Then he takes my flute, sits in the shade of a tree and plays a tune.

* * *

Prayag

I am in a boat headed towards Sangam, which is the confluence of the Ganga and Yamuna, where the two rivers meet like lovers. The two banks are dotted with funeral pyres. Half-burnt corpses are floating in the river. Seeing me horrified at the sight, the boatman points to them and recites a hymn in Sanskrit.

The smell of burning human flesh and the sight of human remains transport me back to the Devika Ghat in Udhampur, where I go almost every evening on my way back home from Link Road. I spend my evenings there, sitting on the steps overlooking the stream. Time passes slowly there. In front of me are the burning pyres of Kashmiri Pandits from the camp. People who weren't supposed to die, but died nevertheless. Some died due to strange ailments and some succumbed to snakebites, sunstrokes, heart attacks and even strokes. And some perished from deep longing, unable to bear the separation from their homes and their roots. There are people who can't take it any longer and simply die because living becomes impossible. Camp life is fraught with perils. In camps, you die if you are not strong enough. You are put to the test. You learn what it takes to survive . . . to stay alive. But then, in the camps, you die even if you are strong. It's survival of the fittest and the luckiest. Because even the most fit can collapse. And these deaths cannot be explained. 'Why did so-and-so die when he was so young and healthy?' everyone whispers.

Sensing my discomfort, the boatman keeps reciting the hymn and eventually begins singing. It's a familiar old Hindi film song! His gaze is elsewhere, but he knows his way both upstream and downstream. He knows how to row. He knows the boat will reach the shore even if he stops rowing. He knows the river as well as a child knows its mother's lap. The current will carry the boat to the shore. He has been ferrying people across the river to Sangam his entire life. He belongs to a family that has done it for generations. The trade was passed on from one generation to another. From grandfather to father, from father to son, from son to grandson, from grandson to great grandson.

The song takes me back to an Udhampur evening at the Devika Ghat. The boatman is singing the song as if he is not going to see me again in this lifetime. As though our paths will never cross again and I'm going away forever.

He joins his palms together and bows when I tell him that I can't pay him more than what he deserves.

'You see, this river gives me more than I deserve,' he says. 'It has given me enough to last seven lifetimes. Ganga is my mother. We come from her; she accepts us back when the world is done with us . . .'

As we reach the shore, he joins his palms again upon seeing a burning pyre. 'I am the one burning,' he whispers to me, with his eyes lowered in deference for the departed man or woman. The wood covering the corpse is not sufficient and the half-burnt bones are black with soot. The body must burn completely. But if some of it doesn't, then it must be immersed in the holy waters.

'I am also you. I am everyone else,' sings the boatman.

Suddenly, I have a realization and decide to take a train back home—first to Delhi, then to Jammu and finally to Udhampur. I've run out of money but my work here is done! Banaras has saved me from doom.

I travel without a ticket in the unreserved compartment. I don't even have the money to buy water. The train keeps stopping because some passengers deliberately pull the emergency chain to get off and some villagers come with buckets of water and ice. The water is smelly. I have no choice but to drink it to keep myself from dehydration. I vomit as soon as I drink the water. I sit next to the toilet in the compartment, trying to wet my lips with a parched tongue.

Sitting next to me is a family of four. The woman offers me her bottle of water. It is the only bottle of water they have and it is meant for the kids. They are migrant workers bound for Delhi. I take a sip from the bottle and return it to her. Her two children—a boy and a girl—look at me, smile and then go back to playing a guessing game as if they've never known hunger, thirst or exhaustion. They are busy in their own world.

'Are you going home?' asks the woman.

The train starts moving again and the passengers begin singing. It is a long song that doesn't seem to end. It goes on and on. It is a happy song because everyone is smiling and laughing and no one wants the song to end. The song will end only when the train reaches its destination the following morning. I close my eyes and fall asleep.

Thirty-six hours later, I'm back in Udhampur.

The next day, I meet my guru and show him the four flutes. I narrate the incident. He chides me for my impertinence. But he is happy that I managed to convince Pandit Bholanath to part with two of his personal flutes.

'You must never repeat the same mistake,' he says. 'Or else . . .'

* * *

19 January 1992
Udhampur

> *Life is coal tar*
> *When it is time*
> *To cast the aged skin off*
> *And smear the forehead*
> *With holy ash.*

Impermanence prevails
Until all youth,
Spent recklessly over hallucinations and mirages,
Is ancient phenomenon.
The boatman awaits me
At the ghat.
Therefore,
Sin, annihilate and conquer.
Holiness is no deliverance.

* * *

April 1995
Udhampur

I'm preparing to leave Udhampur to join Jawaharlal Nehru University in Delhi. I go to see my music teacher, Anil Raina, for the last music class before my departure.

I don't want to leave Udhampur, but what choice do I have? What do I do with myself here? Music has become my life now. It is the only thing that gives me hope and a purpose to live. But I struggle. I sit down in front of my guru and wait for him to begin. What will he teach me today?

He picks up his flute and starts playing. Then he gestures that I should follow him. I hold my flute, waiting for my turn. When he pauses for a breath, I play a note. Then he stops pausing for a breath. There are no pauses in his playing. His world is one long, endless breath.

And then he stops.

'We shall have to start over,' he says, watching me go haywire. 'No, no, that's not how you sit. Look at me. Like this. You need to learn how to sit like this. Like a mountain! Still, yet relaxed! Not like a string about to snap! Not like

water that flows here and there! And this is how you hold the
flute in your hands . . .'

He begins to teach me how to sit and produce the *swara*
'Sa' the way it should be produced and the way it should
sound.

'Your Sa is still shaky,' he says. 'Your breath, fingers,
mind, body and soul are not in harmony. We need to get
them into harmony first.'

What am I to do now? I don't have the time to begin
again. My tickets for Delhi are booked and, in a few days, I
will be gone.

I offer both my gurus some *gurudakshina*—money I have
earned by tutoring my landlord's friend's son. 'A day will
come when you know what gurudakshina is,' my gurus say.

I see sadness in Anil Raina's eyes. He sees sadness in mine.
'Are you sure you want to leave everything and go?' he says.
The silence between us is tormenting. I hear his unspoken
words: 'Don't give up music. Find a guru in Delhi . . .'

Sensing that I'm conflicted and morose, he adds, 'Go to
Pandit Amarnath. Mention my name, fall at his feet and beg
him to take you on as a student. If he agrees, you will have to
walk on fire. Are you ready for it? If not, you must prepare
yourself. The path of music is tough and you will have to
sacrifice many things along the way . . .'

* * *

The Summer of 1995
New Delhi

I'm at Jawaharlal Nehru University, Delhi. Classes have
begun. I don't know what to do. Without a guru, how will I
learn music and what will become of me? My music practice

dwindles as the days go by. How far will I go? How long will I survive?

My guru's parting words continue to haunt me: 'Study in Delhi, then get a job and do something with your life, but don't give up music. Music will follow you if you don't give it up.'

* * *

A Day in the Summer of 1999

I return to Udhampur to see Babuji, who is fading away. His suffering is unbearable. His heart and mind are elsewhere now—a home far away, beyond time, space, dreams and memory. He has lost his sense of time, of relationships and of the true nature of things. I have become his father; his granddaughter has become his wife; his wife has become someone else—his daughter-in-law or a stranger.

He grabs hold of my hand and places it on his cheek. He smiles as I caress his cheek the way he used to caress mine when I was a boy. I helplessly kneel in front of him. Pa asks me to play the flute, hoping that it will ignite a memory of the happy times we spent in our home in Srinagar.

A memory of Babuji humming the hymns of life while looking after each one of us!

'You know,' Pa reveals for the first time, 'Gasha, my uncle, was a wonderful flautist. The melodies he played would make the cows in our cowshed happy . . .'

He turns to Babuji and asks him if he remembers anything about Gasha or our home. Babuji smiles his old smile.

Babi says, 'If this is how you will behave, I don't wish to linger here anymore. Take me with you . . . Take me with you . . .'

Babi oscillates between hope and despair. Hope is her only strength. Left with no other choice, she appears resigned to fate. Her suffering is no less. She prays, 'Take me with you . . .'

* * *

10 January 2020
New Delhi

I am attending the Swami Haridas–Tansen Sangeet Nritya Mahotsav, where Pandit Hariprasad Chaurasia will perform a flute recital. After a long wait, at 10 p.m., he walks in through the door of the concert hall, greets the audience with a graceful smile on his lips, settles down in a chair and begins playing Raag Jaijaivanti. Behind him, his two disciples—a girl and a boy—make sure that the melody remains unbroken whenever their guru pauses for a breath. At the end of the recital, audience entreaties for Raag Malkauns are placed before the maestro. 'Are you willing to wait until the third *prahar* (segment) of the night?' he says, referring to the time when Raag Malkauns is usually played.

The recital ends. Panditji places his flute by his side and joins his palms before the audience. I have this sudden urge to rush to him, fall at his feet and tell him that there was a time when all I wanted was to run away from camp to his *gurukul* (school) in Bombay and beg him to accept me as a pupil. That's all I dreamed of in those days. But I don't have the courage now. I don't have the same madness that made me run away from many places earlier. I am not that boy anymore. I am just a daydreamer now.

I slip into a trance. I am playing Raag Chandrakauns as a shepherd girl dances in the moonlight.

Once, while strolling in the bazaar near his school, my guru, Anil Raina, reminisced about his growing up days in

Kashmir when his father began to teach him music at the age of ten. 'I'm still trying to figure out how to play Raag Yaman well,' he said. Quoting his father, he said, 'A single raag can take you a lifetime to learn. You must be prepared for *sadhana* (devotion) and *samarpan* (submission) if you wish to be showered with the blessings of a raag.'

'What if we can never return to Kashmir?' I asked him that day.

'What makes you think we won't? Of course, we will go back, even if it takes us several lifetimes.'

I have now become a dream and a memory of those whom I loved and lost during the past three decades in exile. Their sadness has now become my sadness.

The road to my home in Kashmir goes through a tunnel of darkness. And the tunnel is becoming longer and longer with each passing day.

What if it really does take me a lifetime to go back? What will I do on the first day of my return? How will I begin again?

I seek solace in the teachings of my gurus. Between the swaras, 'Sa' and 'Re is a long distance stretching up to infinity and it will take me a thousand lifetimes, each lasting a hundred thousand years, to cover even a miniscule.

* * *

A Day in November 2020
New Delhi
A Deserted Street

I am returning from a grocery store. I park my car by the sidewalk to sanitize my hands. Out of nowhere, a flute seller appears with a bunch of flutes attached to a pole he's carrying. Upon seeing me, he starts playing a Hindi film song that sounds familiar. I lose track of time. He stops playing and hands me a flute, pleading with me to buy it.

'Please, Sir, I have no money,' he says. 'During the lockdown, I couldn't earn even a single rupee. I will give you a good discount if you buy a flute.'

I inspect the flute and play a tune. The man looks at me with wonderment.

'Sir, you know how to play,' he whispers.

Me: 'Where are you from?'

He: 'District Budaun, UP.'

Me: 'You should do something else to earn a living. No one is going to buy flutes these days.'

He: 'Selling flutes is family tradition. I won't do anything else, even if the heavens fall. Please buy a few flutes since you know how to play.'

I hand him some money and buy a flute. I play a film song. The same song that I had heard on the ghat thirty years ago.

The man breaks down.

He: 'Sir, I recognize this song. I wish I knew how to play it.'

Me: 'You should learn how to play this song. It will take time, but you will get it eventually. You will be the happiest man the moment you start playing it exactly the way it should be played.'

He: 'Sir, I have no rations to feed my family. Can you buy me some rice and wheat flour?'

Some Days Later

The flautist from Budaun appears in the street once again. He is playing the film song that I played. Apart from flutes, he's also carrying a bunch of colourful balloons for sale.

Had the flute seller not given me his flute that evening at the cremation ghat on the banks of the Devika River in Udhampur, I would not have known anything about life.

I have yet to repay him for his gift. I'm still trying to perfect playing that song.

20

The Certificate Is Your Last Link to Kashmir. Don't Let the Link Snap!

30 June 2016
Jammu

Pa and I are at the office of the relief and rehabilitation commissioner for migrants, Jammu. The office was set up in 1990 to provide relief and succour—cash assistance, free rations and shelter—to Kashmiri Pandits who sought refuge in Jammu and other nearby places after being uprooted from their homes in Kashmir.

The purpose of my visit to the office is to apply for a state subject certificate. It's an important legal document that acknowledges and certifies the special rights and privileges accorded to the domiciles of the Jammu and Kashmir state as enshrined in Article 35A (now revoked) of the Constitution of India. The certificate, once issued, will establish that I am an original resident of the state with the lawful right to employment, property and settlement there. I have no desire to apply for a job there. But I wish to revive an old dream—of buying a small plot of land and building a house in the future.

The state subject certificate is a must-have for this wish to be fulfilled.

The clerk hands us a note listing the documents to be arranged for the certificate to be issued. Pa has kept most of the paperwork ready. There's one document missing—a government record ascertaining our original residence in Kashmir. I am assured that the certificate will be issued as soon as the proof of my residence in my long-lost home in Srinagar is arranged and deposited at the office.

I wonder: 'It's been twenty-six years since I was made to leave Kashmir. Will the record exist? What if I can't produce it?'

We board a bus and reach the migrant voter list office in Jammu. It holds the records of Kashmiri Pandits who voted in Kashmir before being forced out in 1990. My parents' record as voters in Kashmir is expected to be in the registry there.

A rickety staircase leads us to the second floor, where the voter registry is kept. The rooms are dingy and the furniture is ramshackle. A Dogra clerk greets us. I explain that I am there to dig up an old record.

'The records of your entire community are here; don't worry, we will find your record,' says the clerk, pointing to the racks against the walls.

I look around. The entire office is in a state of disarray. The racks are dusty and cobwebbed. Each rack is full of thousands of files containing papers.

We begin searching for my record, with the clerk helping us. 'There was cataloguing until a few years ago, but not anymore. I have no help here to manage the records properly . . .' he laments.

A surreal experience unfolds. Searching for a missing record among thousands arranged randomly on shelves.

The record, if located, will establish not just the proof of my residence—the place of my birth—but also the proof of my ancestry.

We rummage haphazardly through stacks of sooty files supposed to be arranged district-and-tehsil-wise on shelves. Termites have left a trail on several files. Silverfish have made the files their home. The ink on the paper is fading; the files are damp and smelly. I go through hundreds of files with hundreds of names. I could be one of them.

It is a strange place to exist—this ghostly house of records.

I survey the rooms and make a quick calculation. Each room has four wall-to-wall racks. Each rack has sixteen large shelves. Each shelf contains about 100 files. Each file holds the records of around twenty-five people. There are four such rooms. Records of well over 6,00,000 displaced Kashmiri Pandits lie neglected and in abject conditions. These are hard copies. There's no backup or digital archive, nor are there any safe and secure vaults to protect the records from theft or damage. There is absolutely no protection from fire, rain, termites and rodents.

What if the unthinkable happens?

I read name after name and address after address. These are the names and addresses of people who were once traceable but are now scattered in exile. These records are the only proof of their origins. Where are these people now? What has become of them?

I keep searching. Still no trace of the record! What am I to do without the record? What if it is lost? What if I never find it?

A memory of a happy day comes alive. Babuji is walking with a stoop, his hands behind his back. He's going about his favourite pastime—inspecting the kitchen garden in our house in Srinagar. The buds have started to sprout. Babi is sitting by the window and talking to a crow perched atop the sill, something she does often. She's preparing for the arrival of guests from her maternal family, who live in a village. The crow spills the beans about what is going to happen—only good things. The next moment, Babi rushes into her kitchen. Ma is stringing pearls for a necklace she's making for Henna.

'It is for her wedding,' she says. Pa takes me to see the new plot of land he has bought. The plot is atop a plateau near the airport and it overlooks snow-clad peaks.

'We shall build a house here next year,' he says. I have my eyes set on the view from the window of my future room.

At last, after interminable hours of flipping through hundreds of files, I stumble upon a piece of paper bearing the names of my parents and grandparents. The address I've been looking for is mentioned on the paper. Towards one corner of the paper is a glassy impression of a moth's wingspan—telling a story of the insect's fleeting existence.

Having acquired the document, we must rush to the district court to get the record verified and attested by a magistrate. But before that, we must get an affidavit made. The ordeal is unending. Back at the office of the relief and rehabilitation commissioner for migrants, my fingerprints are taken on a blank and unattested certificate. 'I will hand it over to your father after everything has been verified,' says the clerk.

* * *

July 2016
New Delhi

Pa couriers the laminated certificate to me.

It says:

'This is to certify that Siddhartha Gigoo, son of Arvind Gigoo, resident of Khankah-i-Sokhta, Tehsil Srinagar, District Srinagar, is a permanent resident of the J&K state as defined in the constitution of the Jammu & Kashmir Government.'

Pa's letter:

Dear Siddhartha,

Keep the certificate safe. It is your last link to Kashmir. Don't let the link snap.

Papa

I keep the certificate under lock and key at home in Delhi.

* * *

5 August 2019
New Delhi

I wake up to the news of the abrogation of Articles 370 and 35A of the Constitution. People all over the country are now talking about being able to buy land and property in Jammu and Kashmir. A friend from Bihar says he would like to settle in Kashmir after retirement. 'Let's go together,' he proposes.

Stripped of its special status, Kashmir is now a place that belongs to everyone and where everyone can settle.

But can I go there just like everybody else from India? How must I return given the history behind my forced departure in 1990?

In the evening, I take the certificate out of the drawer. The certificate has no legal relevance now, but its emotional relevance will never fade.

Many people have perished over the years. But their records still exist in the registry in Jammu.

I can't take my eyes off the certificate that I thought granted me special status with unique rights and privileges no other Indians born elsewhere had. The special status that was bound by the state's constitution to protect us from persecution in 1990 and then guarantee our dignified return to our own homes before it was too late, but failed to do so, is now gone forever. The yearning for restitution is stronger than ever in my heart. The dream of home persists. The dream of reclaiming everything that was snatched from us lingers on.

Someday, those of us who survived will return to our homes in Kashmir. And that day, we shall take along all records to show our progeny the proof of our survival and of the intrepid journeys we made in exile.

21

This Is Still Your Home, Son

24 June 2009
Srinagar

Deepak and I are in Srinagar after returning from our pilgrimage to the holy cave of Amarnath. Deepak leaves for Delhi while I decide to stay back in Srinagar for a day. My secret wish is to go to Safa Kadal to visit my house there.

I take up a room in Hotel Ahdoos on Residency Road. It used to be Pa's favourite place. Second only to India Coffee House, which was set ablaze by militants in 1990.

Showkat, an old classmate, comes to meet me. I express my desire to go to Safa Kadal.

Before hopping into his car, I smoke a cigarette. We spend some time near Regal Cinema—the same place my dad took me to watch *Lion of the Desert* years ago. The memory of that day comes alive. There were so many other movies that we watched in this cinema hall before it was forcibly shut down in 1990.

We drive past Nalle-e-Maer. I recognize some old shops and houses that are unchanged.

The walls and the shutters of shops are still full of graffiti:

'Azadi!

Go India, Go Back!

Pakistan Zindabad!

Freedom!'

Then we walk towards the house. For the first time in eighteen years, I see my old house. The tin roof is all rusty brown. From a distance, I see the stained-glass latticed window of Pa's room on the first floor.

An old, rickety and rusted wheelbarrow is next to the lamp post. Could it be the same wheelbarrow from my childhood days?

The same wooden lamp post of my childhood.

Babuji's initials—O.N.G.—are still etched on the front door.

I knock at the door. A middle-aged woman opens the door and looks at me with strange eyes.

Me: 'Many years ago, I lived in this house. This used to be our home. My family and I left this house in 1990. May I please . . .'

Woman: 'My husband is not home right now. But you are welcome to come in.'

Me: 'Where is he?'

Woman: 'He is at his shop near Yarbal. He sells vegetables. He comes home late in the night.'

Me: 'Are you sure I can come in? Or should I come back later?'

Woman: 'No, no, son! I believe you. Your eyes have truth in them.'

Her eyes flash a look of compassion and pity.

The courtyard, the veranda . . . the stained-glass window of my room . . .

Woman: 'Have we kept your house in order?'

In the living room, an old woman is quietly sipping her tea.

Woman: 'This is my mother-in-law.'

Then she tells the old woman, 'He is a Pandit, who once lived in this house. He was born here.'

The old woman smiles and says, 'This is still your home, my son. May God bless you!'

A beautiful blonde-haired girl climbs down the stairs and looks at me as if she were expecting me.

Woman: 'She is my Noor.'

The woman complains about how the previous occupants failed to take care of the house.

I move from one room to another. Finally, Babuji and Babi's room. From the window, I look towards Eid Gah and the Tibetan refugee settlement.

The drawing room . . . the almirah . . . still intact . . . the same almirah in which we kept Baijee's books—the books were looted in 1990. Everything is still the same. Everything except the books. But then, books are everything.

The woman's elder daughter offers me tea.

Girl: 'Mother, is he a Muslim? How does he speak Kashmiri like we do?'

And at last, my room. The room now belongs to the girl. The woman opens the door and leaves me there all by myself. She asks her daughters to leave me alone.

Familiar signs are still glowing on the walls of my room.

My name is still visible on the door of the room. A painting I made as a boy is still nailed to the wall. It is *The House of Snails*.

The bookshelf is here too. Everything is where it belongs. All my things are here. As if I never left and were merely waking up from a very long dream.

Shall I ask the woman if I can have my painting and take it along with me? After all, it's my painting. I will show it to everyone! It is a miracle that all these things have survived. As if they waited all these years for me to return and take them back with me.

But something prevents me from expressing such a desire. If *The House of Snails* has survived all these years without me, it will survive and outlive me too. It belongs here. May it never get to leave this room and this house.

The little girl with blonde hair will look after it as if it were hers. It's the girl's *House of Snails* now.

The willow tree that Babuji had planted is gone.

I take out a Rs 100 note and hand it to the girl.

'No,' says the girl's mother politely.

'Please let her keep it. I shouldn't have come empty-handed. She can buy chocolate or anything else she likes.'

Before leaving the house, the woman asks me a strange question.

'Are you here to buy your house?' she asks.

'No, no!'

'Swear to God, because if that's your intent, please don't hide it from me. It is okay if you want to buy this house . . .'

The look on her face changes and her eyes turn moist. This is the look of silent pain and remorse. This is where humanity touches our hearts and souls for the first time and teaches us what it is to be human. To forgive, to cry and to embrace one another's suffering. There are only tears left now. These tears are proof of the humanism buried deep inside her heart and mine. Nobody should see our tears.

The woman bids me farewell as I look at the house one last time before walking away. My house is now hers.

I walk towards the tailor shop that Babuji used to visit almost every day. He would sit at the shop for hours and spend time with his friend, chatting and sharing tidbits about daily life. Sometimes he would sit silently, watching people come and go. The tailor is an old friend of his.

'Aadab! I am the grandson of your old friend Omkar Nath Gigoo, who lived in the house just at the end of this street. Do you remember him?'

The old man looks at me with indescribable agony in his eyes. For a minute, he doesn't speak, as if he has no words.

'How is Doctor Sahab doing?' he says. 'Where is he these days? Is he happy and healthy?'

'He died some years ago. He used to talk about you. I came to see our house and meet all the people who knew him.'

The old tailor looks at the picture of Mecca on his wall. He goes silent for a few moments and mumbles a prayer.

'May God forgive my sins for not even grieving my old friend's demise! He would have died a happy man in his own house. My son, I offer you my blessings for informing me about my old friend.'

'Do you remember that you tailored all his shirts?'

'All his shirts, his pherans and his trousers too! I used to tailor clothes for all the Pandits in this neighbourhood. They trusted only my measurements. My hand was steady then, but that is no longer the case. Sometimes, my fingers tremble. Back then, no one could compare with me in needlework. Now, old age and medicines keep me company. Besides, these days, no one wants to get their clothes tailored at my shop. May God bless you, my son! Thank you for coming to see me.

Pardon me, but I don't remember my last meeting with your grandfather. I waited for him and then got to know that he had left . . .'

With misty eyes, he gets back to sewing a cap.

I walk past the shop where we used to buy milk. The owner's name was Qadir. We called him Qadir Goor. A young man is sitting at the place where Qadir Goor once sat. Behind the shop, there used to be a cowshed where people assembled with their utensils to buy fresh milk and curd every morning.

I reach the pinwheel man's shop. Babuji's best friend in the neighbourhood. The shop is closed. I wonder where the pinwheel man is. He used to make the best pinwheels for me.

The barbershop is next to it.

I borrow a match and light another cigarette.

'You seem to have lost your way,' says the barber, handing me a match. 'Would you like directions? This place can be confusing if you aren't from here.' The man mistakes me for a Muslim. I almost look like one.

'Do you know when this shop opens?' I ask him. 'This is the pinwheel shop, right?'

'This shop has remained shut for years now. It belonged to my uncle. How do you know him?'

All this time, Showkat has been witnessing everything without uttering a word. He is in a state of disbelief. He didn't expect any of this to happen.

The Ram Mandir across the street stands forlorn, dilapidated, ravaged and abandoned.

Someday, I will bring Babi here.

I return to the hotel in the afternoon. At night, an old dream haunts me once again. There are no images, but only voices. I hear screams.

'Allah O Akbar!
Tyrants, leave this land!
We want freedom. We want freedom!'

And then there is the sound I've been dreaming of for years.
The sound of a temple bell. Someone is lighting a lamp inside
the temple at Durga Naag.

22

Get Me Salama . . .
Get Me Salama . . .

24 December 2013
Jammu

Pa shows me his English translation of 'Tyol', an epic poem by Arjan Dev Majboor. 'To the Swan' makes an apt title.

'Majboor likes my work. I am the only one he trusts with the translation of his writing,' he says.

He recites:

I opened my heart to the swan,
sat him on the chariot of my liquid memories,
made him recollect the heavenly green spot.
I wove a wreath of past events,
held a mirror of Time,
showed him the scarred hush of my being . . .
Fetch me a swig of water
for I am parched.

* * *

12 October 2014
Jammu

Pa writes open letters to Kashmiri Muslims and Kashmiri Pandits.[10]

My dear Kashmiri Muslims,

Right from 1947, your leaders and politicians have lied to you, confused you and exploited you. The crafty politicians have used you for their selfish ends and the Indian leadership have taken you for granted. Pakistan played on your religious sentiments. Then some other countries started playing their own games with you. When George Bush condemned Muslim terrorism, you became sad. When Barack Obama praised Muslims, you became happy. When Pakistan mentions Kashmir, you feel elated.

You are a gullible lot. You believe in false promises. Nobody trusts you. Your tragedy is the result of the politicking of your leaders and of those you consider your well-wishers.

Kashmir is an issue of betrayal, blunder, falsehood and mistrust. It is a confusing admixture of plebiscite, Pakistan, India, independence and ambiguous ideas and theories. Once it was 'Jana Gana Mana', then it was 'Nizam-e-Mustafa'. You turned so naive that you thought achieving Azadi was just a matter of a few days. Now, things have degenerated into a miasma of stone-pelting, drugs and things that you have no control over.

In the last twenty years, you've lost hundreds of thousands of people—young boys, men, women and children. You've lost your humanism and your cultural ethos. You've lost Pandits. You are living on lies. You are a victim of depression, repentance, sorrow and defeat.

Pakistanis have a very poor opinion of you. Indians don't trust you at all. Your leaders don't care for you.

Militants, double agents, suspects, informants, spies, looters, freebooters and conmen thrive in Kashmir. Nobody knows who is doing what. You suffer from political and societal schizophrenia and civilizational dementia.

You've lost your freedom of speech. The cunning among you talk about one thing in private and change their stance in public. Some have chosen silence, and silence during a period of political unrest is dangerous. Political blackmailers, extortionists, security forces and greedy opportunists have devastated you. Now you are insensitive to your own suffering and to the suffering of your own people. Rumours and farcical slogans have placed you in a quagmire of directionless aspiration, purposelessness and psychological trauma. You have yet to set your goals.

Your educated youth have intellect, vision and dreams. But unemployment, uncertainty and a lack of opportunity have frustrated them. How long will they and you go on waiting for the outcome of 'meaningful and composite dialogue?'

Answer your own questions. Question your leaders, politicians and think tanks. Everything is in your hands. Shifting loyalties and short-term plans will lead you nowhere. For sixty-three years, your leaders have done nothing for you. Pursue only one goal. The politics of double talk are bound to fail. Kashmir is not safe in the hands of its clever rulers.

* * *

Letter to Pandits 100 years after the exodus of 1990 (to be read on 19 January 2090)

My dear Descendants,

You are rootless. You belong to no place. The base of your life is a vacuum. The language you speak is not your own. Your festivals are borrowed. You live by proxy. Machines and robots wait upon your parents. You are unaware of your children. You visit other planets. There is a place called Kashmir on this planet. Fly to that place and find your scattered selves there. What is your religion? You don't know. You are lost in this world populated with cold and callous half-humans. You have no love or compassion. You don't celebrate memory because you have none. Your life is some digits and speed. What do you want? You will never know. You are non-persons.

* * *

The letters are posted on Facebook and shared by several people.

The next day, Pa starts receiving calls and messages from strangers. Some calls are pre-recorded messages; they are abusive, impolite and distasteful! Some are even threats!

'Why did you expose us?' ask the callers.

One person keeps calling for months.

* * *

21 January 2021
(31st anniversary of our exodus from Kashmir)
New Delhi

Pa is interviewed by Barkha Dutt.[11]

'How do you look back at the last thirty-one years and what is your abiding memory of Kashmir?' asks Barkha.

Pa replies, 'In Kashmir, we had a love–hate relationship with the Muslims. But in 1990, everything changed. We saw horror. We saw fear. All the Muslims came out of their homes and started shouting anti-Pandit slogans. We had to run away. Since then, I've been deeply hurt and angry at my Muslim friends. Now, I divide my time between Jammu and Delhi. It has been a horrible and painful experience. One day, a very close friend of mine, Qureshi, said to me, "You (Kashmiri Pandit) are a poisonous snake." I was shocked. Another friend, Gulam Hasan, was having tea at our place. I haven't trusted them since then. I am sorry to say this, but none of my friendships have survived. I have kissed goodbye to Kashmir. I don't want to go back. Our house is sold. Where do I go and why should I go? In Kashmir, we were under suspicion. One day, I was walking in Srinagar when a close friend questioned me, "Why are you here? Are you an agent of India?" Nobody suspects me anymore. In exile, my father lost his memory; he lost everything. Even in that state of mind when he didn't remember any of us, he used to say, "Get me Salama . . . Get me Salama . . ." The only person he remembered was Salama. He forgot everything except his Muslim friend, Salama. Such a horrible experience! Salama was a tonga wallah whose house was next to ours. He would take us to different places. He is still in Srinagar. My mother lost her mental balance, too. She would repeat everything 100 times. I went to Kashmir three or four times in the last thirty years. It was hell. It wasn't a homecoming. Certainly not the homecoming we wished for. Now I don't want to go back. Kashmir is not my home anymore. You can't imagine how my mother felt. She would only talk about Kashmir. Every single day. Until her last breath. When you meet one Muslim in Kashmir, things are okay. One-on-one is a different thing, but when you meet 500 Muslims, things are different. The psychology in such a situation is altogether different. Nobody wants to go back. There is nothing to go back to. We are stuck here. We will die here. This is the truth.'

* * *

September 2016
New Delhi

I send a Facebook message to Henna, a childhood friend in Kashmir. In the mid-1980s, we were taught by the same teacher, Pyarelal Trisal. Our parents are friends too. Henna teaches English at a college in Srinagar.

'Eid Mubarak to you, Henna!'

Henna replies a few days later. 'Sorry, we had no internet connectivity here for days. You know how the situation is in Kashmir.'

Her delayed response is terse but heart-rending. 'I am in a cage,' she writes. 'There's no escape and I must learn to live with it.'

I feel very sorry for not comforting her in person when she lost her mother.

Earlier, we wrote to each other on occasions and when there was something to say. We would reminisce about the old days. Our wonder years in Srinagar. Meeting each other at Fateh Kadal (the third bridge over Jhelum) on our way to

Trisal Uncle's house. He was more than a teacher to us. Our parents were close friends of his. Sadly, he died of a brain tumour in Bengaluru. I was lucky to meet him a few days before his demise. Chemotherapy had made him weak. For a long time, his family dangled between hope and despair.

For years, Trisal Uncle battled another affliction. Unlike cancer, the affliction known as displacement is curable. But he didn't live long enough to see the cure in his lifetime.

Henna and I shared a deep admiration for stories and art. Once during a long, unending summer, as we walked through the lanes of Downtown Srinagar, we expressed our admiration for autumn. 'I still fancy it,' she wrote to me. 'I hope it keeps its promise.'

I write to Henna again, about the demise of Trisal Uncle and my last meeting with him at his son's place in Bengaluru. I couldn't describe his condition to her. The tumour had eroded his body. Strangely, it hadn't been able to rob him of his memory. When I mentioned Henna, he said he remembered everything. It wasn't a miracle that he did. Teachers seldom forget their students. Especially those they considered their own children. I knew others who could recall only one place when all other memories had faded.

It was because of our teacher that Henna and I became friends. We met every day between 1986 and 1989. Our friendship blossomed during the long walks home. The walks came to an end in 1989. In the twenty-six years since, we've met only once. It was a chance meeting in Delhi in the summer of 2011, at a gathering of some common Kashmiri friends.

The gathering had been organized to understand the violence that had erupted in Kashmir in 2010. All of us were part of a Facebook group whose mission was to bring Kashmiris scattered across the globe together. The motto of the group, 'Let us assemble and tug at the same rope in the same direction' is a line borrowed from one of the *vaakhs* of the great mystic–poet, Lal Ded.

That evening, we were more excited about meeting each other after over two decades than the discussion on Kashmir. Henna and I parted on a sombre note. 'We will meet again, in Kashmir,' we promised each other.

Thereafter, we continued writing to each other. Inevitably, we painted Kashmir as we had always known it. The Kashmir of our childhood. The Kashmir that once was. The Kashmir of promises. For both of us, it remains hidden, unblemished and ineffable. We still inhabit it.

'I hope you come out of the cage soon,' I say to Henna and send her a prayer. I pray for the bad times to end and the good times to return. My prayer is full of hope.

The turmoil should end. Pandits should get to return to their lost homes. Muslims and Pandits should embrace each other, irrespective of their likes and dislikes, prejudices and opinions, affiliations and ideologies.

Muslims did nothing when Kashmiri Pandits were forced to leave their homes in 1990 and made to perish in camps, year after year. Muslims still do nothing to get Pandits back to where they belong. If only they had stood by us and come to our rescue, we would have been saved from ruin.

It isn't too late, even now. Now is the time to defeat those whose sole purpose is to create further partitions. Can the two communities defeat the demons residing within? The demons of hurt created by history.

I imagine a two-line play: *Luck*.

A Kashmiri Muslim: 'Look at me. I am still alive. Nothing has happened to me yet.'

A Kashmiri Pandit: 'Look at me. I survived too. Nothing has happened to me as well.'
What both of them hide from each other is:
The Kashmiri Muslim: 'Ali's son hasn't come home for two days now. But my son has.'
The Kashmiri Pandit: 'Kashi Nath's son has left him at an old-age home. But my son hasn't. He says he will take me to the US.'

I have some more letters to write. To my friends in Kashmir and to those outside, whose near and dear ones are trapped inside a cage there. To children who dream of a beautiful time. To those who don't know what's to come. To those who yearn for the cage door to open. To those who died while dreaming of a glorious future. And to the nameless soldier from Tripura, Bihar or Tamil Nadu, away from home and family, risking his life to guard the jewel state, unsure of whether he will live to see another day. Kashmir is his second home, too.

* * *

A Day in April 1986
Home, Srinagar, Kashmir

I am in the attic, waiting for Halley's Comet to appear in the night sky. The sky is clear. The stars are twinkling and the moon is shining. But Halley's Comet is nowhere to be seen. The previous nights yielded no luck either. For days, we have been hearing stories about the comet.

'It is a once-in-a-lifetime event,' people say. Some people believe the comet's arrival will bring good luck. Others say nothing good will come out of it. And some believe that it will spell doom for some of us. But we children are excited. We can't wait for the comet to appear in the sky. I am the only one with a pair of binoculars (a gift from Mamaji, who lives in Melbourne).

'Is it still around or has it already left?' asks a cousin at midnight.

'There it is . . .'

'Where? Where?'

'There. Follow my gaze.'

'Where?'

'No, no, that's not it. Don't fool us.'

There is hope in our hearts. The comet won't disappoint us. We've heard news reports about people having seen it.

'If not tonight, then tomorrow . . .'

We see meteors and meteor showers. We see stars and we see twinkling objects. We see everything except the comet.

Some Nights Later

'There, there!'

We turn our heads. At last, there it is. A flaming marvel in the night sky.

'Is that it? Is this the comet?'

'Yes, don't talk, don't wink. Just look at it quietly without creating a ruckus. It will disappear in no time and return only after seventy-five years . . .'

'Seventy-five years is a long, long time. But, at least, we will have another opportunity . . .'

'What makes you think we will . . .'

'Which year will that be?'

'Count for yourself. Can't you do even that?'

'Tell us.'

'2061.'

'Really?'
'What if we are . . .'
'I want to see it again. I missed it . . .'
'It's a long wait.'

* * *

18 April 1986
Home, Safa Kadal, Srinagar

It is the final of the Austral–Asia Cup. The Sharjah cricket stadium is the battleground today. India is playing against Pakistan and, to make matters worse, it is Friday. The whole of Kashmir is tuned into the match. Those who don't have television sets are listening to the commentary on the radio. India set a target of 246 runs for Pakistan. When Pakistan starts batting to chase the target, our neighbours start reciting verses from the Quran. Voices blare through loudspeakers in mosques. Muslims start praying for Pakistan's victory. They wave Pakistani flags from their windows. This has been happening for days now.

At the end of the forty-ninth over, Pakistan is 235 for seven, requiring eleven runs from six balls to win. Chetan Sharma is to bowl the last over. The voices grow louder and louder.

'Pakistan . . . Pakistan . . . Pakistan . . .' blare the loudspeakers. So do the people in our neighbourhood. Pandits are praying too, but for India. Their prayers aren't heard. The last ball. Pakistan needs four runs and India needs one final wicket from the last ball. Chetan Sharma bowls to Javed Miandad. The entire area falls silent. And then, suddenly, the roar. The neighbourhood erupts at the very mention of Miandad's six. Miandad has always been a hero for Kashmiri Muslims.

I go out to meet my friends in the evening. A woman stands at the window of her house and screams at me. I look up. She utters something that I wish was easy to forget. The first abuse is thrown at me.

'Serves you right, you Pandit,' she says with an expression of ridicule and profound hate on her face. 'We will defeat you and your India soon. Our beloved Pakistan will crush you . . .' The look on her face changes from hate to joy when she utters the word 'Pakistan'.

Thousands of Muslims are out in the streets of Srinagar, taking victory laps. Pandits curse their luck.

* * *

August 2015
Home, Jammu
Morning

I am in Jammu to conduct a story-writing workshop for a bunch of Muslim, Pandit, Dogra and Ladakhi boys and girls from Jammu, Kashmir and Ladakh. I am conscious of the conflicting political ideologies and nationalistic affiliations of the three different ethnic and religious communities that these teenagers hail from. But I realize that these youngsters are progressive in their outlook towards one another and their immediate environment.

A Kashmiri Muslim boy narrates a disturbing incident of violence, resistance, revenge and transformation. He says he wants to become a writer and that his stories will seek to unite and not divide. He says he has made peace with India and that the pro-separatist movement has become a sham in the hands of conniving and greedy leaders. 'First, we must be human and learn to accept one another, despite our differences. Then we must learn to comfort one another for the predicament we've endured individually and collectively,' he says. 'All of us have suffered in different ways. To hell with India and Pakistan and their petty politics.'

A shy boy from a remote village near Kargil recites a poem about his teacher, a Buddhist lama, who teaches at a *gompa* (a Buddhist prayer site). In the poem, the teacher talks about the philosophy of life. A girl from Ladakh narrates a story about a girl who falls in love with a boy at a bus stop. Another girl from Kashmir narrates a story about her grandmother's love for her husband. A boy from Srinagar's Khankah-i-Sokhta reads a poem in Urdu about a flood that has ravaged a city. He and his family have survived the floods that wreaked havoc in Kashmir in 2014. The boy cries while reading the poem. Tamanna, a Rajput from Gurah Salathian village near Jammu, narrates a story about a girl's love of nature. A Pandit girl recounts her experience of growing up in exile.

Evening

We recount memories of our days in Udhampur. My father and I flip through old photographs in an album. Once again, for the 1000th time, I'm reminded of the day my parents handed over my sister and me to our neighbours. Leaving Kashmir seemed adventurous initially. I was fifteen and didn't care about many things. My parents and grandparents were the last Pandits to leave their neighbourhood in Kashmir. Some neighbours had come to my father and pleaded with him not to leave. They reassured them, saying, 'We will protect you. No harm will come to you.' Ironically, they were the ones who also advised them to leave if the situation worsened. It took me years to understand the humanity of it all. My parents chose Udhampur over Jammu because it seemed less chaotic and was flanked by hills.

I meet Ramesh Hangloo, who operates Radio Sharda, a community radio service for displaced Kashmiri Pandits. He is recording a children's programme. An hour later, some children come out of the studio. A girl holding the hand of a boy her age comes out of the recording room. They blush when I offer to shake hands. Hangloo tells me that the programme is about the dying Kashmiri language, a language he wants to keep alive among the next generation of Pandits, who speak mostly in Hindi.

The irony of it all strikes me. These children, born in camps, will grow up to be the most rootless of us all. What memories will these children inherit and what history will they remember? I wonder if they have any clue about their ancestry at such tender ages. I wonder what they think of the camp where their parents lived for years. Years from now, some of these children will remember and recount their lost histories.

* * *

October 2018
New Delhi

I receive a Facebook friend request from Sudeep as well as a message in my Messenger inbox.

'Are you the same Siddhartha Gigoo I knew in 1990 in Chandigarh? I heard the speech you gave at the Chandigarh Literati. The video clip showed up on my Facebook timeline. Please write back asap.'

A Few Days Later

Another friend request from someone named Mohit. And a message in the inbox.

'Remember me? Your roomie from New Hostel, DAV College. I heard your speech at the Chandigarh Literati. I found the video on YouTube. Where the hell have you been all these years, man? Why did you disappear that day? I kept waiting and waiting. I am now a colonel in the Army and posted in Darjeeling. Meet me soon. You have a lot of explaining to do . . .'

Sudeep is a doctor now. She lives in Ludhiana.

'Come over to meet me and my family sometime,' she says.

23

The Separation of Stars

27 March 2020
New Delhi

I read about Comet NEOWISE and download a stargazing application on my phone to track its path as well as the paths of other comets. Halley's Comet is still somewhere out there in the galaxy.

Babi once said that if you make a wish upon a shooting star, it will be fulfilled. But you must not reveal what you wish for, to anyone. It will come true only if you keep it a secret.

I know what you wished for, Babi! But I won't tell anyone.

* * *

Babi appears in my dream.

'How many days has it been?' she asks. 'Years, not just days, am I right?'

I'm sitting at her bedside with my arms folded. She's in her room, doing the things that she loves to do. 'I dreamed of you,' she whispers. 'Yesterday . . . wasn't it?'

Her hair is auburn, her smile is radiant and her eyes sparkle. I know she's going to narrate the dream as if it weren't merely a dream.

'Come, let me tell you a secret. Don't tell anyone . . . If I ever tell you that I wish to leave, don't believe a word of what I say. I will never want to leave all of you even if, God forbid, we go through the most miserable of times. I will say that I am sick and fed up with all this and would like to go now, but I will not mean it . . .'

'Only on one condition, Babi, you will have to promise me that you will never stop appearing in my dreams. For as long as I am alive.'

Babi and Babuji are taking me to Tulmul. We are on a bus. From Ganderbal, we are to take a tonga. Babi has arranged a room in the temple complex. We are going to spend a few days in Tulmul. The room overlooks a stream and a lush green paddy field. And the window frames the naag* of Mata Kheer Bhawani's temple. The next few days will witness the grand mela.

'When will we go home?' I ask Babi. I start missing my room if I stay away from home for more than two days. The very thought of going away for more than a day is unsettling. I miss my corner. I want to go back to it.

'Go back to sleep. We will be home before you open your eyes,' says Babi.

* * *

'To discover life and its beautiful mysteries,' Pa says, presenting me with a book, 'you must learn how to read and enjoy poetry.' I hold *The Faber Book of Children's Verse* in

---
* A holy pond.

my hand and flip through the pages. The stamp says: Kashmir Book Shop, Residency Road, Srinagar, Kashmir. 'I will give you another book once you finish reading this. But this isn't a book that can ever be finished . . .'

The title page of the book bears Pa's message, my name and a date. It says: 'Home, Kashmir, 10 June 1982.' Pa's belated birthday present to me.

The book contains poems from across the world. Poems meant for children. Poems about poetry and music and dancing and seasons and beasts and birds and children and kings and queens and heroes and magic and fairies and gods and angels and travel and home and love and heaven and history and time.

'If you memorize some poems, you will never feel alone in the world,' says Pa. 'You will never feel bored and sad in life. You will roam the world and unravel the most beautiful mysteries . . .'

Thirty-three years later, I show Pa the books he presented me with when I was eight years old.

'Do you feel bored while reading and writing?' I ask Pa, sensing his dwindling interest in books.

'I have never known boredom in life. And I never will. But were it not for my weakening eyesight, I would still be reading books. I read a page or two every day. On some days, a paragraph. Do you read these days? What have you learned about life?'

I'm still trying to discover life . . . knowing that the process is ongoing—it could take a lifetime. Maybe one lifetime is not enough.

Everything is possible in the blink of an eye.

* * *

Of the times gone by and the years spent in exile, especially the 'camp years', I remember many people who, towards the end, lost their memory. They remembered nothing, neither the bad nor the good times. But they remembered things, places and people that no one else did. Those things didn't exist. They transcended time, memory, reality and dreams.

Is it a boon or a curse to be thrown into a situation that makes you lose your memory? You forget everything. You are not even able to recall the easiest-to-remember things. The names of people, for instance. Or the names of places and things. The names of your son, daughter, wife, husband, mother and father. The name of an ancestor—your namesake. You were named after him or her. You can't even recall the name you inherited. Your own name.

This happened to thousands of us, including my grandfather. It might happen to me as well. I live with this fear every single day. What if it happens to me? But even if it does happen, I won't even remember. It is not a boon. It is a curse. What if I forget the name of my own ancestor? What if I forget my own name?

I forget the name that was once on my lips. I don't know what to do or whom to ask. I search for it everywhere. It is nowhere, yet everywhere. It abandons me like life abandons a man on the brink of death. I look in the mountains, in the seas and in the dead memories of dead people. I knock at the doors of old dreams—every door shuts on me as if I were a ghost. I peep into a black hole that is said to carry the ashes of stars long dead and gone, separated from us by infinite lightyears—their black light lost forever in the universe.

And then I remember a photograph. On it is written a name, which was once my life.

So it all comes back—that we once did something together. Something that can never be done in life or in a dream.

How beautiful you are at this moment! Your eyes . . . they make everything stop. The hands of all clocks come to rest on top of each other. Even time feels cheated because it can't conjure you up the way it conjures everything else up. It can't do things that you do. It can't touch a dead man, bring him back to life and give him another chance in this world.

You sing to the mountain breeze. The mountain breeze sings back to you: 'Make me yours; take me with you.'

Years from now, people will shun their memories and disown their ancestors because they won't be in their lives or in their dreams.

I cling to a forgotten name like an orphan clings to someone else's mother. And, at last, as if by magic or witchcraft, you pass by me like a young comet passing by a dying planet one last time, leaving it with a scar for the rest of its descent.

Everything comes back to me. The day we met and the day we separated. Our separation—the separation of stars.

Once, we wrote our names on the withered leaves of Chinar trees and buried them in the earth in our courtyards, thinking that they would become fossils. We thought that years from now, people would chance upon these fossils and know our names.

Once, we spent the entire winter looking at the stars and thinking that they spoke our language. 'Look at the way they hold each other's ashes even when they are dead and long gone,' you said. 'They will never let go of each other. For they are one now.' We saw them in an embrace in the galaxy—fading, fading, fading. Are they going away from us or coming back to us?

What if happiness is sadness and sadness is happiness? What if we are mistaking fear for love and love for fear?

It was predicted that a day would come when someone else would weep my tears and laugh my laughs. It was foretold that someday you would rid me of this curse—this curse that leads to estrangement, obscurity and forgetfulness. That separates you from me.

* * *

'It is absurd to beget children,' says a camp-dweller. 'What kind of life can we offer them after bringing them into this sordid world? Where will we keep them? They will curse us once they realize where they are.'

'Not only should we beget children, but each married couple should produce at least seven children, if not more. We are dwindling. We should procreate to grow in numbers. Otherwise, we will become extinct in some years,' says a poet.

For the first ten years (1990–2000) in the camp at Udhampur, there weren't any marriages. There was no room for basic things, let alone marriage and married life. There was no privacy in the tents. You can live without privacy for a month, a few months, a year or a couple of years. But imagine living without privacy for twenty years. Women and teenage girls were the worst affected. If you were a married woman, imagine having to share one cramped tent with several male members of the family! You would constantly have your father-in-law, brothers-in-law or other males around you, leaving you with no personal space or privacy. Their mere presence is unsettling. Where do you go in such a situation?

All you have is a 12ft x 12ft second-hand canvas tent as your home until some messiah comes to take you back to your palace of dreams. The tent is all you have. It is a world unlike the one you have seen or known.

Inside the tent:

A 4ft x 4ft kitchen, a kerosene stove, some utensils and containers for rice, wheat, sugar and spices.

A wooden charpai or a folding bed with nylon straps for the person who needed it the most, usually an elderly grandfather or grandmother.

Tin trunks or leather attaché cases containing some belongings from Kashmir (those who were able to salvage things had them).

Most tents were partitioned into two areas using a bed sheet or a large drape, separating one end from the other. One side had a wooden cot with nylon straps. That's all. The other side had a rug on which the family members sat, slept and did everything else. You can't even spread your legs. You sit cross-legged. Men, women and children. Everyone. Day after day, month after month and year after year.

Then there are the essentials:

A plastic chair or stool, a small rack and a table fan.

A tarpaulin sheet on the floor and a rug to cover it.

Plastic sheets to prevent rainwater from seeping into the tent.

A radio set and a portable TV set in some cases.

A small corner that serves as a temple. Idols and framed pictures of gods and goddesses. A box of joss sticks. A bell. An almanac. And a book of scriptures.

No shelves. No furniture. Nothing that takes too much space. What more can a tiny tent hold inside?

A box containing medicines, a sewing kit and coins.

And the most important thing—the very life force—two large plastic drums to store water. One contains drinking water and the other holds water for washing purposes. And two earthen pots to chill the drinking water during summer.

On average, three generations live in one tent. They are joint families with eight to ten members. Grandparents, parents and children!

If you pay attention, you will notice, to a great extent, an uncanny order and hierarchy of things inside a tent. From utensils and idols to bedding and a box of clothes and a tin trunk containing valuables such as cash, bank passbooks, photo albums, migrant registration cards, ration cards, educational certificates and papers (mostly ownership papers of houses and land in Kashmir), all the things inside a tent have their own place, relevance and stature. These are the only things that really matter in the long run. Nothing else matters! Years from now, they will be the only signs of our lives in these camps. They will bear witness to a lost time that very few will remember. Especially when nobody else will believe that we lived such a life.

Men and women have their own peculiar habits. Women are largely concerned with keeping the kitchen area clean. They fret about auspiciousness, as they always have. They keep reminding the men and children not to bring shoes inside the tent. They are very particular about adhering to the same rules that governed their kitchens in Kashmir. No matter what, these rules must be adhered to and followed, even if there is barely any space. These 4ft x 4ft kitchens must always be kept sparkling clean, whatever be the circumstances. The floor must be swept twice a day. The women have also built small wooden or cardboard perches outside the tents to feed the birds. But the only birds around in the camp are crows. There are neither sparrows nor mynahs. This isn't the land where you will find sparrows, mynahs, woodpeckers, nightingales and bulbuls.

Imagine yourself as a teenage girl living in one such tent in the camp for ten years. The wounds that 'tent-women' carry on their hearts and souls will always bleed and cause pain. They can't even express the horror of having gone through such predicaments and lived such lives.

If you were five and forced to live in that tent in 1990, you lived there until you were fifteen. If you were ten, you

lived there until the age of twenty. If you were twenty, you
lived there until you turned thirty.

Outside the tent:

A constant haze! Dust storms! Outsiders stare at you
pitifully. Men salivate. Crows, kites, foxes, snakes, scorpions
and centipedes.

Six toilets for 1200 families living in tents. The families
whose tents are next to toilets suffer the most. They are forced
to live with the stench all the time. However, they have found
a way to keep the stench at bay—joss sticks! Day and night,
the fumes of joss sticks make it easy for the children to stay
inside the tents.

* * *

I haven't had the courage to spend a full day or night with
Pamposh in his tent. We meet outside, in the camp compound,
by the roadside or in the market. Pamposh invites me for
lunch. 'Mother has made lunch for you,' he says. 'Come over
for some time. Have lunch and then leave. Mother will be
happy. She keeps inquiring about you . . .'

Aunty never tires of asking me over, though I have a
feeling she knows I will never agree. I don't want to be the
cause of their embarrassment.

'Tomorrow,' I say, yet again.

'You and your tomorrows,' says Aunty.

'I will come over to your house when we are back in
Kashmir.'

'In that case, you must stay over . . .' says his mother.

The tent next to Pamposh's tent houses another family.
Two men and two women live here. An elderly couple with
their son and daughter-in-law. I feel drawn to the family for
some strange reason. I don't know them, but I have always

wanted to greet the man to make his acquaintance. And there comes a time when I find myself inside the tent as though I belong to the family. I keep going there from time to time on some pretext or another. After all, I've been a student at the camp school here. My friends and teachers are from here.

I sit in a corner, pretending to study. I have a book in my hands, but my gaze is fixed on the people. You can't tell if it is day or night. A Hindi film song is playing on the radio. It is from a movie that ran in the cinema halls in Kashmir in 1989, before all the movie theatres were made to shut down. I remember watching the movie at Neelam Cinema. The song has stayed with me ever since. This is one of those moments where I feel trapped between two eras. Like a dead moth caught between the two pages of an old book. I am unable to escape. The song goes on and on endlessly.

In front of me is the woman. She is lying on the wooden cot. She is unaware of where she is. She doesn't know that something is not right. She is not supposed to be on the cot. She is supposed to be on the floor next to her mother-in-law and husband. The expression on her face turns frightful the moment she opens her eyes. She turns sideways and, to her horror, she sees her father-in-law lying next to her. 'How did this happen?' she wonders. She is supposed to be sleeping on the floor, sandwiched between her husband and mother-in-law. I pretend to be asleep too.

The woman can't even hide her shame. Her husband and mother-in-law are asleep on the floor. Her husband is wearing a vest. The heat is atrocious. The woman wants to know if it is morning already. It is dark outside. The crickets have gone silent—a good omen. Dawn is around the corner.

The woman can't even hide. Where will she go? What will she do? At least, no one has seen her in this condition and position. She places her right hand over her lips, cursing her luck. She wants to strangle herself. She wants to slash her wrists. She wants to die. She prays for instant death. But she is helpless. It is not her fault. She is not to blame. She can't even die in this position and state. It will bring her shame. It will bring shame to her family. She is virtuous and pious. She musters strength. She gets off the cot quietly, tiptoes next to her sleeping husband and sits down in a corner of the tent. Her father-in-law has a smile etched on his face. She takes a small mirror out of her satchel and brings it closer to her face. She examines her own reflection as though it weren't hers. She runs her fingers across her cheeks, nose, chin, forehead, eyes and lips. She closes her eyes, unable to accept her own reflection.

Her hands are rough and leathery, as if she has been kneading stones with them. She takes a jar of moisturizing cream out of a bag and applies some to her hands to soften them.

She throws a blank, meaningless look at the man sleeping on the floor next to his mother. In Kashmir, they were inseparable when they were first married. They roamed in their orchards and spent days and months thinking of names for their future children and grandchildren. Now, the distance between them is growing wider and wider. Soon, they will be so far apart from each other that they won't even be able to see each other or feel each other's existence.

She puts the mirror down and covers her face with her hands. She sobs as though she has been robbed of the most valuable possession. Once, she was beautiful. But now . . . the beauty is gone and it will never come back. Her face isn't hers any longer.

She knows she will never get a second chance. She will never have her life back. But she won't stop dreaming.

She is still looking at me with those eyes and with that inscrutable look in them. The eyes that know only one language—the language of desperation, the language of silence.

'What are you looking at?' her look conveys. 'This is me. This has been my fate for ten years. This will be my fate for the next ten. I was not born here, but I will die here. I will never give birth here. I will never see motherhood. This is what you do. You will just peep like the devil and go away . . .'

Lost in a reverie, she smiles for a second, but then returns to the present moment. She shudders as she whispers to herself, 'I am not used to so much happiness . . . I must not allow myself such liberties . . . May I die if this happens to me again . . .'

She rummages through her bag again and again. She finds a tiny box barely containing some kohl. She applies whatever is left of it on her eyelids. She finds nail polish. Most of it has dried up, but there are still some remnants. She tries to paint the toenails on her right foot. Her heels are cracked. Those feet were once beautiful. Before her is a young woman in bridal attire. It is her from just a few years ago. But it seems like a lifetime ago. From another life that was cut short. She wants to get dressed, but her bridalwear is gone.

At last, she gives up. The moon, her only constant companion, holds her in its light until it hides behind a cloud. The moonlight having left her, her face is now covered in darkness.

This strange ritual continues night after night for several nights. One day, she musters courage and begs her husband to take her somewhere else. She says this land is cursed and it is making her do strange things. She can't see eye-to-eye with her mother-in-law on many things, but she falls to her feet and begs for forgiveness. The father-in-law doesn't know anything—he is beyond knowing anything at all.

Dawn brings relief, but with night comes fear. The woman has no one to talk to. Except for one person. No one knows what they talk about. Every evening, the two of them go behind a tree and sob when no one is around.

The nameless, faceless woman who doesn't know what dreadful and ignominious curse has befallen her is looking at me and begging me to rid her of the curse. Her shadow is still in the camp. It will haunt the place for years. It will haunt me. This is where she wasted the prime years of her life.

The next day, many camp-dwellers distribute sweets to one another. The results of the matriculation examination are out. An old man stands at the camp entrance, holding a box of sweets in his hands. He can't contain his happiness. He has the smile of a man who hasn't smiled in years. He can't chew anymore. His dentures are nowhere to be found. Even his spectacles are beyond repair. The tremor on his lips reveals a different story. 'My grandson has passed the matriculation exam,' he goes on and on. 'He is a matriculate now . . .' For the rest of the day, the man doesn't abandon his position, like a sentry making sure that the news of his grandson's achievement reaches everyone and that not a single person passes by without having a sweet. Passers-by who walk past stop briefly to look at him. They exchange greetings. 'Mubarak,' they say. Everyone offers blessings to children. 'They will save us someday . . . They are our only hope . . .'

Inside the tents, there is the aroma of food and the sounds of chit-chat, laughter and tears. Happiness is finally here, after a long, long time. Yet some people are crying. At dinnertime, people sit inside their tents and eat the way they sat and ate in their homes in Kashmir.

Inside one tent, a girl is teaching her younger sibling how to play noughts and crosses (tic-tac-toe). After several games, she lets him taste victory. He is all smiles.

There is a pigeon nest atop a bamboo fixture on their tent. A pigeon is nurturing her two chicks. The hungry chicks are cooing constantly with their tiny beaks open in front of their mother. The siblings look at the pigeon chicks and place a handful of corn kernels in a bowl.

Two siblings are floating paper boats in a puddle of water. A young woman is teaching the kids how to create an embankment around the small puddle. Nearby, around some other tents, a stream has formed due to incessant rain in the night. The woman stares at it as though it were a river to be crossed. She was to get married in Kashmir. She left her trunk behind, which contained her bridal attire and other things her grandmother had kept for her. Things the girl had collected and preserved for years. Had she not fled, all her inheritance would have been safe with her. Now look at her. She has lost the will to live. But she goes on.

* * *

Pamposh is gone now. The keeper of the deepest secrets of the camp in Udhampur is nowhere to be seen. I miss him. I don't know where he is. Many people have shifted from the camp to Sailan Talab, where they've rented two-room sets. Pamposh and his family must be there, too. I feel happy for Pamposh's mother and grandmother. At least they won't have to go through any more horrid nights in the camp. Nights mean all sorts of delusional disorders. Disorders that should never happen to humans.

Pamposh didn't want me to be the cause of people's embarrassment. That's why he never wanted me to be in the camp. He knew I wouldn't understand many of the things that took place. No one would. But now I worry for him.

What might he think if he found out that I disregarded his advice? I worry for myself too.

Will Pamposh ever forgive me for my flaws and mistakes? I may never get to meet him again. He had said he would rather die than go anywhere else. Neither Jammu nor Delhi nor any other city. The only place he would ever go is his home in Kashmir. Nothing interested him more than the life he was forced to part with. Nothing gave him more energy than the dream of his home. While I regretted not clearing any of the competitive examinations and landing the dream job of a postman or a Life Insurance Corporation agent, he worked towards planning how to give back to his parents all they had lost. The plan to restore everything fuelled his life.

'I will wait here until I take them back home,' Pamposh had said. 'I won't go anywhere else.' He rarely talked with others. I was his only friend and confidante.

How beautiful it is to die with a bunch of secrets buried in your heart! Secrets you don't even tell yourself. But there are days when those secrets haunt you. Then you shudder and wonder why. You think they are beautiful secrets, but are they? They will consume you. They will not let you be at peace. They will drive you insane.

At home, in Kashmir, we had four seasons in a year. Here, in the camp, we reap nothing but ashes. Here, wives lament the absence of their husbands and long for their return, even when they are next to them. And husbands make love to their wives only in dreams. Parents turn their gazes away, seeing their sons and daughters on the precipice of adolescence.

'Time will carry us on its shoulders to a place we don't want to go,' said the most sought-after person in the camp. He was an expert in performing rituals.

There was a time when 'What is the time?' was a frequently asked question in the camp. Camp-dwellers asked this question to one another almost every hour. People looked at their wristwatches. Some of the wristwatches weren't even working. Some people looked at the sun while others looked at the shadows and the birds and the strays to tell the time. At night, people looked at the moon.

And then came a day when an elderly man, fed up with this 'time checking' ritual, sighed. 'This is a refugee camp. Time has no time for us,' he said.

Once, when we were kids, we were stranded on the Srinagar–Jammu national highway for three days. It was winter and the national highway was blocked due to heavy snowfall. Babi and other women sprang into action. They created makeshift kitchens by the roadside. They created snow shelters for us to spend the night in and keep warm. They lit stoves under the trucks. After three nights and four days, we turned back and went home.

When we expressed sadness over not being able to go very far, we were told we were never meant to leave home. And we were fortunate to be back so soon. We were told that one should never get to leave one's home. Home meant everything to the elders. They never wanted to go away, even for a day. Such was their emotional dependence on their homes.

* * *

2017
New Delhi

Pa has lost his mobile phone on a metro train. We are now in an autorickshaw going back home after buying a new phone. Pa wipes his tears.

'What happened?' I ask.

'Do you remember when you were twelve years old and you wanted a new jacket but I could not afford to buy you a new one? I kept you waiting. And then I went to the Bangladeshi market in Forest Lane and bought a second-hand jacket. You loved it, but you didn't know it was not a new jacket . . .'

'I loved that jacket.'

'There was a time I had nothing. Very little money . . . I was unemployed for years. But I wanted to see you happy. I wanted happiness for all of us . . . I am happy today. That is why I am crying . . .'

I say to Pa, 'I see Kashmir through your memory, not mine.'

* * *

Summer 2018
Delhi

Boxes sent by Pa arrive by courier from Jammu. Four boxes contain books. One box contains the letters that I'd written to Pa and Babuji from Delhi. Pa has preserved everything. In another box are old photographs and certificates. Babuji's two microscopes and prescription booklets are in another box. In another box are birch manuscripts. The writing is in the Sharada script. Dr Toshkhani, who is one of the very few people who can read Sharada, says these manuscripts chronicle accounts from Maharaja Ranjit Singh's life and times.

'They are priceless and possibly nobody else has these,' Pa says. 'If you wish, you can donate them to some museum where they will be preserved and taken care of.'

We should get them digitized and then give them to the National Archives or the National Museum, I think.

In another box are Babi and Babuji's things: spectacles, a magnifying lens, earrings, pens and coins. Each of these possessions has a history behind it and a story to tell. Stories of their own journeys and how they have been witnesses to an unfolding history too.

Everything is in immaculate condition. Every letter, paper, certificate, document, photograph and possession.

'It is time to hand over everything to you,' says Pa. This is one of the very few times I disagree with him. But he insists.

'We are old now and it's better if these things remain with you than with us. I have couriered some boxes to Henna too. When we are forgotten by everyone and when I may also have no recollection, then you will remember everything and pass on the remembrance to your children so that it never vanishes. It should be carried forward.'

24

1990 Is Back

'There is still so much hatred in my own town,' says the Jewish Holocaust survivor, Irene Zisblatt, who features in the 1998 Academy Award-winning documentary film *The Last Days*. 'I didn't want the world to see how much hatred is still going on after all of this suffering,' she says.

Like the four other Jewish survivors of the Holocaust featured in the film, Irene recounts stories about her time in a Nazi concentration camp—going back and forth in time, and revealing a horrifying account of persecution and extermination under the genocidal Nazi regime in Hungary. She talks about the life she lived in the concentration camp, her miraculous survival and escape from the camp and a strange homecoming to a homeland that once was hers and from where she was deported. Hers is a journey from days of joy and glory to days of darkness and horror. That horror is still encased in her heart, as if it were a trophy. It has now given rise to a void and out of that void springs forth abundant humanity, goodness, goodwill and a desire to dedicate the rest of her life to the memory of those who perished, including her own family.

* * *

30 August 2021
Srinagar, Kashmir

Hundreds of Kashmiri Pandits assemble in the streets of Srinagar and bring out Krishna *jhankis* (tableaus) to celebrate Krishna Janmashtami. This coming together of Kashmiri Pandits in the Valley for the first time in three decades to celebrate Janmashtami in the traditional way is an act of courage. It signals an intent to reclaim lost time and a lost way of life. The message being conveyed is: 'This is our land and we will no longer be fearful.'

At the heart of their celebration and gaiety shines an ardent desire to return to their long-lost homeland, from which they were ousted thirty-one years ago. This celebration has been long overdue. People have waited for this day.

The sight of Kashmiri Pandits bringing out jhankis and singing devotional songs in the streets of Srinagar brings back old memories, having been part of such happy festive occasions during my childhood in Kashmir. Everybody greets each other. It isn't the usual greeting; it is accompanied by the airing of optimism and hope. There is a growing feeling that our thirty-one-year-long exile might end soon! Perhaps this will usher in a new dawn and we will be able to return and do everything we used to do when we lived there. Everyone praises the government for some reason.

Some see signs of normalcy, while others sense a lull before the storm.

* * *

15 August 2021
Srinagar, Kashmir

It's the seventy-fifth anniversary of India's Independence Day. The *ghanta ghar* (clock tower) at Lal Chowk is draped in the *tiranga* (tricoloured national flag of India) for the first time in history! That clock has been a silent witness to the goriest of events and bloodshed.

Another unusual sight: two tall flags are flying high on the Hari Parbat Fort and Shankaracharya Hill.

Earlier in March, a fashion show was held in Srinagar. Imagine a fashion show in a place where cinemas are closed.

* * *

20 September 2021
Kashmir

It is Anant Chaturdashi. Many displaced Kashmiri Pandits travel from Delhi and Jammu to Kashmir. They perform puja and hawan in the temple at Nagbal (the sacred pond), Anantnag. A few days earlier, many prayed on the banks of Jhelum to celebrate Vyeth Truvah, the birthday of the river goddess Vitasta, also known as Jhelum.

The revival of age-old customs in the land of my birth fills my heart with hope. Henna and her husband are also in Kashmir to spend a few days there.

'How is everything there?' I ask them.

'A new beginning,' they say, sending me video clips from their visit to Hari Parbat, the Bhadra Kali temple and Nagbal, rekindling hope in my heart. 'We shall soon come back to our homeland for good. This is our only prayer . . .'

Yet I sense a strange silence, an uneasy calm. An old memory comes alive at the sight of a floundering Downtown by the Jhelum. As though something ominous is about to unfold.

But then, the sight of so many Pandits in Kashmir is reassuring—the good old days seem to be back. The Muslims are all smiles and wish Pandits on auspicious occasions. This bonhomie isn't unfamiliar.

Is this the light at the end of the tunnel? The light we have been dreaming of day after day, night after night, for the past thirty-one years!

* * *

3 October 2021
Anantnag

Locals desecrate the Mata Bargheshekha Bhagwati temple, which is located on a mountain ridge in District Anantnag. Our hearts sink yet again.

* * *

6 October 2021
Srinagar

A well-known Pandit pharmacist is shot dead by terrorists outside his shop on Srinagar's bustling Hari Singh High Street. The news of his killing sends shivers down the spines of the entire community. It's reminiscent of the murders of Lassa Kaul and Justice Neel Kanth Ganjoo. Yet again, we are made to relive those dark days.

The unfolding of familiar horror! Our worst nightmare comes true once again. Killing the very person who selflessly serves people is akin to dehumanizing the entire community that the person belongs to. Such a thing didn't take place even in the dark ages.

In the preceding months, we continue to struggle to come to terms with the killings of Pandits in Kashmir. In June, Ajay Pandita, a forty-year-old Kashmiri Pandit sarpanch, meets the same fate when he is shot dead by terrorists while he is serving the people there. His house in Jammu wears a sombre look now. It was once a residence of happiness and laughter. In September, Police Constable Bantu Sharma is killed. The killers are still at large.

* * *

Morning, 7 October 2021
Srinagar

Terrorists sneak into a school's premises in Downtown Srinagar, separate the Muslims from the non-Muslims, single out Principal Supinder Kour (a Sikh woman) and Deepak Chand (a Hindu) and shoot them dead. Their fault: they don't belong. Their only mistake—celebrating their nation's Independence Day in school. It becomes the cause of their killing.

'Kill one, scare ten, the Muslim mobs chanted and ten were, indeed, scared . . .' writes Salman Rushdie in *Shalimar the Clown*.

The ploy always works. It worked in 1989 in Kashmir.

This premeditated and targeted killing of religious minorities in Kashmir is not just any other killing. This is a language. The only language Pandit-haters have known since 1989.

'Genocide, after all, is an exercise in community building,' writes Philip Gourevitch about the Hutu genocide of the Tutsi minority ethnic group in Rwanda in *We Wish to Inform You That Tomorrow We Will Be Killed with Our Families*.

I'm afraid for other Kashmiri Pandits who are still serving in Kashmir. It's as though the final shred of hope is being snatched at the very last moment. Imagine the condition of about 6000 young Kashmiri Pandits who are employed in various parts of Kashmir under the prime minister's Employment Package for Kashmiri Pandit migrants. The very words in the name of this scheme—'package' and 'migrant'— are so inept and cruel. Package employees! That's what these youngsters are called in their own homeland and in state government circles.

These youngsters, living in mortal dread, along with their spouses and children—most of them barely even thirty—are children of exile, having been born in camps in Jammu. Those 'camp homes' still exist in Jagati and Buta Nagar in Jammu. The displaced parents and grandparents of these youngsters live there.

What, then, is home? Where is home? Kashmir, where these youngsters are forced to work as 'package employees' or Jammu, where their parents live in camps, longing for a dignified return to the land of their birth and to their ancestral homes?

What will they do now in the wake of these killings of Pandits? And what about those Pandits who, despite all odds, chose to stay behind in 1990? They have paid a huge cost for staying back. With their freedoms snatched, an uncertain future looms large! The fear of extermination once again gives rise to thoughts of leaving everything behind and fleeing their homes in Kashmir.

We are the nowhere and no-place people.

My father recalls spending time at the pharmacist's shop in the 1980s. He knew him quite well. Almost everyone in Srinagar knew him for his selfless service to the underprivileged in the worst of times.

Within hours of the pharmacist's killing, the mayor of Srinagar proposes to name a portion of the road near Iqbal Park after Bindroo.

It's a new fad the government seems to have acquired from somewhere. To name roads and institutions after Kashmiri

Pandits. The government has now set up a committee to name places in Kashmir after Kashmiri Pandit poets, scholars and even martyrs.

Imagine, we will have roads, bridges, parks and even museums named after us. There will be a Kaul lake and a Gigoo mountain. Our cut-outs will adorn the slopes of Zabarwan. And Muslim kids will ask their parents, 'Who are these people?' We will be nowhere. Neither here, nor there! Twice banished from our homeland! And all that will remain is an odd signboard in a street in Srinagar flashing our names, relegating us to the past, long erased from history. This will be the government's doing.

Summing up the strange yet indescribable plight of Kashmiri Pandits, Pa says, 'We weep laughs, we laugh weeps.'

Almost every Kashmiri Pandit living in Kashmir is at risk now. Anyone could be next.

'It happened; therefore, it can happen again; this is the core of what we have to say,' says Primo Levi about the genocide of the Jews during the Holocaust.

The fate of 6000 young Kashmiri Pandits working in Kashmir as part of the prime minister's Employment Package hangs in the balance now.

Once again, Pandits find themselves on the hit lists of Kashmiri terror outfits.

* * *

Evening, 7 October 2021
New Delhi

I give Sushant a call. He is posted in a government office in a remote village on the outskirts of Anantnag. His wife is a government school teacher there.

'We are caught between the devil and the deep sea,' he says, terrified. 'The government has left us to fend for ourselves . . . what happened to all those tall promises made by the current government? We have been forced to live in cramped spaces in transit quarters made of asbestos sheets . . . in far-flung areas with no security . . . our own government has betrayed us . . . we are being massacred again one after another . . . the leaders are clueless . . . we don't know what to do . . . our existence here is under threat once again . . . it is going to be a long, dreadful night . . . there is only one option now . . .'

'You mean you will leave? When?' I ask.

'Tomorrow, at the crack of dawn,' he says.

'What have you decided?'

'We will demand safety and security! We will demand transfer to safer zones. If we go back to Kashmir and to the remote districts where we are posted, where there is risk to our lives and where we are exposed without security, we will be killed. It is clear now. The government must act now. It is up to the government to save us now.'

The Next Day

Yet again, our pleas fall on deaf ears. Yet again.

* * *

'There are 3,50,000 survivors of the Holocaust alive today and I implore all the educators to not allow the Holocaust to remain a footnote in history,' said Steven Spielberg in his 1993 Oscar acceptance speech for his movie *Schindler's List*. 'These 3,50,000 experts just want to be useful for the remainder of their lives. Please teach this in school and

please listen to the words and the echoes and the ghosts . . .'
he adds.

* * *

A Day in the Winter of 1988
Home, Kashmir

The film *Escape from Sobibor* airs on Doordarshan Kashmir.
We sit still in front of the television set, watching the
horrifying scenes of the mass escape of Jews from the Nazi
extermination camp at Sobibor. It is my first encounter with
world history, especially the extermination of the European
Jews during the Second World War.

If someone tells me that we too will be made to go through
horror two years later, I will die laughing.

* * *

December 1993
Sri Fort Auditorium, New Delhi

Panun Kashmir, an organization of Kashmiri Pandits founded
by poet and activist Dr Agnishekhar, is hosting a conference.
The purpose of the conference is to inform the world about
what we are going through. Pa and I have come to Delhi to
attend the conference. The only famous personality to address
the audience is Anupam Kher. The press is here because of
him. Samdhong Rinpoche, the former PM of the Tibetan
government-in-exile, is there to express his solidarity. He
talks about his own exile. He speaks of hope and home. 'We
must never lose hope. We must dream of home. No other
dream is worth dreaming . . .'

Lectures are delivered to empty seats in the Siri Fort Auditorium.

* * *

February 1994
New Delhi

Representatives from the Kashmiri Pandit community inform the United Nations High Commissioner for Refugees (UNHCR) in Geneva that Islamist militants have driven them away from Kashmir.[12] They beg the UNHCR to take note of this persecution and displacement, and to send a fact-finding mission team to Kashmir to investigate the ethnic cleansing and genocide of the Kashmiri Hindu minorities. This is the community's first appeal to world conscience. 'Listen to us, look at us . . .' they implore. Letter after letter and memorandum after memorandum go unnoticed.

* * *

What will become of us and our progeny? How will our progeny know what happened to their own ancestors?

Day after day, year after year and decade after decade, we have pleaded for justice. Some people took note, others expressed sympathy and some didn't even care to listen. The result—nothing. There was no fact-finding mission, even though the truth was out there. All that was needed were visits to the camps to witness the conditions of the people there. There were more than fifty such camps all over India. Some camps exist in Jammu even now.

We were thrown into a long exile and forced to live in subhuman conditions in camps. How will we ever forget all that we were made to go through?

'Yours is going to be a long struggle,' says Pa. 'Language will play an important role. Don't forget to tell your story correctly. Don't let anyone dilute it or take the truth away. The only thing we have now is truth. Nothing else! It is our only heirloom! But if you choose to be silent, make sure even your silence doesn't go unheard and that it reaches far and wide . . .'

Words like identity, displacement, home, exodus, exile, genocide, camp, refugee, migrant, memory, space, time and hope define us now and give meaning to our lives.

I watch *Escape from Sobibor* for the second time. We went through a similar situation—trying to escape persecution and extermination. Had we not fled Kashmir, we would have been slaughtered.

We didn't realize our own horror at the time because we were busy keeping ourselves alive.

In his seminal 2001 essay, 'The Exiled Tongue', Imre Kertész speaks of the impossibility of writing about the Holocaust. He goes on to add that, 'because of the paradoxical impossibilities, it is impossible not to write about the Holocaust. The Holocaust cannot be repaired, avenged, assuaged or even understood. All one can do is to look it in the face and recognize it.' This becomes the fulcrum of the moral dilemma the protagonist of his novel, *Fiasco*, is faced with.

There is deep humanity in being a silent sufferer—to not give up hope while battling all odds, especially when you find yourself surrounded by people who deny you your own history and won't care to know it even when you are going through it. And then comes a time when you, as a silent sufferer, find yourself face-to-face with your brutal past once again, with images from your history coming alive one after another.

I see myself once again. Helpless, begging for mercy, alone and about to die.

It is absurd to even imagine such a situation. Beyond the absurdity of that horror is the morality of a people long suppressed by a nation's apathy and the apathy of their own compatriots.

An entire generation has grown up in the shadow of the horrors inflicted on their own ancestors.

On his deathbed, Babuji implores us to take him home to Kashmir, but he knows he will not live to see that day. Therefore, he wants us to take his ashes there. And then he dies a lonely death, unable to even dream one last happy dream of homecoming.

* * *

12 May 2022
Kashmir

Rahul Bhat, a young man employed in Kashmir under the prime minister's Employment Package for Kashmiri Pandits, is killed in his office in Chadoora, Budgam. His friends and colleagues come out to protest and demand security. 'Send us back to Jammu,' they cry again for the hundredth time. 'Give us a Jammu posting. Is it too much to ask? Here, we are being targeted, threatened and killed once again . . .'

The youngsters have been desperately pleading for eight years. Just a simple plea. Transfer to a safe zone, which will give them a sense of dignity and security! A sense that they are being cared for and not left to die and that they won't have to undergo persecution over and over.

Little do they know that not only will their demands be ignored, but they will also be teargassed and lathi-charged in full public glare. They endure the humiliation.

Dear people, the least you can do is empathize, listen and comfort us. Acknowledge that we are being wronged once again.

* * *

31 May 2022

One more Hindu teacher, Rajni Bala, is killed on her school premises in front of her students and fellow teachers.

'Even the shadows cannot be trusted here,' says the Lt governor of the union territory of Jammu and Kashmir to the protesting youths.

Everyone is saying the same thing. We live in constant fear. The Lt governor is right. He understands the fear more than we do. We are fearful even of a shadow. We are trapped inside a cage. We are not the perennial migratory birds, Mr governor. We belong here. But this isn't the home we dream of; this isn't the homecoming we long for.

* * *

1 June 2022

In 1990, the militants gave us thirty-six hours to leave our homes in Kashmir.

Today, on 1 June 2022, we give the Jammu and Kashmir administration and the Government of India a thirty-six-hour-notice before fleeing Kashmir once again to save our lives.

A long silence from the administration and the people in power and authority, whose conscience falls silent and dies only when a Kashmiri Pandit is killed. In all other instances, they are the conscience-keepers of the nation. Now that one more Hindu has been killed because he was a Hindu, they are without a conscience. The government has no empathy left for us. They have shut their doors on us. We are on our own. We have always been on our own. This has been going on for decades.

Ours is not a service or employment issue, as is being deliberately portrayed. It is not even about justice right now. Justice will be useful if and only if we manage to stay alive to see it. Right now, it is about the looming danger to our lives. The very idea of our existence as Kashmir's original inhabitants is being questioned once again. Not for the first time, though. We are now the 'once again' people. It is about life and death now. It is about being forced to become cannon fodder. We are sitting ducks in our own homeland. We must save our lives.

Yesterday, it was Rahul. Then Rajni! Tomorrow, it could be you and me who are forced to serve in Kashmir with neither safety nor security.

'Don't send us there forcibly to get us killed,' say the employees.

But we Kashmiri Pandits are not even a problem for the government. We have never been a bother to anyone. We are disposable entities. Nobody is going to spare a thought for us. They use us for their own gains and vested interests when it suits their agenda. You use us when you have your own axe to grind.

They have now locked us up in our own quarters. So that we can't even leave, protest, plead with joined palms, or even be seen or heard in the streets. How absurd can this get? Our entire existence is absurd now. You think these cages are a substitute for our lost homes? This isn't our home any longer. You have allowed it to be converted into a slaughterhouse and a house of hate and violence. Where its own people will never be allowed to stay. Where they will be killed for even calling it their home or for thinking of it as their own. At the very thought of its existence as part of our lives.

What if this doesn't end for another fifty years? We asked the same question thirty-three years ago? We've been asking the same question day after day, month after month, year after year and decade after decade. Will it even end? What will it take to end? What will it take to give us and our progeny justice? All we want is to be safe. It has come to this. Jammu is our home now. Let Kashmir be the home of our dreams and memories—beautiful, pristine and flourishing— with us living happy lives with all those who perished in the camps in exile. But now, even the dreams are turning ugly and gory.

I dream that I am being chased by someone who is hell-bent on killing me just because he wants me dead. What is it that has corrupted the souls of these people who come out of their houses, walk into schools or offices, shoot people dead and then return home to carry on with their daily lives?

* * *

3 June 2022
Kashmir

Hundreds of young Kashmiri Pandit employees flee Kashmir. Frustrated, exhausted, dejected and angry, they have no recourse but to leave and rejoin their parents and grandparents in Jammu. Their parents and relatives have been living in mortal dread and terror all these months. We sum up our plight in just four words.

Morning: Kashmir
Evening: Jammu

Kashmir will always be in our hearts and we will always dream of going back with dignity when we will not be humiliated and targeted. Where we will have safety and security. Where our children and parents will not live with constant fear.

This is the eighth exodus in our history. And India should never forget this. This should be a blot on the nation's history. Where is the civil society in India? Where is everyone? Why is everyone silent even after seeing what we are being made to go through?

'I have reached Jammu,' says a friend.

The next day, warning letters and death threats are issued and circulated. Something along the lines of: 'Hindus, keep out of Kashmir. Anyone who rents out rooms to Hindus will not be spared.'[13]

January 1990 is back. The same language. The same warning.

One more ultimatum is issued. Something along the lines of: 'All Hindus must leave Kashmir within thirty-six hours.'— Kashmir Tigers

In 1990, it was Allah Tigers that issued the ultimatum to us. Thirty-two years later, it is Kashmir Tigers.

* * *

4 June 2022

The tourism department of the Government of Kashmir issues advertisements.

'Want to undertake a trip of a lifetime? A trip to remember! Visit Kashmir this summer.'

'Kashmir is open for film shoots.'

'*Welcome to Kashmir*' reads a banner just outside the Srinagar airport. Tourists start arriving in Kashmir. Preparations are underway for the Amarnath yatra.

'We are living in transit quarters in our own homeland,' says a young Pandit employee who is about to leave Kashmir for Jammu. 'You think this is true rehabilitation and return? Do you want to see the home the government has given us? Look at this! This is a prefabricated metal shed. Its shelf life is seven years, but we have been forced to live in this shed for the last twelve years. Six families are forced to share a shed. The 5ft x 5ft kitchen is to be shared by six households. Look at the roof. Asbestos sheets. What do you want us to call this place? Transit quarters? A shed? A camp? A home? We have been turned into bonded labour. We have been divided and separated from our families. Parents are in Jammu; we are here; children are neither there nor here. My home is just a ten-minute walk from here, but I am afraid of going there. I can't even take my wife and child there. We are stuck here with no safety and no security. What kind of life is this? This is worse than death. I am leaving this place now. I don't know what will happen. But I can't live here like this anymore . . .'

'Our children are the worst sufferers,' says his father, who lives in the camp in Muthi, Jammu. 'They were made to sign on a dotted line. We were helpless then. We are helpless now. After all, what did we have then? What do we have now? Nothing except educational degrees and a dream! We lost everything in Kashmir. Our homes, our culture and our future! The government gave us this employment package as compensation, but it is designed to humiliate our children. Our children were forced into a cruel pact: that they wouldn't demand a transfer under any circumstances. If they leave

Kashmir for whatever reason, they will be terminated from government services without notice. They must remain quiet no matter what.'

According to Sub-rule 6 of Rule 6 of the Jammu and Kashmir Kashmiri Migrants (Special Drive) Recruitment Rules, 2009, the appointee must work within Kashmir and will not be eligible for transfer outside Kashmir under any circumstances.

There is another absurd and oppressive rule that applies to the 'package employees'. According to Sub-rule 4 of Rule 4 of the Jammu and Kashmir Kashmiri Migrants (Special Drive) Recruitment Rules, 2009, in case the appointee migrates from Kashmir for any reason whatsoever, he or she shall lose the job without any notice and shall stand terminated.

Both rules clearly jeopardize the lives and safety of the employees.

'This is not a step towards rehabilitating us,' the man continues. 'The government cheated us. They are the ones without a conscience or a soul. They are using us to prove a point: since we are back, Kashmir is normal and they have succeeded in rehabilitating us. They are celebrating their victory and our silent suffering. We are a lost cause. Once again, we appeal to the Government of India to talk to us to understand what we are going through. We have tried everything. We are still trying and we will keep trying. What else do you want us to do? Immolate ourselves on the streets?'

The government of the union territory of Jammu and Kashmir issues a statement: 'Accommodation for Kashmiri Pandit employees posted in Kashmir to be completed by 2023.'[14]

We've been hearing such tall promises for the past twelve years. Every year, a promise is made to us to keep us happy and quiet.

'Land has been identified for you. The plan has been approved. Construction will begin in the spring. You must wait for some more time,' says a government official.

Why does everything have to wait until spring? When will the spring of our homecoming arrive?

We know we can't have our lost lives back. We don't want accommodation in Kashmir. We want our homes back. We want our Kashmir.

'But the government hasn't given us even a single home yet, let alone an entire homeland that once was ours,' says Sushant.

Imagine the plight of thousands of such people. They have strange addresses.

Their address in Jammu: Kashmiri Pandit Migrant Quarters, Buta Nagar.

And in Kashmir: Kashmiri Pandit Transit Quarters, Anantnag.

The words—'migrant', 'transit' and 'quarters'—are now etched into their very being. This is the burden they carry. For some, it is a matter of shame, of stigma and of injustice. For others, it is a matter of unresolved social identity.

* * *

The streets where we once walked and where our shadows once fell are empty again. Not even the faintest sign of our lives remain there. The houses are empty. The rooms where, until yesterday, we huddled, looking at our old, deserted houses through the windows, dreaming of going there and rebuilding them and living in them, are empty. Even the songs won't be heard anymore. What traces of our existence will we leave behind before we leave once again, so that years from now our progeny will find them and know what we were made to go through? Don't allow the world to turn you into a nomad, a homeless or a dreamless person. Take what is rightfully yours. What was mine is now yours. Claim it.

My dear children,

Can a dream ever be found? Will you someday dream my dream? The dream that was snatched from me; the one I was not allowed to dream.

Yours,
An exiled father who has nothing to offer you except a dream. The dream of new roots.

* * *

**Dawn
8 June 2022
New Delhi**

It is Zyeth Aetham today. Today, Kashmiri Pandits go to Tulmul to pray. They have been going to Tulmul on this day every year. It is a tradition. I tune into a Facebook Live broadcast from Mata Kheer Bhawani Temple in Janipur, Jammu.

'We feel we are home,' says a devotee. 'Even if we spend thirty minutes here, those thirty minutes equal thirty years or even thirty lifetimes . . . Goddess Kheer Bhawani is our *isht devi.** She will take us home someday. When I close my eyes, I am already in my home in Kashmir, next to our Tulmul. The goddess has blessed me. Look at the holy pond. For years, the water in it was black. The water now is cerulean, the right

---

* The presiding deity.

colour. It is a sign of the good times to come! Auspicious times! We will go back . . .'

The temple bells are pealing. A woman sits in a corner with her eyes closed. She is happy.

* * *

August–September 1982
Eid Gah, Srinagar

Babuji has brought me to Eid Gah to teach me how to fly a kite. Hundreds of kites are flying in the sky. The Tibetan refugee colony is nearby. Kids from the refugee colony are flying kites and playing cricket and football. Some women are knitting sweaters and some are selling winter clothes. Men are idling. The smell of water chestnuts wafts by. The leaves of poplars and willows have started to change colour, signalling the arrival of autumn shortly. Kites are dancing in the sky. The summer has been one of happiness, but now a strange melancholy seems to have crawled out of nowhere.

I am learning how to fly a kite. Babuji has taught me how to make kites. I prefer one with colourful long tails. One of my kites is saffron, white and green, but all the other kites in the sky are green and white.

Every weekend, we come here to fly kites. My kite now knows how to soar high above the clouds.

One day in September, Babuji's friend from the neighbourhood brings some news. 'Sher-i-Kashmir is no more . . .' he says. 'Sheikh Abdullah has attained Jannat-ul-Firdaus . . .'

All of Kashmir has taken to the streets. Babuji and his friends decide to be part of the funeral procession. The look on their faces is one of dejection and despair. For years, they took pride in the belief that Sheikh would always do what was best for Kashmiris. And that whatever Sheikh did would always be for the benefit of Kashmir.

'What will happen to our Kashmir now?' people say.

'They say his son is going to take over as chief minister . . .'

I have never seen Babuji this distraught. It seems to be the worst day of his life. He keeps on talking about Kashmir's tallest leader. The people's leader. He remembers his speeches and utterances. 'You know what he used to say . . .' says Babuji, describing Sheikh's speeches.

Outside in the streets, everyone is waving red flags. The flags bear images of a plough, the symbol of the National Conference. But the Valley has been painted green.

* * *

A Day in 1987

There is talk of a surprise picnic. We students are instructed to assemble outside the gates of the school. We are taken on buses to another school and given instructions. We are told this is part of the civics practical and that a day will come when we, as grown-ups, will be required to cast our votes.

We are taught what to do upon entering the rooms. By evening, all of us have cast our votes in an 'election'.

In his lifetime, Babuji didn't get to realize that the leaders he and his friends believed in and glorified were the ones who betrayed them. It would have caused him immense pain.

* * *

And now, I want you to close your eyes one last time before everything ends. We won't get a second chance at this. It's now or never.

There must be no words between us. Nobody and none of the things that surround us should get to know anything. Not even you and I. Everything between us will be an unspoken heart-to-heart.

I am not me. You are not you. We are other people who have come and gone and who are yet to come. The people who have some of me and some of you. The people who will have some of me and some of you. We are our own ancestors. We are our own progeny. We are those people who once were and who will be. They will sing our songs, dream our dreams. The songs and dreams we left incomplete and couldn't finish.

We begin now. This must be done very carefully and slowly, as if death masquerading as life were at our doorstep, waiting to deal the final blow. Time, in its dying moments, has chosen us to be the sole recipients of the last remnant of its own flesh and blood. Who knows—it could be a boon? We could live off it as slowly as possible to prolong its end indefinitely and until infinity.

25

New Roots

19 January 1990–19 January 2024
New Delhi–Srinagar

19 January 1990,
the colour of fear,
an unvoiced decree,
and the last journey.
Afar—
A sunset on the stairs,
Blood dripping on the saffron bud,
Fear,
Shrieks,
The deafening curfew,
A gaping wound on the forehead
And the paralysis of the shadow.
Exile shakes the pillars of our conscience.
We have no seasons,
No walls to hang pictures
Of our ancestors.
History weeps through the eyes of the old,

And children,
Housed under canvas
Play mute.
A snakebite
A sunstroke
An accident
And then the curtain.
A civilization dangles between
The horoscope and the computer.
The young see visions
Even at the crematorium.
Dreams of permanence flow.
A new strangeness
A new land
And the exiles discover
Some new roots.

* * *

March 2022

I have known Bhaviya for over three years now. We follow each
other on Instagram. She writes about books and music. Her bio
says she is doing her master's in English literature. She wants my
suggestions about what she must do next. On the phone, she
says she is interested in doing a PhD. And that she would like
to study the exodus and exile of Kashmiri Pandits. But will her
identity as a Kashmiri Pandit come in the way of her independent
research and prevent her from being objective? Her father has
seen uprootedness. I don't think she should abandon the idea.
This is an important subject. 'I was born outside Kashmir and
all I have are memories and stories told to me by my father,' she
says. 'He knows you and wants to talk to you.'

Me: 'What is your father's name?'

She: 'Bushan Lal Kaul. He knows you from Udhampur days.'

Me: 'Udhampur days? What does he do?'

She: 'He was a professor of music at the Government Degree College, Udhampur. Your father's colleague and friend too!'

My heart skips a beat. She is my guru's daughter and it has taken me three years to find out.

She: 'I am passing the phone to Dad.'

Masterji: 'Do you remember your Udhampur days? Are you still learning music?'

Masterji asks question after question. He wants to know everything about me. I want to know everything about him. He passes the phone to his wife. Aunty still treats me like her son. Her voice turns heavy with emotion.

'Come home,' they say. 'We divide our time between Jammu and Delhi now.'

'What should I do, Masterji? How should I learn?'

'Listen to raags that evoke feelings of compassion and peace,' he says. 'Listen to Kirwani and Alhaiya Bilaval.'

* * *

I am listening to Pandit Hariprasad Chaurasia's Raag Kirwani. It's a vintage recording. Panditji was young at the time he played it live for an audience. According to the description, Raag Kirwani evokes moods of love, devotion, melancholy and longing. It should be played and listened to at night. Each musical phrase brings alive an old, lost memory. And it blossoms as if it's not just a memory but a moment that I am reliving again. I feel as though I have been granted a boon.

My guru appears before me for the first time in thirty years. 'I forgive you for not keeping your word,' he says, seeing my tears and sensing my guilt. 'I knew from the very first day that you didn't have the qualities required to be a student of music. You always talked about wanting to do this and that . . . In music, there is no wanting. There is only surrender . . .'

The window opens to a new dawn. Thirty years have passed. The world outside has the same glow. The same madness and desire continue to grip my heart. To want everything. To wish for beauty. To experience love.

'To learn music is to be perennially thirsty . . .' my guru goes on. 'The oasis is far, but it exists. What you sometimes see is a mirage, not an oasis. It is because you can't bear the thirst anymore. But if you learn how to see properly, you will reach the oasis and quench your thirst. You will taste nectar . . .'

'O thirsty wanderer, come and quench your thirst. I am the oasis you are searching for . . .'

'But what if?'

'I knew you would bring in your pet phrase, What if . . .'

'What if I am the water the parched oasis seeks . . .'

'And what if you are the parched oasis the water seeks?'

26

The Ghosts of History

May 2022
New Delhi

Me: 'Pa, you must resume writing your diary again.'

He: 'I am trying . . . I wrote a few sentences some days ago . . .'

Ma: 'He has lost interest now. He says he gets tired soon. Something's happened to him.'

Me: 'Do you remember the years we spent in Udhampur?'

He: 'Every single day.'

Me: 'Write about those days.'

He: 'I am reading a book these days.'

Me: 'What about the translation of Lal Ded's poetry? It's been almost two decades in the making now.'

He: 'I will go through it one more time.'

Me: 'I have our domicile certificates. Shall I send them to you?'

He: 'Keep them with you.'

Me: 'Do you remember the exact date and month when you sent Henna and me away with Ratni Aunty and family? Was it February, March, April or May in 1990?'

Pa: 'It was a winter day.'
Ma: 'It was spring.'
Me: 'But the diary says there was snow on the highway . . .'

Henna has inherited Pa's memory. She was nine years old when the two of us left our home in Kashmir. She remembers that day. She reminds me too—Muslim neighbours arriving at our house early in the morning to carry our luggage to the truck parked on the road near the house of the Kaw family. Little would have been possible without their help. They made leaving easy. We didn't need to lift the heavy things ourselves, not that there were too many of them.

'Remember the day in 1990 when Pa fractured his toe in Jammu because a minibus ran over his foot,' asks Henna. 'We met him by chance at someone's place. We had been searching for him for days when someone informed us that he had been injured in an accident but there was nothing to worry about. We had no idea where he was at the time. Such were those days when we were scattered . . .'

It is only now—when I am approaching the end—that the memory of many incidents has begun to resurface, layer by layer and image by image. After all, memory works in the strangest of ways. Henna recalls incidents and experiences that I don't remember, while Ma adds some other details from her memory. Pa recalls things that he has never told anyone else. He doesn't remember whether or not he has eaten in the present day, but he remembers what he used to feed Babuji day after day for over a year, when Babuji was unable to eat with his own hands.

This is what has become of us in exile. This is who we are now. We have become ghosts of history. The memory of our own history has become disjointed, partitioned, broken, hazy . . . but at the same time, it is alive and throbbing. Those who remember everything but choose to remain silent are one half of it and I am the other half.

This 'exile memory' has begun to consume me. I fear a day will come when I will have no recollection of my own past. Perhaps not even of myself.

Over the last two years, I have spoken to Pa and Ma every day about everything that happened to us to ascertain that I remember everything correctly and completely. Sometimes, during conversations about the past events that shaped our lives, we remember other people's experiences more vividly than our own.

All the incidents are important because they've determined people's destinies and impacted the course of their lives and those of their children. I owe the preservation of this memory to each one of us. To those who wish to understand the nature of the human condition and of suffering. However, several memories could be lost forever. And many can never be recalled, for it is their fate to be lost. Our lives will be equally defined by these un-memories, no matter how hard we try to conjure them up. There is no count. There can never be a count.

The loom of memory and un-memory spins in the strangest of ways. Years from now, some memories will resurface even when I am gone. They will come alive in the minds of our descendants.

'What do you make of everything that we endured?' I keep asking Pa, knowing full well the ramifications of asking such a question. It has now started to impact his memory. He doesn't talk much. I observe his silence. It is not an ordinary silence. It is the silence of each one of us who, for years, witnessed the suffering of others while suffering ourselves. Pa has come to personify our collective silence.

He has laughed and cried. He has endured pain. He has held it inside as though it were a treasure.

Throughout the camp days, Babi kept us engrossed by narrating riddles and challenging us to crack them. We were never good at cracking them. Often, these riddles concealed memories from her own past and stories about her own youth. Memories and stories that pertained to our own lives too. She kept reminding us about the good times to come. Even in the most desperate of circumstances, she always sang of arrivals and never of departures. I realize now—all arrivals are departures too.

'I want you to be with me at the time of my death,' Babi said to Pa one day. She kept saying it day after day and night after night. 'I want you to light my pyre.'

All he lived for from that day onwards was to fulfil her last wish. And he did. He was the saddest of us all when he lit Babi's pyre. That sadness will never go away.

I can never forget his words: 'This madness will save us from ruin.'

Elie Wiesel, the Nobel laureate and Holocaust survivor, says, 'Sometimes I am asked if I know "the response to Auschwitz". I answer that not only do I not know it, but that I don't even know if a tragedy of this magnitude has a response.'

Yet once again, I explore the prospect of taking Ma and Pa to Kashmir for a few days this summer. What kind of trip will it be if we do get to undertake it? I worry. I am fearful of the psychological impact it might have. What will we do there? We will sit by the window of a hotel room and look at the world outside. Like a boy marvelling at the sights and sounds for the first time.

'He looks for you and keeps on asking when you will be coming over, even when you are nearby,' Ma says to me about Pa.

Memory, after all, is a book of faces.

* * *

We are in a garden. It is springtime. An aroma of togetherness has engulfed each one of us. There is music all around. A woman is applying henna to a girl's hands and feet. A boy is sitting on the branch of a tree, listening to songs on a transistor. Men and women are eating and laughing. The girl is narrating a dream she had. In the dream, she is sad because she sees spring coming to an end and she doesn't want it to end so soon. Her mother laughs and whispers into her ear a secret about spring and its passing. The girl gets up and starts running around the garden, crying and laughing, because she is happy that it was just a dream, after all. Her mother smiles too, because she knows the dream wasn't just a dream.

27

The Paper Domiciles

24 June 2022
New Delhi

It is 24 June today.

Babi went to Srinagar on 24 June 2012 and never returned.

On 24 June 2007, for the first time, during an impromptu visit to Srinagar, Aishwarya and Amia see our old house from a distance. Amia was three then.

On 24 June 2009, destiny conspired to take me to my old home after nineteen years.

And today, on 24 June 2022, Henna has gone to the house once again. She rings me up from there.

'The house has changed,' she says, describing everything. 'The owners have renovated it. The cobbled courtyard is a garden now. Your room looks different. It has new woodwork. Babuji and Babi's room looks different, too. The windows don't face the street now. There is a new almirah in their room. The old almirah in Ma and Pa's room has been converted into a window. The bathroom on the ground floor

414

looks different. The attic, however, is unchanged, but it seems to be up for renovation . . .'

'What about the old bathhouse in the courtyard? Is it still there?' I ask, referring to the house of snails.

'It is gone,' says Henna.

'What do you mean gone? Gone where?'

I realize my stupidity. What kind of questions am I asking her? I am being unreasonable. I am not ready to accept the fact that our house is no longer ours. It's not just a house, after all. I realize it has come to assume the most significant location in our lives. It is still the cradle of our lives. It has become the very fulcrum of our existence, memory and history. And how can we allow that fulcrum to change? How can we allow that cradle to be altered by people who took over? Nobody has the power to take the cradle away from us. That cradle is ours and ours only. We were born there and we will die there.

But this is all just wishful thinking. All this dreaming about and believing in a past that is dead and gone comes to naught. Dreams, belief and hope are one thing; reality is quite another. The cradle is gone; gone forever. We can't change reality by turning our heads away. We can't keep nurturing the same dream again and again.

'I am sending you the video clips of everything I saw,' says Henna. 'Don't show them to Ma and Pa. They will be sad.'

For how long will we keep visiting Kashmir every summer or winter? How long until we return to our homes for good?

Ma says Henna should not have gone there. 'Did you know she went to Safa Kadal? It is not safe for her to keep going there. Anything could have happened. She should be more careful and responsible now that she's a mother herself. And how on earth did they allow her to enter the house?'

I watch the video clips over and over. Nothing has changed. Everything is as it was.

'But what about the past we've lost?' Henna asks, looking at the photographs.

Everyone is scattered now. Ma's aunt lives alone in Jammu. She is eighty-eight years old. Her only wish is to see Ma more often. 'Even if I see you for a brief time, it is enough,' she says to Ma. 'Maybe we will relieve those beautiful days, laugh a little and I can hug you and kiss you . . .'

* * *

1 July 2022
New Delhi

Our applications for domicile certificates for Ma, Pa, Aishwarya, Amia and myself have been rejected by the government of Jammu and Kashmir, owing to a lack of proof. Sushant's brother helps us file another set of applications. The applications are accepted and, after a few days, domicile certificates are issued in our names.

Aishwarya understands the relevance of the domicile certificate. I show Amia her newly issued domicile certificate. It bears her name, my name and an address.

The certificate reads:

'This is to certify that Amia Gigoo, daughter of Siddhartha Gigoo, of Khankah-i-Sokhta, District Srinagar, of Kashmir, Pin Code 190001, whose photograph is attested below, is a domicile of the Union Territory of Jammu and Kashmir. That the applicant is eligible in terms of the following clause of Rule 5 of the Jammu and Kashmir Grant of Domicile Certificate Rules, 2020.

Signature with the seal of Relief and Rehabilitation Commissioner (M), J&K, Jammu.'

'But,' says Amia, 'I wasn't born there. The address mentioned isn't my address. I was born in Delhi and this is my home now.'

I've had an explanation ready for years now:

My dear Amia,

This is precisely why you must take the Kashmiri Migrant domicile certificate seriously. It is not just an ordinary paper or document. The text on the certificate is the most important text in my life. It constitutes a very important part of my existence. And now, it is an integral part of your identity.

One day, years from now, if the Government of India declares compensation or establishes a commission to record testimonies, you must step forward and stake your rightful claim to whatever is placed before you. It is very important. My history is your history now. Your history to claim, to remember, to embrace, to protect, to preserve and to give to your children. Never forget what happened to your father and what he was made to go through when he was your age. The domicile certificate bearing your name entitles you to a stake in the process. It entitles you to seek justice and to be the beneficiary of justice, if, at all, it is delivered someday.

I don't want you to remain a 'paper' domicile, like me. My wish for you is to reclaim your rightful place in Kashmir. Whatever is lost is gone, but whatever exists must be protected from further erosion.

What I may not be able to achieve, you must and you will . . . Our story will go on and on.

There are many things etched in my memory and some of them are terrible. The time spent in the camp and the camp itself did strange things to our hearts and minds. I feel the impact now, much more than ever. I wish I had the courage to recount those things, but I don't. Maybe the memory of those things should remain hidden or a closely guarded secret, even though it will never fade. That memory will burn with me.

Towards the end, my grandfather and your great-grandfather, Babuji, didn't remember who he was. He had become a stranger to himself. But, for fifteen years in Udhampur, he polished our shoes every night. He kept our clothes ironed and ready for us to wear. When we asked him why he did so every day, his reply was, 'What if we are asked to go home tomorrow? What if the government asks us to report back to Kashmir? We should always be in a state of readiness.' He never got to wear the polished shoes and the ironed shirt and trousers. He never got to go back home or to his laboratory.

The day I left Udhampur for good, I had no idea that I would never come back. I made a wish that day: before I die, I should be able to come to Udhampur at least once and spend one night by the ghat at Devika.

The greatest source of happiness now is remembering the smallest things: who we are, where we have come from, what we lost, what we gained and what we have become!

From now on, every day is Memorial Day. We will remember all those who came and went without being noticed or remembered. Nothing remains of their existence—no traces, no photographs, not even memories.

And someday, when we reach the end of memory and of time, we will sit by the windowsills of our houses and flip through the leaves of old photo albums. We will pause at each faded photograph and rewrite the story of that day when the people in the photographs were happy. And we will take an oath to build the palace of our dreams once again in the place we still call home.

With unbounded love,
Yours forever,
Poppy

*　*　*

5 August 2022
New Delhi

Caller: 'Am I speaking to Siddhartha Gigoo?'
Me: 'Yes.'
Caller: 'My name is Anil Raina. Many years ago . . .'
Me: 'Guruji, not a single day goes by when I don't think of you. You saved me.'
Guruji: 'I have been looking for you. Where were you all these years?'
Me: 'I want to meet you and tell you everything.'
Guruji: 'My daughter sent me a video clip of someone playing Raag Marwa and Raag Lalit on the *bansuri* (flute). I realized it was you. I noticed some mistakes in your playing of Raag Lalit.'
Me: 'All that I know of flute playing and of music is your teaching.'
Guruji: 'After you left in 1995, your father asked me to come over and gave me all your flutes. I was sad that day. I missed you.'
Me: 'I carried two flutes with me to Delhi. The same flutes that Pandit Bholanath had given me. Do you remember my trip to Banaras? I got some good-quality flutes from him . . .'

Guruji: 'I remember better than you do because I had asked you to go there. We didn't have many avenues to buy good-quality and well-tuned flutes in those days. But you also brought along one flute that wasn't well-tuned.'

Me: 'Thank you for completing my memory.'

Guruji: 'I remember everything. You had started picking up music quite well, but then you had to leave . . .'

Me: 'After I came to Delhi, I practised for a few years and then I stopped . . . I curse myself.'

Guruji: 'We shall resume tomorrow. Take me with you to Udhampur if you decide to go back there again.'

28

A Dream of Justice

Summer of 2022
Jammu

The protests by Kashmiri Pandit employees employed in various parts of Kashmir under the prime minister's Employment Package continue in Jammu. No one pays heed. So far, the administration has refused to talk to them. Every day, the protesting Pandits go to the Office of the Relief and Rehabilitation Commissioner in Jammu and submit letter after letter to the authorities. So far, they haven't heard anything.

Sushant hasn't given up hope. 'We will not give up until our demands are met. What are we demanding? Transfer to Jammu or other safe zones outside Kashmir so that our parents don't have to live in fear of repeatedly seeing their children persecuted and killed in Kashmir. That's all. Is it too much to ask?'

He shows me some photographs from 1993. One photograph is of the Holi celebration in a camp in Garhi near Udhampur in 1993. Sushant's uncle and his three friends are posing for a photograph. It is a happy picture. Behind the four happy people is a vast camp with tents all over.

The roads in Udhampur are teeming with Pandits pretending to share the joy of the local Dogras celebrating Holi. Dogras invite the Pandits to play Holi. After all, Holi is a festival of colours and joy. But the Pandits had refrained from playing Holi in Kashmir due to the ridicule they faced for celebrating it. Being an Indian festival, it was considered alien to Kashmir.

What do the exiled Pandits do now that the Dogras have invited them to come out and play Holi? They come out of their tents and rented accommodations. Children splash colours. Elders watch them. They close their eyes, hoping that when they open them, they will be back in the courtyards of their homes. But none of that happens. The nightmare is endless and so is the night. The morning of their hope never arrives.

A video clip of a camp in Jammu shows up on Facebook. It is time-stamped July 1993. A man is talking about life in the camp. The screen goes blank every two or three minutes. The audio fades, but the man persists. He is a schoolteacher. In front of him are his two children—a boy and a girl. They are sitting cross-legged and studying. In front of them are books. The man is fanning them with a hand fan. The man's wife is cooking. Smoke from the stove fills the tent. The flaps are left open for the smoke to escape. Outside, a storm is raging. 'I want my children to remember this day throughout their lives,' he says. 'A day will come when they will be grown up and living somewhere else. They will tell their children about this day. I want them to become teachers . . .'

* * *

15 October 2022

One more Kashmiri Pandit is killed in an apple orchard in Shopian, proving yet again that no matter what, Kashmiri Pandits living in Kashmir will be killed.

* * *

The Pandits employed under the PM's package in Kashmir are cannon fodder and sitting ducks. They are soft targets, easiest to kill to make a point in this tit-for-tat game. We pay the price for being Kashmiri Pandits.

Once again, hundreds of Kashmiri Pandit employees refuse to go back to Kashmir. They continue to demand transfers to safe zones outside Kashmir.

The administration threatens them to resume their duties in Kashmir or else face disciplinary action. Notices and warning letters are issued to the employees. And then their salaries are stopped. The employees don't stop their protests. They continue to plead, seeking the attention of the prime minister and the home minister, hoping that they will pay heed to their woes and address their concerns.[15] But nothing of that sort happens. Hoping that they will come to see the conditions is wishful thinking. Neither the prime minister nor the home minister utters a word about the issues.

'You want to force us to go back to Kashmir so that we get killed one by one,' say the Pandits. 'We are being killed there and you refuse to even acknowledge our continued persecution and genocide . . .'

Once again, I read the sentence written on page eight of the 2014 Election Manifesto of the Bharatiya Janata Party. It reads: 'The Return of Kashmiri Pandits to the land of their ancestors with full dignity, security and assured livelihood will figure high on the BJP's agenda.'

Then, on page twelve of the 2019 Election Manifesto of the Bharatiya Janata Party, the party in power at the Centre: 'We will make all efforts to ensure the safe return of Kashmiri Pandits.'

Year after year, we keep submitting memorandum after memorandum to the Supreme Court of India to take cognizance of the genocide of the Kashmiri Pandits, and to institute a probe into what was done to us in Kashmir in 1989 and 1990 to determine why it happened in the first place, so that the truth is revealed about who is actually responsible, including those in power and in the establishment who were meant to protect us. We were compelled to live in camps for twenty years. Why? Why didn't the government do anything to help us? We kept pleading, crying and screaming. Are we a dispensable community?

All we demand is that the Government of India acknowledge what happened to us and the price we've paid for it over the last three decades. To admit to the historical wrongs and injustices done to us. To acknowledge the fact that what we were made to go through is nothing short of ethnic cleansing and that had we not fled to save our lives in 1990, we would have been slaughtered and the government, having abdicated its duties, would not have even batted an eyelid, let alone done anything to prevent the atrocities. We didn't even demand monetary compensation for all the losses we were made to incur.

Is it too much to ask for a free and fair probe into the events that took place? Are we making an unreasonable demand by requesting a dignified return to our homeland? Is it not our right to demand safety and security for those of us working in unsafe areas of Kashmir for the government of J&K?

Isn't it the government's moral duty and obligation to at least acknowledge successive wrongdoings? All we desire is a healing touch and a humane understanding of the problems we've been facing over the past thirty years. The same healing touch and humanism that former prime minister Atal Bihari Vajpayee promised the people of Kashmir, including the militants.

The BJP has been in power for over nine consecutive years. When will the day come when they fulfil the promise made to us? When will the government listen to us?

* * *

10 September 2022
Office of the Relief and Rehabilitation Commissioner
(Migrants)
Jammu

Standing under an awning in the sweltering heat amid hundreds of protesting Kashmiri Pandits is a little, ten-year-old girl. In her hands is a placard that reads: 'We want justice.'

Her mother, an employee under the PM's package for Kashmiri Pandits, is chanting, 'We want justice. We want justice. We want justice.'

The protests of the PM package employees, who have fled Kashmir and returned to Jammu in the aftermath of the targeted killings, have entered Day 159.

It starts raining. The little girl holds the placard aloft. Her mother places her hand over her head like an umbrella.

'What if no good comes out of your protests?' asks a journalist.

The girl's mother smiles as she replies, 'This is the very first time in our history that we have taken to the streets. What choice do we have now? It is a question of our existence and dignity. The dignity and existence of our children more than ours. If we are forced to go to Kashmir to resume our duties in unsafe areas, we will be killed and it won't matter to anyone. For how long will the mighty Indian government ignore us? A day will come when our cries will awaken those in power and compel them to come to us and listen to our woes. We have lost everything, but ours is not a lost cause. A day will come when we will be heard . . .'

Bringing the microphone closer towards the little girl, the journalist asks, 'Why are you here and what do you want?'

'We want justice,' the little girl says.

'Only solution, relocation!' chant the protesting youths. 'Don't force us to resume our jobs in Kashmir. Transfer us to Jammu.'

Not wanting to return to Kashmir right now doesn't mean we don't belong there or that we wish to stay away forever. But we need to be alive to work towards the cause. It involves a long fight. This time, we won't allow ourselves to be killed by anyone there. We owe our lives to our parents and grandparents, who sacrificed their well-being to keep us alive.

* * *

December 2022

Hit lists are back and so are warnings and death threats to Kashmiri Pandits working in Kashmir.[16] Newspapers carry reports citing threats issued by the dreaded blacklisted terrorist organization Lashkar-e-Taiba's affiliate, The Resistance Front.

'Kashmiri Pandits, Stay out of Kashmir or else . . .'
'We will turn Kashmiri Pandit colonies into graveyards.'

The same old hatred. The same old venom.

These threats are issued on the very day the Lt governor inspects the progress of the ongoing construction work on the transit accommodations for the Pandit employees.

After seeing their names on the militant hit lists, the Pandit employees and their families intensify their protests. Out of desperation, they now appeal to the Government of India, citing Article 21 of the Indian Constitution, which guarantees the right to life and protection of life for all citizens under all circumstances.

A silent protest is held. The placards read: 'Transfer us to Jammu. We will give our blood to serve the people of Kashmir. Don't force us to go back to Kashmir to get killed. Release our salaries. We have no other means to sustain our elders and children. Give us just this much.'

The government and the administration are adamant. The demands for transfer to safe zones in Jammu are denied.

* * *

Simran Koul is pursuing a PhD in English Literature from Sharda University. Her parents live next to the camp in Muthi. The topic she has chosen for research is 'Kashmiri Pandits: Then and Now'. 'This isn't any ordinary study; this is trauma studies,' she says.

She wants to know everything. Every single detail. All that happened to Kashmiri Pandits in Kashmir in 1989 and 1990 and why almost everyone was forced to flee. She wants to know how people lived in the camps. There is very little research available and very few testimonies! No one has documented it yet. Simran wants to be the first person to carry out in-depth research. Dr Pallavi, her PhD guide, understands the relevance of the research from sociological, psychological, economical and historical perspectives.

'My parents were among those who . . .' Simran says, pausing because she is unable to complete the sentence. 'But I want to meet all the survivors and record their testimonies. I also want to do something for them . . . help them . . .'

Simran's parents lived in the camps initially. Her father wants her to complete the research and write a book. We will need a thousand books to cover the impact of a year. Sadly, an entire generation perished in the camps without anyone taking note of their experiences. I share the blame as well! Much of our contemporary history is lost. But young researchers like Simran are our only hope.

Someday, Simran should do what I have been wanting to do. Document the lives of martyrs—those who were killed and those who died while serving and saving people who were on the brink of death. Nobody knows about them.

Now that I am talking to you about that strange time in the camp, some more memories are coming back to me. Of certain people and all that happened to them. Most of them are gone, but many are still alive and are scattered all over the country. They are my age and their children are around my daughter's age. We sometimes 'like' one another's posts on Facebook, but I dread to even talk to them about those days. They don't wish to talk about the past and I can't stop talking about it. It haunts me every single day. I feel like telling you everything. Some life stories must be told a thousand times for us to understand life and human nature.

Before we part, Simran asks me a question: 'Shouldn't the government have stopped it or done something about it? Why were we made to go through this hell? Will we ever come out of it? What should I do?'

'It is your duty to find out,' I say to her. Each of us has had the answer ready for thirty-three years.

* * *

4 December 2022
Faridabad

Babli Didi's son is getting married. I meet the boy for the first time. Babli Didi whispers into my ear: 'I have told him everything about you . . .'

The boy introduces me to his life partner. She too seems to have a sense of our history. Both work for multinational companies now. I am happy they will soon be well-settled. But maybe someday, I will get to hear from them their stories.

Kuka Bhaiya gives me his business card. He works for a newspaper in Jammu. The conversation is interspersed with pauses and silence.

29

The Last Wish

Sunday, 2 October 2022
Jammu–Udhampur

I am driving Ma and Pa to Udhampur. I haven't been able to go back to Udhampur since I left in 2003. It is going to be a day's trip.

At the traffic check post (TCP), where the Dhar Road merges into National Highway 44, I stop by the narrow lane leading to the open ground that once housed the camp with 1200 tents. It is now a different place altogether. It is a playground once again, just like it was before 1990.

You will be lucky to come across someone in Udhampur who still remembers the camp. The young have no clue. Those who were in Udhampur in the 1990s may know, but will they still remember? They never stepped inside the camp those days. You won't find a single photo of it on the internet. What does it take for people to walk past the camp without stopping to even look at life inside it? To decide to turn one's head away in the opposite direction as if nothing important is going on there? What does it take for people to not step inside even once for ten years? The camp is next to their houses. What does it take for people to forget all that and never talk about it or even mention it as if it were only worthy of forgetting? Isn't it as much about their experience as it is ours? They are a testament to our existence too. This is the story of those people too, for when they remember those days, they will get to know themselves better.

Raj Cinema Hall is no longer there. The building is now a swanky mall. The TCP is bustling with energy. Almost everyone you see at this place is going to Kashmir. Tourists, traders, pilgrims, investors, film crews, politicians and businessmen. Everyone except us Kashmiri Pandits. Thousands of trucks carrying apples are parked along the national highway. They are waiting for the green signal from the traffic police so that they can resume their journey to other parts of India.

The camp site should have been made into a museum or a memorial. It is a symbol of our recent history, after all. We are the children of that camp. The camp is our lived history. But that history is partly lost and partly on the verge of extinction. How do we preserve it? How do we keep it from further erosion? How do we prevent it from vanishing from our collective memory?

If you happen to read the obituaries published in the *Daily Excelsior*, you will see that they still refer to Kashmir as the permanent home of the dead. 'Mr So-and-so, permanent resident of so-and-so village in Kashmir, now living in so-and-so place in Delhi or Mumbai left for . . .'

(Those days, obituaries were the only news. Every day, there were pages and pages of obituaries of Kashmiri Pandits.)

Near the TCP is a lane leading up to a small colony consisting of thirty or forty houses. The name plates on the doors read: Rainas, Dhars, Panditas, Kouls . . . It's a happy sight. A Kashmiri Pandit settlement has come up.

We go to the Bhatiyal residence. The house where we stayed for twelve years. The Bhatiyals made us feel at home. They kept spreading cheer even when there was nothing but despair in our lives. Mrs and Mr Bhatiyal live all by themselves now. Their children are settled in Delhi.

'We will never leave Udhampur,' they say. They still see a faint trace of that old silence on our faces. Perhaps it will never go away. It will always live within us for as long as we are alive. It is this inscrutable silence that has come to define our history and existence. But I hope our children don't inherit it.

'You have come this far,' say Mrs and Mr Bhatiyal to Pa. 'From now on, there is only one path in front of you—the path of happiness. It leads to freedom. You are already on that path. Visit your old house more often. This is your home. This will always be your home. Spend more time with us. We will laugh together . . .'

I take Pa to the Government Degree College. Back then, it housed the camp college where he taught for fifteen years. He sits on a bench outside his old classroom without saying a word. A lone gardener is tending to saplings and removing weeds and deadwood.

At last, I am next to the pink house in Chabutra. The house we rented and lived in from 1990 to 1992. The compound in front of the house used to be vacant every day except Sunday, when a hawker would park his bicycle by the house and sell fried kalari (cheese made with buffalo milk). Now, the compound is teeming with vehicles and hawkers. This is the same place that once took me to the summit of despair when I felt I had nothing left to live for. I was stripped of everything. I was left with nothing, not even hope.

I can't muster the strength to go inside. Ma and Pa decide to look at the house from a distance and remember the time we spent here. A time we will never forget, no matter how hazy our memories get. There is something about that experience that even a fading memory can't snatch from us.

Do you know when people are the most beautiful? It's when they are dying and about to close their eyes forever; when they are on the funeral pyre about to be consumed by flames. *That* is when they are the most beautiful.

I remember my grandfather's face as he lay dying—he had an enigmatic smile! It was as though he were trying to unravel a mystery or solve the most difficult riddle of our lives.

I saw ugliness in this pink house, while I longed for one glimpse of beauty. I discovered things I didn't know even existed. I was sixteen years old and full of dreams. I discovered music for the first time in my life. And music often took me beyond the realms of suffering, time, longing, life and death.

When I leave this world, I will leave with the thought of having felt something that can't be touched and of being touched by something that never touches a human.

The memory of an old night comes alive. I am sitting on the terrace of the pink house, waiting for a meteor to flash in the skies. So that I can make a wish and send out an intention. And I spot a familiar constellation. The brightest of the stars is about to die. At that very moment, I close my eyes and make a wish, praying that it is fulfilled, even if for a day or a fraction of a day.

Now, almost two decades later, my wish has been fulfilled. It has taken me years, but I am back here. The only question that has been tormenting me is: What if I am unable to remain faithful to my memory? What if my memory can't remain faithful to me from now on? I may not be able to hold on to the memory of those times for long, but I wish to be in the memory of those times forever.

I am now at a stage when everything around me—people, events, stories and incidents—reminds me of the camp days and of Udhampur, as if Udhampur were not just a place but a person with whom I spent half my life.

Our part of the story has not ended—not yet, at least. It must never end. Tomorrow, you might hear about us once again. And you will once again ask the same questions: Why does it keep happening? When will it end? When will we get to return?

I don't want to stop. This is not the end. This must not be the end. I dream of a tomorrow when we won't be written about in the past tense—that we once were . . .

A day will come when someone's diary entry will read: 'Today, I am back home, where my parents and grandparents once lived. And it is going to be the longest day ever, with so much to do and so much to remember . . .'

But this time, it won't be a dream.

* * *

I walk past the ground where, until some years ago, hundreds of Kashmiri Pandits lived in ORTs. It is a ten-minute walk from my parents' house in Lower Roop Nagar, Muthi, Jammu.

Some nomads and gypsies have made this place their temporary abode now. Next to the nomad dwellings are the shanties of migrant workers working at construction sites nearby. Next to the ground is a swanky new apartment complex overlooking a stream, which was the source of water for the ORTs in the camp.

Remnants of a life that once existed here can still be seen. If you inspect the rubble on the ground, you will come across name plates made of wood and plastic. On them are engraved surnames and ORT numbers.

Rainas
ORT No. 347
Walis
ORT No. 640

You will stumble upon household items such as utensils, plastic ware, clothes hangers, broken stoves, the wooden legs of a cot and a myriad other things that were once prized possessions in households. This site is a museum of sorts. It is also a war zone where people battled deprivation and death every single day and where history has left a trail.

'What will you do with my things after I am gone?' Babuji asked me once. 'I want you to keep the two microscopes, my wristwatch and my shaving razor. Use them and then pass them on to your children. I will die a happy man.'

* * *

I am sitting in a plane that is about to take off for Srinagar. Deep within is a familiar sinking feeling.

From the airport in Srinagar, I take a cab to Ishbar. Swami Lakshmanjoo's ashram is nearby. The smell of almond blossoms and rain fills the air.

From the Zero Bridge, Shankaracharya Hill looks transformed. It seems to be spinning on its top—its peak resting on the ground and the base touching the sky.

Next to the gate of the temple at Durga Naag, a boy is kicking pebbles. He's singing a song much like I used to do when I was his age.

The next morning, I start running from Ishbar to Dal Lake. I pass by the Shalimar Garden. I reach Dal Lake.

The boy from last evening is sitting next to his turquoise bicycle. He looks at me and flashes me the most enigmatic smile. It is the smile of a boy whose only wish in life is about to come true. He's probably younger than ten years old, with a glint of hope in his eyes and on his face. He points to a house on the other side of the lake.

I imagine the boy's mother and father, grandfather and grandmother celebrating the boy's birth. They are planting a willow tree in the courtyard of the house.

The scene changes. The boy is ten now. His grandfather has taken him to the woods near Ishbar. He is teaching him how to talk to birds.

The scene changes again. The boy's grandfather is picking up bullet shells that have fallen from the sky after an air raid. Years later, he narrates the story of an air raid to everyone.

I close my eyes. The boy is preparing his bicycle for the ride. He invites me to sit behind him on the carrier rack. 'I will take you to your old garden. The forget-me-nots are in full bloom these days.'

Many years ago, here, at the same place, an autorickshaw driver had said to me, 'Don't come back, ever . . .'

The boy is now singing an old, familiar song: 'Don't go away, ever . . .'

A strange force is trying to prevent me from leaving. It is pulling me towards the place the boy calls home. 'Stay,' he says. 'This is our last chance for the promised reunion.'

Remember the comet I told you about? The comet I saw while sitting in the attic of our house when I was a kid. We'd waited for days for it to appear in the night sky. It is going to be back, but it will take years. It must be out there on its finite passage from one galaxy to another. Someday, it will pass by the home we call Earth again and we will wish for our last wish to come true. Until then, we will continue to divide our time between a real and an imagined home.

I close my eyes. All I see is a photograph of a boy standing next to a lake.

It is evening. But the light is neither glowing nor fading. It is just still, unlike any light I have ever seen.

How will I return the love you bestowed upon me when I had nothing left to live for?

And one day, I will be gone, just like that, never to return the way I returned, day after day, night after night, mistaking dream for reality, reality for dream. I will be gone, just like that, leaving everything behind. It will feel like the kiss of the autumn breeze.

Do you think the long season of ashes will end that day?

* * *

I am within striking distance of everything I've ever lost.

One day, years after she was gone, Babi said to me, 'Close your eyes and count to ten. When you open your eyes, you will find me sitting in front of you.'

This isn't the end. I am going to close my eyes and count to ten. Slowly, very slowly. When I open my eyes, I will find my home in Kashmir before me.

Acknowledgements

I'm indebted to:

Dhanawati Gigoo and Madhu Ram Gigoo (paternal great-grandmother and great-grandfather).
    Uma Shori Gigoo and Omkar Nath Gigoo (paternal grandmother and grandfather).
    Dwarka Nath Gigoo 'Rajkamal' (granduncle).
    Pushpa Dhar and Pushkar Nath Dhar (maternal grandmother and grandfather).
    Sarla Gigoo, Arvind Gigoo and Savita Raina (mother, father and aunt).
    Dr Prasanna Pillai and Balakrishnan Pillai (parents-in-law).
    Aishwarya Pillai (*es muss sein*-er and fellow traveller), Amia Gigoo (daughter), Mishima (MM) and General Katu.
    Henna Gigoo–Koul, Rakesh Koul and Aashray Koul (sister, brother-in-law and nephew).
    Paro (BB), Sheeba, Motu, Mother, Gauri Shankar, Radhe Shaam, Mud, Chandu, Sweeti, Bholu, Fox Lady, Choti and Whitey.

Ashok Pillai, Ragashri (Reenu) Pillai, Arvind Pillai, Kaavya Pillai, Jaidev Pillai, Puja Pillai, Mahika Pillai and Khenesha Pillai.

Gigoos, Dhars, Kaks, Dewanis, Watals, Pajnus, Trisals, Mozas, Jaggis, Pillais, Ratni and Chaman Lal Koul and family, Kouls, Guptas, Bhatiyals, Aimas and Tikus.

Bhawna Gupta, Deepak Tiku, Sheetal Tiku, Chander Aima, Rita Bhat, Jaspreet Raina and Manisha Prakash.

Dr Bushan Lal Kaul, Pandit Anil Raina and Pandit Omkar Nath Raina.

Mehdi Hassan, Pandit Bholanath Prasanna, Ustad Bismillah Khan and Pandit Hariprasad Chaurasia.

Tota, Anita Koul, Sushma Koul, T.K. Koul, Dileep Gigoo, M.L. Kak, Sachin Dhar, Rajneesh Dhar, Shilpa Raina, Smriti Kak, Virender (Monty) Watal, Anil, Rahul Bhat, Showkat, Susheel Panju, Monika Koul, Sunil Koul, Neetu Razdan, Dr Agnishekhar, Kshema Kaul, Ramesh Dhar, Dr Kulbushan Razdan, Professor Mohammad Amin, Dr Kundan Lal Chowdhury, Professor Amar Malmohi, Pandit Arun Kaul, Kaka Ji Pandita, Professor Vijay Prakash, Professor R.K. Aima, Professor Ashok Aima, Professor Vinay Handoo, Professor Giridhari Lal Bhat, Dr Kapil Kapoor, Dr G.J.V. Prasad, Dr Harish Narang, Dr Meenakshi Mukherjee, Hari Nair, Saon Bhattacharya, Neelu George, Sanjay Kumar, Dr Anil Raina, Dr Amrita Ghosh, Professor Henna Amin, Muhabit ul Haq, Dr Khalid Mir, Vivek Raina, Amandeep Sandhu, Vinod Veerakumar, Sajiv Pillai, Anirban Dutta, Neeru Kaul, Kirti Koul, Kapish Mehra, Himanjali, Renu Kaul, Arunava Sinha, Namita Gokhale, Shashi Baliga, Patrick Cotter, Raghu Karnad, Elizabeth Kuruvilla, Chinki Sinha, Barkha Dutt, Ratan Kaul, Neha Thakur, Ritu Mehra, Nishtha Gautam, Indira Basu, Jaya Srinivasan, Anukriti Upadhyay, Sumant Batra, Vandhana Choudhary, Upasana

Sinha, Swati Chopra, Nazma Ali, Gunjan Veda, Manmeet Narang, Srishti Koul, Priyanka Dubey, Kunal Mehra, Arnab Chaudhuri, Varad Sharma, Sushant Dhar, Mandeep Kaur, Madhu Shrivastava, Gaurav Mongga, Pratyush Koul, Adarsh Ajit, Satyarth Pandita, Manisha Gangahar, Geetanjali, Kumar Akash, Aashna Narang, Aman Saurav, Kanika Batra, Tapan Kumar, Somya Sharma, Jigyasa Singh, Christina Tudor-Sideri, Shantanu Ray Chaudhuri, Veer Munshi, Vidushi Sharma and Pradeepika Saraswat.

The Imperial Clinical Laboratory (Maharaj Gunj, Srinagar), Government Degree College for Boys (Anantnag), Sri Pratap College (Srinagar), DAV College (Chandigarh), Camp School (Udhampur), Happy Model Higher Secondary School (Udhampur), Air Force School (Udhampur), Government Degree College for Boys (Udhampur) and Jawaharlal Nehru University (New Delhi).

People who were forced to live in displacement camps in Udhampur and Jammu. People who perished and those who survived.

Karthik Venkatesh (executive editor), Aparna Abhijit (copy editor) and everyone else at Penguin Random House India.

Kashmiri Pandits and Kashmir: A Historical Timeline[17]

1500 BCE–1000 BCE: Kashmir is inhabited by the Pisachas, a tribe of the early Vedic period. Rishi Kashyap arrives in Kashmir and his son, Nila Naga, becomes the first king of Kashmir. Kashmir is named after Kashyap. Snake worship is introduced by the Nagas. (The present-day Kashmiri Pandits trace their ancestry to the Nagas.)

Third Century BCE: The Maurya King Ashoka introduces Buddhism to Kashmir. Many Buddhist stupas and temples, such as the Stupa Jayendra Vihar at Ushkur near Varahamulaksetra (present-day Baramulla) and the Vijayeshvara temple in Bijbehara, are built. Ashoka establishes the city of Srinagara, near modern-day Srinagar in Kashmir.

First–Third Century: Kushans rule Kashmir. Kanishka, an emperor of the Kushan dynasty, establishes Kanishkapur (near present-day Baramulla). He convenes the Fourth Buddhist Council in Kashmir. Kashmir becomes the seat of Buddhist learning and practice.

Third–Fifth Century: Kashmir is under the Gonanda dynasty and other rulers.

Sixth–Seventh Century: Gonanda reign is restored in Kashmir. The Gonanda II dynasty takes over Kashmir.

Sixth–Eighth Century: The *Nīlamata Purāna*, the most ancient text about Kashmir's geography, culture, society, politics, economics and way of life, is composed. It also sets out the legend about the origin of Kashmir. The book describes several ancient rituals and festivals that are part of the Kashmiri Pandit way of life even today.

Seventh–Eleventh Century: Kashmir flourishes economically and culturally under the Karkota and Utpala empires. King Lalitaditya Muktapida of the Karkota dynasty builds the Martand Sun Temple near Anantnag, Kashmir. He invites Hindu scholars like Attrigupta to practice and propagate Shaivism. Utpala's grandson Avantivarman establishes the Utpala dynasty. He establishes many towns, including Avantipur and Suyapur and builds many Hindu temples dedicated to both Vishnu and Shiva, notable among which are the Avantiswara and Avantiswami temples. Queen Didda (daughter of Simharāja, the King of Lohara) rules Kashmir in the second half of the tenth century. She marries King Ksemagupta, thus uniting the Kingdom of Lohara with that of her husband's empire in Kashmir. She adopts her nephew Samgrāmarāja who establishes the Lohara dynasty, thus heralding the rule of the Loharas in Kashmir.

Tenth–Thirteenth Century: Kashmir is under the Lohara dynasty. It experiences the revival of Shaivism and Shaiva philosophy because of Acharya Abhinavagupta's efforts.

Eleventh Century: Mahmud of Ghazni attempts to invade and conquer Kashmir twice but fails because of Samgrāmarāja and his army's efforts.

Twelfth Century: Kashmiri Hindu historian Kalhana writes *Rajatarangini* (The River of Kings). Written in Sanskrit, *Rajatarangini*, is the oldest and most comprehensive record of the history of Kashmir—starting from the Mauryan times until the eleventh century. Kalhana cites the *Nīlamata Purāna* as one of his sources.

1313–42: Shams-ud-Din Shah Mir, a descendent of the rulers of Swat, invades Kashmir during the reign of King Suhadeva (1301–20). After the deaths of Suhadeva and his brother, Udayanadeva, Shah Mir proposes to marry Kota Rani, the reigning queen of the Lohara dynasty, to take over the kingdom. Kota Rani turns down the proposal and resists Shah Mir's aggression. After Kota Rani's death, Shah Mir establishes his own reign in Kashmir (in 1339) and establishes the Shah Miri dynasty. Rinchana, the Buddhist refugee king of Kashmir, is forced by Shah Mir to embrace Islam to set an example. Shah Mir starts spreading Islam in Kashmir. The Shah Miri dynasty lasts until 1561. Shah Mir also orders the demolition of the Martand Sun Temple (built by Lalitaditya Muktapida) and the Avantiswami Temple (built by Avantivarman). Both temples are now in ruins.

1389–1413: The first exodus of Kashmiri Pandits takes place during the rule of Sikandar 'Butshikan', the sixth ruler of the Shah Miri dynasty. 'Butshikan' means the destroyer of idols. Like his predecessors, Sikandar continues to destroy the Hindu and Buddhist places of worship and centres of learning in Kashmir. He forces Pandits to convert to Islam and levies jizya (poll tax) on those who refuse to convert. The Pandits who refuse conversion are tortured and killed. Sikandar establishes Sikandarpora on the ruins of the ancient temples. To evade conversion, thousands of Pandits leave Kashmir and seek refuge in Kishtwar and Bhaderwah. The Hindus who live there now still trace their ancestry to Kashmiri Pandits.

1379–1380: Sayyid Ali Hamadani, a religious preacher from Hamadan, Iran, returns to Kashmir during the reign of Qutub'd-Din, father of 'Butshikan'. He and his followers start an organized movement to spread Islam in Kashmir. They issue repressive codes for the Pandits to follow.

1420: Sikandar's son Zain-ul-Abidin becomes the Sultan of Kashmir. He takes over from his brother, Noor Khan. At the behest of Pandit Shri Bhat, a physician who cures him of a disease, he takes a compassionate view towards Pandits. He abolishes the jizya and allows Pandits to rebuild their temples and live peacefully in Kashmir. He comes to be known as 'Budshah' which means 'great king'. His rule lasts about fifty years.

1480–1515: Kashmiri Pandits are forced into a second exodus when Mir Shams-ud-din Araqi, a Shia zealot from Herat, arrives in Kashmir with a mission to force conversions and spread Islam. During Fateh Shah II's oppressive regime, from 1505 until 1514, the subjugation of Pandits continues.

1585–1620: Mughals, under Jalal-ud-Din Muhammad Akbar, annex Kashmir. Departing from his father's policy of religious tolerance, Jehangir starts persecuting Kashmiri Pandits.

1617–1675: Under Aurangzeb's rule, the repression of Pandits continues. Pandits seek the Sikh Guru Teg Bahadur's help. The confrontation eventually leads to Guru Teg Bahadur's beheading on Aurangzeb's orders in 1675. Left with no choice, thousands of Pandits flee Kashmir yet again, triggering their third mass exodus from Kashmir.

1753: Ahmad Shah Durrani of Afghanistan seizes control of Kashmir. The Durranis unleash a reign of terror and terrorize Pandits. Pandits are compelled to leave Kashmir once again. Many choose to settle in Poonch.

1819: Maharaja Ranjit Singh, founder of the Sikh empire, defeats the last Afghan governor of Kashmir and takes charge of Kashmir.

16 March 1846: The Treaty of Amritsar is signed between the British Government and Maharaja Gulab Singh, the ruler of Jammu and Ladakh. The British Government transfers Kashmir to Gulab Singh for an indemnity of Rs 7.5 million. The princely state of Jammu and Kashmir is formed.

1931: Muslims revolt against the Dogra ruler Maharaja Hari Singh. Thousands of Pandits across Kashmir are targeted, their shops looted and their properties destroyed because they are thought to be supporters of the Dogras. Fearing for their lives and safety, thousands of Pandits flee Kashmir once again, triggering their fifth exodus from Kashmir.

October 1947: Tribal militias (called Kabalis) from Pakistan's north-west frontier province supported by the Pakistani army invade Kashmir. They kill hundreds of Pandits and Sikhs in Baramulla, Sopore and other towns. Pandit properties such as houses and shops are destroyed. Maharaja Hari Singh, ruler of the princely state of Jammu and Kashmir, signs the Instrument of Accession. Jammu and Kashmir becomes part of the Union of India. The Indian Army enters Srinagar to counter the aggression by Pakistani tribal militias. India emerges victorious. Both countries declare a ceasefire.

1950–80: Pandits continue to be discriminated against. The J&K Land Estates Abolition Act of 1950 gives the government the authority to seize landlord-owned private property. Thousands of Kashmiri Pandits are affected.

April–September 1965: Pakistani infiltrators cross the ceasefire line into Kashmir, resulting in the India–Pakistan war. The war ends with a ceasefire.

January 1986: Anti-Kashmiri Pandit riots erupt in Anantnag and adjoining villages. Thousands of Muslim rioters attack Kashmiri Pandits, looting and destroying their properties. The rioters set fire to two main temples in Anantnag, causing panic and fear among Kashmiri Pandits across Kashmir. Pandits start leaving for other parts of India, thinking that it is becoming increasingly impossible for them to stay and prosper there.

1989–90: Thousands of Kashmiri Muslim youths cross the Line of Control (LoC) into Pakistan and undergo training in jihad and how to wage war against the Indian state. They return as trained militants with arms and ammunition. A mass uprising and armed insurgency erupt in Kashmir. Thousands of Pakistani terrorists infiltrate Kashmir to wage war against India. Kashmiri Muslims advocate the establishment of Nizam-e-Mustafa (administration based on Sharia) in Kashmir.

14 September 1989: Tika Lal Taploo, a prominent Kashmiri Pandit lawyer and vice-president of J&K State's Bharatiya Janata Party (BJP), is shot dead by terrorists in Srinagar.

19 January 1990: Jagmohan arrives in Srinagar to take charge as governor of the state. Terror outfits, including Jammu Kashmir Liberation Front and Hizb-ul Mujahideen, ask Kashmiri Muslims to defy curfew en masse and launch protest marches.

December 1989–April 1990: Kashmiri Muslims chant anti-India and anti-Pandit slogans. Declarations are issued to the effect that Kashmiri Pandits are kafirs and informers. Militants start assaulting, terrorizing, abducting and killing Kashmiri Pandits. *Aftab*, a local Urdu newspaper, publishes a press release issued by Hizb-ul Mujahideen, set up by the Jamaat-e-Islami in 1989, to wage jihad for Jammu and Kashmir's secession from India and accession to Pakistan. *Al Safa*, a local Urdu daily, publishes a press release issued by Hizb-ul Mujahideen warning all non-Muslims to leave Kashmir within thirty-six hours or face death. Many other local dailies, including *Srinagar Times* and *Chattan*, print warning letters (issued by terror outfits) threatening Kashmiri Pandits to leave Kashmir. Several prominent and common Kashmiri Pandits are killed. The mass exodus of Kashmiri Pandits starts. About half a million Kashmiri Pandits leave Kashmir and take refuge in Jammu, Delhi and other parts of the country.

1990–91: Many makeshift camps are set up in Jammu and adjoining districts to give refuge to the displaced Pandits. Some of the prominent displacement camps are Garhi Camp, Stadium Camp and Battal Balian Camp in District Udhampur, and Muthi Camp, Transport Nagar Camp, Purkhoo Camp,

Stadium Camp, Jhiri Camp, Nagrota Camp and Mishriwala Camp in and around Jammu. Some of these camps are next to factories producing toxic waste. In 2000, the area next to Battal Balian Camp is declared an industrial zone by the government. Living there is a health hazard because factories that produce cement, bricks and plastic generate a lot of industrial waste, resulting in a high prevalence of diseases among the camp-dwellers.

1990–2011: Thousands of displaced Kashmiri Pandits are forced to live in abject conditions in tents and ORTs in camps. Thousands perish because of extreme conditions with minimal facilities for survival in camps.

21 March 1997: Militants slaughter seven Kashmiri Pandits of Sangrampora village, Budgam.

25 January 1998: Militants massacre twenty-three Kashmiri Pandits, including women and children, in Wandhama village, near Ganderbal.

1999: Pakistani troops intrude into strategic positions through Kargil on the Indian side of the Line of Control. India fights back and emerges victorious.

23 March 2003: Twenty-four Kashmiri Pandits are shot dead by terrorists in Nadimarg, Pulwama.

2008: The Government of India announces a package of Rs 1600 crore for the rehabilitation of Kashmiri migrants and other victims of militancy. The package covers West Pakistan refugees and PoK migrants, including displaced Kashmiri Pandits. The Government announces jobs for 6000 Kashmiri

Pandit youths in various departments in Kashmir. Part of the plan is to rehabilitate the displaced Pandits in Kashmir. The government announces an aid package (capped at Rs 7.5 lakh) for the reconstruction or construction of Pandit houses in Kashmir. This aid is applicable to those Kashmiri Pandits who sold their properties between 1989 and 1997, when the J&K Migrant Immovable Property (Preservation, Protection and Restraint of Distress Sale) Act was enacted.

2012: The Government of India inaugurates a large camp complex consisting of about 4000 flats in Jagti, near Nagrota in Jammu. Around the same time, two new camp complexes are inaugurated in Buta Nagar, Jammu. Kashmiri Pandit families living in tents and ORTs are allotted two-room flats in these new camps.

2015: The Government of India approves the creation of 6000 transit quarters for the displaced Pandits serving in Kashmir under the prime minister's Special Employment Package for Kashmiri Pandit migrants. This scheme is part of the plan to rehabilitate the displaced Pandits in Kashmir.

August 2019: The Government of India revokes Article 35A and Article 370 of the Constitution. Article 370 granted the state a special status, enabling the state to make laws on all aspects of governance except three—foreign relations, defence and communications. Article 35A gave the state full discretionary powers to decide who 'permanent residents' of the state were. It allowed the state legislature to impose any restrictions on persons other than the state subjects. It restricted people outside the state from buying property or claiming employment. The sudden revocation of these articles causes backlash against the Kashmiri Pandits employed in

Kashmir. Many Kashmiri Pandit transit quarters across Kashmir are targeted by locals.

2022: The 'PM package' employees still await the allotment of transit homes in Kashmir. Many Kashmiri Pandits living and serving in Kashmir are killed by terrorists. Terror outfits issue warnings to Pandits. Hundreds of Kashmiri Pandits are forced to migrate once again, triggering the eighth exodus. They start protesting in Jammu, demanding relocation to safer zones in Jammu. The administration stops paying the salaries of those who don't resume their duties, even in the wake of targeted killings of Pandit minorities in Kashmir.

March 2023: Hundreds of 'PM package' Kashmiri Pandits call off the 310 day-long agitation and resume duties in Kashmir.

22 May 2023: Srinagar hosts the G20 Summit, which becomes the first-ever international event in decades. It is the biggest gathering of foreign delegates so far. About fifty-seven high-profile delegates from twenty-seven countries participate. The focus is on the promotion of tourism in the state.

23 October 2023: The Lt governor of Jammu and Kashmir addresses a rally of displaced Kashmiri Pandits in Jammu and talks about how the government is making efforts for their permanent resettlement in Kashmir. He says, 'Kashmiri Pandit employees serving in Kashmir will be given land at subsidized rates for constructing houses in Srinagar. A nodal officer has been appointed in the Secretariat to address the issues and concerns of the Kashmiri Pandit community.' Mata Bhaderkali Asthapan Trust Wadipora Handwara announces a plan to construct a *Shaheed Smaarak* (memorial) to honor the martyrs of the Kashmiri Pandit community, police and paramilitary forces.

Notes

1 The first exodus of Kashmiri Pandits took place between 1389 and 1413 during the rule of Sikandar 'Butshikan' of the Shah Miri dynasty. He was an iconoclast and ordered the destruction of the Hindu and Buddhist temples in Kashmir, forced Pandits to embrace Islam and levied *jizya* (poll tax) on those who refused to convert. Those Pandits who refused conversion were tortured. To evade conversion, thousands of Pandits were forced to leave and seek refuge in Kishtwar and Bhaderwah.

The second exodus occurred between 1480 and 1515, when, once again, Pandits were forced to convert to Islam when Mir Shams-ud-din Araqi, a Shia zealot from Herat, arrived in Kashmir with a mission to force conversions and spread Islam. During Fateh Shah II's oppressive regime from 1505 until 1514, Pandits continued to be persecuted and tortured.

The third exodus took place between 1617 and 1675 during Aurangzeb's rule, when the repression of Pandits continued. Aurangzeb and his administrators targeted Pandits and the Pandits were forced to seek the Sikh Guru Teg Bahadur's help. The confrontation eventually led to Guru Teg Bahadur's beheading on Aurangzeb's orders in 1675.

The fourth exodus occurred during the rule of Ahmad Shah Durrani of Afghanistan, who took over Kashmir around 1753. The Durranis too unleashed a reign of terror and Pandits were compelled to leave Kashmir once again. Many chose to settle in Poonch at that time.

The fifth exodus happened in 1931, when Muslims revolted against the Dogra ruler, Maharaja Hari Singh. Pandits were targeted, their shops looted and their properties destroyed because they were thought to be supporters of the Dogras. Hundreds of Pandits fled Kashmir at that time.

The sixth exodus took place from 1950 until 1980, when Pandits continued to be discriminated against. During this period, Pandits kept leaving for other parts of India, knowing that it was becoming increasingly impossible for them to stay and prosper there.

2   'Crime Against Kashmiri Pandits: SC Dismisses Plea Challenging 2017 Order on "Genocide" Probe', *Indian Express*, 9 December 2022, https://indianexpress.com/article/india/crime-against-kashimiri-pandits-supreme-court-dismisses-plea-challenging-2017-order-on-genocide-probe-8314570/.

3   Sanjoy Hazarika, 'Muslim–Hindu Riots in India Leave 93 Dead', *New York Times*, 10 December 1990, https://www.nytimes.com/1990/12/10/world/muslim-hindu-riots-in-india-leave-93-dead-in-3-days.html; 'Communal Fires Rage Across India As Ayodhya Issue Drags on Unnecessarily', *India Today*, 31 December 1990, https://www.indiatoday.in/magazine/cover-story/story/19901231-communal-fires-rage-across-india-as-ayodhya-issue-drags-on-unneces sarily-813417-1990-12-30.

4   I have sourced this information from three standard works of Kashmiri history: M.A. Stein, *Kalhana's Rajatarangini: A Chronicle of the Kings of Kashmir* (New Delhi: New Bharatiya Book Corporation, 2019); Jogesh Chunder Dutt, *Rajatarangini of Jonaraja*, (New Delhi: Gyan Publishing House, 2012); P.N.K. Bamzai, *Culture and Political History of Kashmir: Ancient Kashmir* (Srinagar, J&K: Gulshan Publishers, 2007).

5   Information for this story has been sourced from two books: Jia Lal Kilam, *A History of Kashmiri Pandits* (New Delhi: Utpal Publications, 2004); P.N.K. Bamzai, *Culture and Political History of Kashmir: Ancient Kashmir* (Srinagar, J&K: Gulshan Publishers, 2007).

6   'Martyrs Day: Forgotten Pandits Killed by Terrorists in Kashmir', ABP Live, 15 September 2016, https://news.abplive.com/blog/martyrs-day-forgotten-pandits-killed-by-terrorists-in-kashmir-415495.

7   Muzaffar Raina, 'Pandits Get Back Temple With Muslim Help—Valley Bond', *Telegraph* online, 30 January 2010, https://www.telegraphindia.com/india/pandits-get-back-temple-with-muslim-help-valley-bond/cid/556394.

8   'Healing Touch: 50,000 Temples Closed, Vandalised During Islamist Assault On Kashmir To Be Surveyed For Restoration', *Swarajya*, 23 September 2019, https://swarajyamag.com/insta/healing-touch-50000-temples-closed-vandalised-during-islamist-assault-on-kashmir-to-be-surveyed-for-restoration.

9   'Make return of Pandits to J&K part of state policy', *Times of India*, 10 June 2007, https://timesofindia.indiatimes.com/india/make-return-of-pandits-to-jk-part-of-state-policy/articleshow/2112305.cms.

10 My father's open letters were published by a local daily, but I cannot locate them online. However, my father has posted them on Facebook and the letters have also been shared by others on Facebook, largely in the Kashmir groups.

11 Barkha Dutt, 'Exodus of Kashmiri Hindus: Insurgency, Families and Justice in Jammu and Kashmir', Mojo Story, 21 January 2021, https://www.youtube.com/watch?v=93EeAKvdVsY.

12 'Kashmir Documentation: Pandits in Exile', Panun Kashmir Movement (PKM), 12 February 2010, https://panunkashmir.org/publications/Kashmir%20Documentation%20-%20Pandits%20in%20Exile.pdf.

13 Sunil Bhat, '"Will Turn Transit Colonies to Graveyard": Kashmir Fight's Fresh Threat to Kashmiri Pandits', *India Today*, 15 December 2022, https://www.indiatoday.in/india/story/terror-group-kashmir-fight-fresh-threat-kashmiri-pandit-government-employees-2309293-2022-12-15.

14 'Construction of Only 17% of 6000 Houses for Kashmiri Pandits Done in 7 years, Shows Centre's Data', Scroll.in, 20 March 2022, https://scroll.in/latest/1019916/construction-of-only-17-of-6000-houses-for-kashmiri-pandits-done-in-7-years-shows-centres-data.

15 'Kashmiri Pandit Employees Seek PM Modi's Help After Fresh Terror Threat', *Outlook*, 8 December 2022, https://www.outlookindia.com/national/kashmiri-pandit-employees-seek-pm-modi-s-help-after-fresh-terror-threat-news-243460.

16 Sunil Bhat, '"Will Turn Transit Colonies to Graveyard": Kashmir Fight's Fresh Threat to Kashmiri Pandits', *India Today*, 15 December 2022, https://www.indiatoday.in/india/story/terror-group-kashmir-fight-fresh-threat-kashmiri-pandit-government-employees-2309293-2022-12-15.

17 I have largely developed this timeline by referring to these three books: M.A. Stein, *Kalhana's Rajatarangini: A Chronicle of the Kings of Kashmir* (New Delhi: New Bharatiya Book Corporation, 2019); Ved Kumari, *Nīlamata Purāṇa* (J&K: J&K Academy of Art, Culture and

Languages, 1968); Jia Lal Kilam, *A History of Kashmiri Pandits* (New Delhi: Utpal Publications, 2004). The more recent events are a matter of public record and have been sourced from various newspaper and magazine reports.

References

Prologue

Bhan, Prof. K.L. 2003. *Paradise Lost: Seven Exoduses of Kashmiri Pandits.* Kashmir: Kashmir News Network. https://ikashmir.net/exodus/index.html.

Tikoo, Col. Tej K. 2013. *Kashmir: Its Aborigines and their Exodus.* India: Lancer Publishers LLC. https://www.amazon.in/Kashmir-Its-Aborigines-their-Exodus-ebook/dp/B00DTX8VIS.

Dixit, Sanjay. 2021. The Seven Exoduses of Kashmir Valley. *The Jaipur Dialogues.* 5 June 2021. https://www.thejaipurdialogues.com/itihasa/the-seven-exoduses-of-kashmir-valley/.

Panda, Chandan Kumar. 2022. Kashmir Pandits: Militancy, Migration and the Question of Resettlement. *International Journal of English Literature and Social Sciences.* Vol.7 (2). Mar–Apr 2022. https://ijels.com/detail/kashmir-pandits-militancy-migration-and-the-question-of-resettlement/.

Scan QR code to access the
Penguin Random House India website